YANKEE MIRACLES

For Debbie—
Love reconnecting
with you!

YANKEE
MIRACLES

Life with the Boss and the Bronx Bombers

RAY NEGRON
and SALLY COOK

 Sally 2021

LIVERIGHT PUBLISHING CORPORATION

A Division of W. W. Norton & Company

New York • London

Page 203: Photograph by Charles Wenzelberg

For information about permission to reproduce selections
from this book, write to Permissions, Liveright Publishing
Corporation, a division of W. W. Norton & Company, Inc.,
500 Fifth Avenue, New York, NY 10110

For information about special discounts for bulk purchases,
please contact W. W. Norton Special Sales at specialsales@
wwnorton.com or 800-233-4830

Manufacturing by Courier Westford
Book design by Judith Stagnitto Abbate / www.abbatedesign.com
Production manager: Devon Zahn

Library of Congress Cataloging-in-Publication Data

Negron, Ray.
Yankee miracles : life with the boss and the Bronx bombers /
Ray Negron and Sally Cook ; introduction by
Hank Steinbrenner. — 1st ed.
p. cm.
Includes index.
ISBN 978-0-87140-461-9 (hardcover)
1. Negron, Ray. 2. Sports personnel—Biography. 3. New York
Yankees (Baseball team) 4. Steinbrenner, George M. (George
Michael), 1930–2010. I. Cook, Sally. II. Title.
GV865.N42A3 2012
796.357092—dc23
[B]
2012021858

Liveright Publishing Corporation
500 Fifth Avenue, New York, N.Y. 10110
www.wwnorton.com

W. W. Norton & Company Ltd.
Castle House, 75/76 Wells Street, London W1T 3QT

1 2 3 4 5 6 7 8 9 0

To the Boss, forever.

Cirilo and Jenny, you are always the greatest parents.
Nancy, Naomi, and Angie, you are my heart.
Toni, my chérie amour.
Jon-Erik, Joe, and Ricky, my three sons.
Theresa, you were always by my side.
Jerry and Barbara, thank you.
Aris, Adam, Deni Lamar, Lucky, and Lenny, helping me change
the world.
Sally, my personal Hemingway.
Elvis, John, Paul, George, and Ringo.
Marvin, Frankie Valli, Gladys Knight, the Stylistics, the Temp-
tations, Andy Gibb and the BeeGees, Jolson, Tony Orlando,
Donna Summer, Whitney and Michael, your music helped me
go back to those wonderful times.
Randy Levine, thank you for understanding the Boss's heart.
And, of course, to the New York Yankees and the Steinbrenner
family, thank you for giving so many of us a second chance.

—RN

For Bob, Liz, and Alex—and in memory of my parents.
And for Ray, thank you for sharing your story.

—SC

CONTENTS

Contents

INTRODUCTION

by Hank Steinbrenner

Growing up in Cleveland, my dad had a fascination, some might even say an obsession, with owning sports teams. One of his early purchases was the Cleveland Pipers, the basketball team he bought in 1960. There he learned how to fire and hire to get the right mix to make it work. Later he gathered a group of investors to purchase our hometown baseball team, the Indians. Even though that deal did not go through, my dad, in classic George fashion, would not give up on his dream of owning a baseball team.

I can still recall that January day in 1973 when, to my family's surprise, he burst through the door and announced to us, "I just bought the New York Yankees." Four years later he was presented with the first of his seven world championship trophies.

The on-the-field stories of the Yankees during my dad's ownership are well documented, but like many things in life, what is visible is not always all that is there. As I read *Yankee Miracles*, I reminisced about the events in Ray's poignant recollections that until now have stayed out of the public eye. It was these very stories that brought back vivid memories of my childhood.

Baseball fans will come away with their own memories, but I particularly loved reading about John Lennon and Paul McCartney in the "Birth of Mr. October," the Reggie Jackson chapter. I was reminded of that magical day when the Beatles invaded Cleveland, and my dad and I almost got trampled by the insanity of the crowd when the "Fab Four" took the stage. I also smiled and laughed when I read about "Sweet Lou" Piniella, or when Bucky Dent swung his way into immortality. I couldn't help shedding a quiet tear when I read about Billy and Thurman. *Yankee Miracles*—like a time capsule—not only brought me back to the best times of my father's life but also allowed me to relive those moments. What equally pleased me was reading about the new miracles being performed by today's Yankees, such as A-Rod, Jeter, Rivera, and Gardner.

Ray Negron has been a loyal Yankee employee for thirty-nine years. But more importantly, he is a friend who has captured the heart and soul of the Bronx Bombers. The New York Yankees have always been an organization of champions, but Ray's portrayal captures the essence of the human side of my dad's incredible buy.

There have been many books written—some great, some not so great—about the Yankees, but I felt this one hit a home run. The championship trophies from my dad's era are a symbol of my family's competitiveness, yet the memories and friendships that are captured in these pages are a stronger representation of the true meaning of this storied franchise. My hope as you read this book is that your personal memories of the Yankees will flood back to you as they did for me.

—Hank Steinbrenner

March 2012

YANKEE MIRACLES

PROLOGUE

I STILL FEEL CHILLS, as I will all my life, when I listen to Lou Gehrig's farewell speech at Yankee Stadium on July 4, 1939. As a boy growing up in Brooklyn, I watched *The Pride of the Yankees*, the story of his life, every time it came on television. I not only marveled at Gehrig's baseball talents but was awed by his ability to connect, in one visit, with a hospitalized boy.

It's been a humbling experience to have walked on the same field as this greatest of Yankees, and a privilege that at one time I, too, wore the pinstripes, if only as a batboy, that Gehrig so proudly wore. Even when he knew he was dying, he called himself the "luckiest man on the face of the earth," never surrendering to self-pity, always determined to give to his fellow Yankees, the fans, and the game of baseball his best.

While he knew he was lucky to wear this uniform, Gehrig also understood it came with an obligation—that of serving as a role model for those less fortunate. Through the power of his bat and the generosity of his spirit, he achieved miracles that truly made him "the luckiest man on the face of the earth."

For me, every day has been a miraculous journey since I arrived inside the Yankee clubhouse. I've learned important lessons from everyone involved with the team, from the batboys to the owner. I, too, consider myself the "luckiest man on the face of the earth" and have always known that I also have a responsibility to those less fortunate than I. With the support of our president, Randy Levine, general manager Brian Cashman, and the Steinbrenner family, I have arranged for players to visit hospitals and schools. For years the Boss always said the same thing, "This is what we're supposed to do."

Here is the story of how I learned that lesson.

1

The Boss and the Batboy

As the moon glowed high above the bleachers, I felt that
the stadium was all mine.

M ICKEY MANTLE SMILED at me.

On a blistering August afternoon, he stepped out of the dugout, clutching his bat over his broad shoulder. In the loudest voice a twelve-year-old could muster, I yelled, "Mickey, Mickey! Over here, Mickey! Over here!"

I paced the aisle from one side to the other screaming, but he didn't seem to notice. He clenched that trademark muscular jaw as he strode toward the on-deck circle. It was after my fifth, maybe sixth ear-piercing shout that he finally looked up, searching the stands with those shining blue eyes. There it was, that famous grin. The Mick flashed a smile at *me*.

I never expected to be at Yankee Stadium that day, but my father, who understood my worship of the Yankees, had surprised me with a ticket just a few hours earlier. "Don't bother delivering groceries for me today, Kiki," he said, using my nickname. "I'm sending you to see the Yankees. You're going with Julio and his sons. Remember them?" I shook my head.

"The little one's name is Papo, and the other heavier one, he's Pee Wee. They're about your age. He's taking that Tony Diaz kid, too, that other boy you're always with." I sat there in shock. "What are you waiting for? They'll be here in a few minutes. Get going."

That afternoon, a summer day in 1968, my first ever at a professional baseball game, Mickey Mantle became real. I sat so close that I could see the Mick's dimples and Chiclet-white teeth. His wide smile seemed to light up the field that afternoon. The Yankees weren't exactly filling up the stands in the late '60s, but I didn't notice. My God, my hero, was smiling at me.

"Mickey! Mickey! Look, right here!" I continued, sounding like some crazed Beatles fan. And why not? The Mick was a cult figure. In his best year, 1956, a year after I was born, Mantle had been a switch hitter with unmatched power and blinding speed, running faster and throwing the ball farther than any other player. He played the game with a life-and-death intensity that I had never seen before.

As I inched closer, Number 7 knelt inside the on-deck circle. Then he turned and picked up his bat. With his other hand he placed his helmet over his blond hair. His number 7 stretched over the broad expanse of his back as he stepped up to the plate, adjusted his stance, and blasted a line shot into the lower seats of the grandstands, his second homer of the game.

During the top of the first inning, Papo, Pee Wee, Tony, and I had sneaked out of our bleacher seats when Julio wasn't paying attention. We dashed through the huge stadium, past the concession stands, over to the empty box seats on the first base side, and waited for one of the ushers to turn his back before we slid down to the closest seats to the field we could find. In those days there were usually only fifteen thousand or so fans at a game—so we parked ourselves a few rows back from the field for the rest of the afternoon.

THE SUMMER OF 1968 was not only painful because of the Yankees' collapse, but it was a dark and depressing time in so many other ways. Martin Luther King had been assassinated in April, and Bobby Kennedy was gunned down two months later. The feelings of despair ran so deep that Elvis Presley, my idol, would eventually have a song written in Kennedy and King's honor. He would sing "If I Can Dream" in a December 1968 special, his first appearance onstage after a seven-year hiatus. With its message of peace and the hope for a better land, it became my theme song. Some of my friends' older brothers and cousins were being sent to Vietnam, many never to return. No wonder we all looked to Mantle to distract us.

He was the only thing on my mind as we watched that famous "Mickey Mantle trot." I was in awe of the way he ran with his head bent down so he wouldn't embarrass the opposing pitcher, limping slightly as he rounded the bases. A true team player, the Mick never took away the glory from the others, and he played right through serious knee injuries that he suffered early in his career from playing so aggressively.

As Mickey crossed home plate, he glanced up at me. It was like he was saying, "That's for you, kid!"

Leaving the stadium that afternoon, I heard Phil Rizzuto's voice, unforgettable with that nasal Brooklyn accent, blaring from a nearby transistor radio, "Holy cow, what a day! Minnesota Twins 3, Mickey Mantle 2!" I didn't realize it at the time, but it was remarkable that Mantle, in the twilight of his career, could still hit two home runs in a game. It was enough to get a depressed crowd to clap and holler as if the Mick were young again. I still have vivid memories of a black guy, wearing a Yankees cap, standing in the middle of the cheering crowd. Raising his tightly clenched fist high in the air, he shouted, "Mickey Mantle Power!"

On the subway back to Brooklyn, where my father owned a small bodega in Williamsburg, I thought about how often I had watched the news and witnessed the black radicals—Angela Davis, Huey Newton, and Stokely Carmichael—waving their fists chanting, "Black Power!" My mother was the color of coffee with just a smidgeon of cream. Pop's skin was sand-colored. My skin tone was like my mother's, and I felt lost somewhere between the white and black worlds.

At school, classmates challenged me, "Wow, your hero is Mickey Mantle, a white man! You crazy?" Yet I finally understood something that afternoon: baseball, more than anything else I would ever know, could transcend race.

For years, I actually believed that Mickey Mantle had smacked those two home runs just for me. No matter what his reason, it would be the last time that he would ever hit two homers in a game. The following spring he announced he was leaving baseball forever.

"I don't hit the ball when I need to. I can't steal when I need to. I can't score from second base when I need to." When I read the news I threw the paper across the room. After all, this was the man who had changed my life on a Saturday afternoon. I no longer simply *liked* baseball; I was now completely hooked on the game.

After that I couldn't stay away from the stadium. Even the hour-and-a-half commute from Queens—where my family had recently moved—to the Bronx couldn't stop me. Over the next five years I never became bored, never jaded. Each time I set foot in that stadium it was pure magic: a patch of urban grass had become a vast emerald field to me.

In some respects, I was a little jealous that my half-brothers, Marco and Miguel, lived near the stadium. Along with my cousins Christopher and Ed, who lived in Brooklyn, we all began to meet up on 161st Street. None of us had money for tickets, so we had to rely on the ushers, many of whom would look the other way and let us pass. Other times we would just hop the fence when no one was looking.

Once we were inside, it was clear to everybody except us that the team we were cheering for was not the Murderers' Row of old. We treated Horace Clarke, that little second baseman with the big glasses, Roy White, the steady left fielder, and Joe Pepitone, the first player to bring a hair dryer into the clubhouse, as if they were Ruth, Gehrig, and Joltin' Joe.

Eventually we became friendly with some of the guys on the cleaning crew. "Hey, you kids, come on over here," a scrawny crew member called to us one night. "Don't go telling anybody this, but we usually keep the floodlights on after night games until it's really late. That way we can get ready for the next day's game. Listen, why don't you kids come back tomorrow night and we'll let you in?"

The next evening, after the third inning, we snuck in through one of the gates, when you could still do that kind of thing, by the bleachers, just as we would do on so many other nights. We watched the Yankees beat the Washington Senators, before they became the Texas Rangers. As the stadium was emptying out, the cleaner called, "Hurry up, no one's looking." He must have had kids like us.

While the cleaners hosed down puddles of beer and swept up piles of crumpled napkins, half-eaten hot dogs, Cracker Jack boxes, and peanut shells, our lives were transformed in the summer glow of a Bronx evening on that most hallowed of major league fields. We pitched fastballs to each other, lofted up fly balls, and ran the bases just as our heroes did. Rounding first, then second and third, wearing T-shirts and dungarees, we could hear the roar of the crowd, could smell the popcorn. We weren't just touching the famous monuments, deep into center field, 457 feet away from home plate; we were in that place called Death Valley, feeling the spirits of the greatest players in history.

"Wow, man, the Babe is buried right here! Right *here*," Christopher shouted as he tapped the bronze plaque, which was mounted on an upright granite block that looked like a tombstone.

"Ya think so?" I placed my hands on the plaques of Miller Huggins, that midget of a former Yankees manager, and Lou Gehrig, the Iron Horse, and then crossed myself. It was a portal into another realm, no longer one known as the South Bronx, but a safe world where miracles could actually be realized. Free from the problems of being poor New York City kids, we became the stars of the Yankees. Late on hazy summer evenings Yankee Stadium belonged to us.

A FEW YEARS LATER I was a junior at Springfield Gardens High School, a racially mixed school notorious for its high dropout rate and low test scores, when I decided to cut my last day of school and head to the Bronx. The teachers were so overwhelmed with large classes and bad behavior that they rarely noticed when a kid skipped school. That morning, the late June sun blasted into my bedroom through half-open venetian blinds.

The day before, my half-brother Marco had called me up. "Yo, Ray, we got a half day of classes tomorrow. Got one, too?"

"Forget school," I said, trying to sound as tough as he was. Only a month before, Marco had scolded his friend for pulling out a shiny revolver from his jacket pocket. "Put that shit away," Marco yelled as we sat watching television in his Bronx apartment. I tried not to stare at Marco, his friend, or the gun.

"I'll call the cousins," he said. "Meet us at the park tomorrow."

I was lucky enough to live in Queens, but Ed and Christopher lived in a hellhole, the East New York section of Brooklyn. They'd often argue about which place—East New York or Hunts Point in the Bronx neighborhood where my brothers lived—had more murders. That was their badge of honor.

A year earlier my cousins' parents, Aunt Olga and Uncle Roman, had fallen on hard times. "*Mi familia, mi casa.*" My mother invited her brother, his wife, and their nine children to move into our home in Queens until they could get their own home back in Brooklyn. I liked all of them, but Ed and Christopher, close to my age, were my favorites. They, too, were obsessed with the game of baseball. I brought them to my sandlot practices, and a few times the coach played them in games. After they moved back to East New York, we continued to see each other. After all, they were family.

Maybe five or six years earlier my father had walked out on my half-brothers, just as he had with my mother and me, when I was almost four. My half-brothers, dark, tall, handsome, and confrontational, so closely resembled my father that my mother forbade me to see them.

I had grown all too used to her daily scoldings. "*Muchacho,* you're not going to the Bronx. I don't ever want to hear that you're going over there. You're different from those hoodlum brothers, *los salvajes.* They are nothing but trouble, Kiki," she said, calling me by my nickname. "*Siempre muchos problemas. Muchos problemas!*"

I should have listened to her, but instead, like a self-absorbed seventeen-year-old kid, I threw on a pair of dungarees, a T-shirt, and a button-down shirt over my tee—I looked like I was going to school—and laced up my sneakers. Grabbing a banana, I shouted, "Good-bye!" to Mom, who was upstairs helping my younger sisters, Nancy and Naomi, get ready for school.

Walking quickly up 147th Avenue, past the rows of two-story redbrick houses, set on postage-stamp-sized lawns, I passed a neighbor who was rolling her trash can down the driveway for the Friday morning garbage truck pickup. She waved and smiled. "It's gonna be a scorcher!" she said as she wiped her brow.

Pulling my Yankees cap down low over my eyes, I waited incognito at the bus stop. After a few minutes the bus arrived. I boarded, found a seat, and when I looked out the window I recognized Lee Edwards, my best friend from my baseball team. He was heading toward school. The bus stopped at a red light. *Should I get off at the next stop and go to school with Lee? No, forget it. The teachers at school don't give a shit. Besides, I've only cut twice this year. But if Mom finds out I'm doing this she's gonna jump my ass. She'll scream and yell and say no television for a week.* Still, the thrill of cutting the last day of school, the possibility to hang with my cousins and brothers in the Bronx, kept me sitting right there.

At the Parsons Boulevard stop in Jamaica, a street still lined with coffee shops, pizzerias, and newsstands, I hopped off the bus and ran down a flight of stairs to the subway station. Racing down the stairs, two at a time, I caught the E train. The windows were sealed up tight, covered with a swirl of graffiti that defined the look of the New York subways at that time. The lights flickered on and off, as the train swerved and barreled into the Briarwood/Van Wyck Boulevard station, then on to 75th Avenue, Long Island City/Court Street, 51st Street, and the 50th Street station. The ceiling fans whirred and clattered but did nothing to cut down on the unbearable humidity. I peeled off my button-down shirt and tied it around my waist. The heat in the train was unbearable, made all the worse because I couldn't get a seat. It was no better when I switched to the D train.

By the time I came out of the subway, I was drenched in sweat. There was a party mood on 161st Street that day, and the younger kids doused themselves in gushing fire hydrants while a bunch of teenagers jumped out of a second-story window onto an old garbage-soaked mattress. Marvin Gaye's "I Heard It Through the Grapevine" was blasting out of stereo speakers propped up against open apartment windows. I stood and watched, admiring the kids' moves. Grabbing an old mop from a garbage pile, using it like a microphone, they belted out the chorus and screamed "honey, yeah" at the top of their lungs.

The steady uplifting beat brought some lightness to the darkness of the Yankee neighborhood: boarded-up, burnt-out buildings; trash-filled lots. Squealing with delight, some neighborhood kids had stripped off their torn shirts and were running around in only their dungaree shorts and sneakers. They cursed and shouted to one another—"Maria, *mira* bitch, watch out! Holy shit, get the hell over here, Ramona. Juan, you fuckin' *loco*?"

A few kids raced up the street and jumped on the bus's back bumper. The driver, unaware, just kept going. When a police cruiser passed by, the boys hopped off and tore to safety behind a tenement building. As the cruiser turned the corner, the boys reappeared and began opening up the hydrants, or pumps as we called them, with a borrowed wrench.

Skipping through the cool spray, I crossed the street to the park, where my cousins and brother were playing handball. With my wet sneakers, I cleared shards of glass and candy wrappers off the courts before taking my place next to my slim, light-skinned cousin Christopher, who was smiling, as he always did. His smile hid the pain of the tough street life he witnessed daily. We fell into an easy rhythm of handball.

"This one's for your mother!" We batted the small pink Spalding ball against the dirty wall with the palms of our hands.

"Kiss my ass," I yelled back. I always thought the breakneck game of handball—furiously banging the ball into the wall—helped sharpen my skills as a shortstop.

"Hey, I got this!" Christopher smacked the ball. We played until we reached twenty-one, and then it was my brothers' turn.

Later on that afternoon we emptied our pockets of change and scrounged up enough nickels and dimes to buy a few thirty-cent burgers at the McDonald's on the corner of 161st and River Avenue. At the Off Track Betting parlor next door, a few old Latino and black guys, along with a couple of grounds crew workers from the stadium, sat outside on folding chairs, talking about Secretariat, who had won the Triple Crown a couple of weeks before.

After we ate, we headed over to Macombs Dam Park, across the street from the stadium, for pickup baseball with some of the neighborhood kids who were hanging around. We had played with many of them before, and we knew which guys could run fast and which guys could throw. We divided up into teams and started a game.

Next to us a large group of kids, from ages seven to sixteen, took chalk and drew a board with thirteen boxes and numbers on the side of the street. They darted in and out of traffic, scooping up melted tar with bottle caps, getting ready to flick them on the chalkboard for a game of skellies, a kind of street pool we played in the Bronx and Brooklyn at the time. The hydrants, the stickball, the taunts from other kids, all put together, gave me the feeling of being slightly out of control. I swore more, ran faster, laughed louder, and was completely in the moment. This was the Bronx of my youth, the Bronx I knew and loved.

While my brothers, cousins, and I waited for Yankees games to start, we began tagging buildings in the Bronx. All of us did it at the time. It created, for lack of a better expression, a sense of danger and excitement. The guys usually scrawled words like "mothafucka" or "shit," the basic words in their graffiti vocabulary. But I always wrote the same word, "Stick," a tribute to New York Yankee Gene Michael, a skinny shortstop, just like me. He was a smooth and stylish player, one so graceful, with his long flying limbs, that he resembled a ballet dancer on the field. I sprayed his nickname in fat bubble letters, even while I had second thoughts. My mother seemed to be speaking to me, my other half saying, "Slow down, Ray." However, I'd end up convincing myself that the Bronx was one big mess of graffiti anyway. So what if I write a little on one more burnt-out building?

In the summer of 1973, spray paint was easy to get. It wasn't kept locked up in stores at that time, and kids from all over the city were pinching paint and using it to cover every surface they could find— subway cars, apartment buildings, school windows. The graffiti was all over the place, some so spectacular that we called them "pieces," short for masterpieces. There were huge multicolored eyeballs, American flags in three colors, black-and-white portraits of figures smoking or dancing. Sometimes an entire subway car would be sprayed from top to bottom in bright reds, oranges, and pinks with words like HATE! POT, EARTH IS HELL, or an artist's name, CLIFF! L'IL JUDGE, LIBRA 182, or COMET 161. We greatly respected the few who could create such magic with only a can of paint.

The city had essentially become a billboard for kids who liked to express themselves. Perhaps we were publicity seekers, or maybe we just wanted people to know we existed.

"See, you ain't a scared-ass no more," Christopher, a few years younger than the rest of us, would tell me as I tagged another building. I would feel good, accepted by my brothers and cousins. They meant a lot to me.

But that afternoon in June, the guys were daring me, driving me to tag Yankee Stadium. I had never touched the place with paint. It was sacred, and I didn't want to do it, but they kept pushing.

"What you waitin' for? Come on, Ray, do it," Ed, my other cousin, yelled. "Tag the goddamned stadium."

Since it was baseball, not graffiti, that was keeping me going, I just wanted to get the spray-painting over with and then sneak into the stadium. Even now, I remember that the Yankees were playing the first of a three-game home series against the Cleveland Indians that night. I didn't want to miss a second of that game, or any Yankee game for that matter.

I shook up the spray paint can and popped off the top. Nobody was paying any attention to us. It was just that dirty stadium wall and me; an artist's canvas, the biggest billboard that the Bronx could offer.

I have to confess I wasn't naïve. I knew what I was doing. The word was out on the street about the police department's graffiti task force, which had been formed earlier that year. I heard about the guys who lived in the area who weren't paying enough attention and got busted. My cousin Ed said he knew guys who were thrown in jail for tagging, some for up to a year. The stakes were high and my nerves were jangling, yet I had a lot to prove to the rest of the pack. This was the "Big Leagues." The stadium, looming like a massive gray fortress, was special to me, so I had to do something different. *I ain't gonna write my name or scrawl a bunch of swear words like most guys do. I'm gonna spray a big* NY—*just like the Yankees wear on their hats. It's gonna be beautiful. I'm paying tribute to the team I love.*

So at 3:35 P.M. in the afternoon of June 29, 1973, I began to spray. As I did, a surge, an incredible high, raced through my brain. *This isn't my thing, it's not really me, but I gotta show the guys I'm cool.*

I felt invincible. I was soaring as the guys egged me on. Then with a suddenness I'll never forget, a navy blue town car slid up beside us. *Cops! Undercovers!* I froze as I heard my cousins yell, "Oh, shit, run!" The car screeched to a halt as the guys peeled off.

I tried to flee with them, but my body wouldn't move. I wanted to run, but I was stuck right there in front of that massive hulk of Yankee Stadium—as an imposing man wearing a white shirt, blue and gray striped tie, and navy blue blazer jumped out and slammed the car door. He was a much neater version of the popular television detective Columbo, played by Peter Falk. His full sandy hair was parted on the side and precisely combed. His slacks, perfectly creased down the middle of each leg, were cuffed and fell just to the right length. Red with a rage I hadn't seen since my mother was about to whip my ass after she caught me taking quarters from my father's pants pockets, the man marched toward me. His hands were clenched into tight fists, his lips curled and nostrils flared.

Before I could make a dash, the man grabbed me by the scruff of my neck. My hand went lame and the can of paint crashed to the ground. It started rolling. A security guard, a tall bald man who had jumped out of the sedan with the large man, quickly stopped the can with the tip of his shiny black shoe. He bent down, scooped it up, and pointed the half-empty can in my face. The security guard's eyes had a fierce intensity to them. For a minute I thought he might spray my eyes. I flinched.

"You no-good piece of crap, you're gonna pay a price for this," he said. Now his eyes were glazed and they bulged. He looked like he couldn't wait to beat the living crap out of me.

Oh, God! He's gonna punch me. I'm caught with the evidence.

Everyone else is outta sight—and they're supposed to be my lookouts. What is Mom gonna think when she finds out?

"How dare you deface Yankee Stadium?" the man in the suit shouted. He ripped my treasured Yankee cap off my head and threw it to the ground. "Kid, don't you know who I am? You don't deserve to wear this hat!"

Before I could mumble a reply, he dragged me by the sleeve inside the stadium. The security guard with his bald head and nasty strut obediently followed, muttering, "You're nothing but a lousy punk."

I looked around from left to right, scanning every direction of 161st, hoping that a guardian angel might appear. I prayed that my brothers and cousins were on their way back to help me. I twisted my body and looked up at the deep horizontal lines in the man's forehead. I could feel myself shaking as he yanked me harshly, dragging me down a flight of steps and through a long, narrow corridor. Many times I had slipped into Yankee Stadium, but I'd never seen anything like this. We were deep into its bowels, where the dingy gray cement corridors seemed to wind on forever. *Where the hell is this guy taking me? I've really fucked up big this time. Why me? How did the brothers and cousins run away so fast? Mom and Pop are gonna go crazy once they find out that I was tagging the stadium. Mom's gonna say over and over again, "No! He's not supposed to be there." I can just hear her when they call her and tell her what I did. "Por qué? Por qué? No entiendo este muchacho."*

Mom had married for the second time ten years earlier. Cirilo Negron was a devoted husband and father, an honest man, and had adopted me when I was eight. I called him Pop.

"One day you're going to be a big-time lawyer. What an *abogado* you'll be!" he would say. "You can do English and history real good, Kiki. *Mi Dios*, you can argue your way out of anything."

No way I'll be going to law school after this. How am I gonna face Mom and Pop now? I thought back to my favorite movie, *The Pride of the Yankees*, and how Lou Gehrig's mother always told him he'd make a great engineer. I had always thought that Lou's mom and mine were alike, both hardworking disciplinarians who wanted the best for their sons. Pop spent twelve hours a day in his little bodega so I would have a good life.

Even some of the most die-hard baseball fans don't know this, but deep inside the old Yankee Stadium there was a small police station. It even had a little holding cell where they took drunken bleacher bums who got into fights or ran out onto the field during games until a police car came and hauled them off to the 44th Precinct. I thought I knew the stadium inside and out, but the windowless police station was new to me. The man dragged me headfirst into a room lit by a cold fluorescent light, with two desks on each side. *This is gonna be an interrogation. They're gonna force me to squeal.* Three beefy police officers, guns in holsters, were standing there, looking me up and down. In the back of the room I saw a grubby cell, big enough for two people. I crumbled as if I had been kicked in the gut.

"Hey, it wasn't me. I didn't mean to. I'll clean it up. Please, mister, look at this cap. I'm a Yankee fan. C'mon. I won't do it again. I promise. Just give me another chance, please?"

The man in the suit ignored me. As my pop always said, I had a gift for gab and thought I could talk my way out of anything. But this guy was different. He wouldn't give me a chance.

"Stay still!" he barked. "I'm sick and tired of this spray-painting bullshit. You're gonna pay the price. You think you're a smart kid, don't you? I'm gonna teach you a lesson. This is *my* stadium now, and nobody spray-paints on the great Yankee Stadium and gets away with it."

He demanded my wallet, which I handed over. I could see he was searching for some piece of identification in the clear plastic case that I had gotten when I joined the Student Government Association at Springfield Gardens High School. Now I wished I hadn't been so quick to fill out the blank ID card with all that stuff—my name, telephone number, and address. Beads of sweat trickled down my face. The man didn't say another word and turned me over to the guards. They shoved me in the cell and slammed the heavy screen door. I had never been locked up before. *Oh, God, if you get me through this one, I swear to you, I'll never do anything wrong again.*

The man started to walk away.

"Please, mister, please," I cried. "I'm so sorry. It won't happen again. C'mon, give me a break, please. Open the door!"

The man was gone. The cell stared back at me, smelling like old piss and vomit. The burly guards stood outside, so close I could hear them laughing at me.

"You're in big trouble now, kid. Who's gonna bail you out?" The cops cracked up. "You're gonna go to court, tell the judge what you did."

One of the cops snorted as he peered at me menacingly through the heavy screen. I sat on the floor, covering my face with my hands. I knew I couldn't lie because I had gotten caught in the goddamned act. They even had the evidence, the white can of paint, which my cousin Ed had handed me.

Given the epidemic of spray-painters who had been vandalizing the Bronx that year, tagging was a serious matter. But that was just the least of it. The Bronx was literally going up in flames, with the gangs setting fire to trash cans and tenements daily. Tagging just added to the chaos in the Bronx.

They're gonna make an example out of me—prosecuting me, as if I could have stopped the entire Bronx from burning. They won't believe me when I tell them it was the first time I painted the stadium. Every offender says that. They'll probably blame me for all the other times it got tagged, too. I'm going to jail on the last day of my junior year of high school.

More than anything, I was concerned about what this would do to my poor mama. She and Pop got up at 5:00 A.M. every day. She cooked us *plátanos* and eggs for breakfast, packed bologna and cheese sandwiches for my father, my sisters, and me, and worked tirelessly at helping Pop at his store. She was also going to college while caring for our house and us. Often, she didn't go to bed until well after midnight.

I sat and waited. I closed my eyes. I thought about my Uncle Hector, my mother's younger brother by eleven years, who had been the badass in her family. A Golden Gloves boxer, he was tall, wiry, and muscular with wavy dark hair and a big easy smile. I sometimes visited his apartment on the Lower East Side, where I would parade around with his boxing trophies. "You can earn these, too, someday," he used to say. "Just keep boxing and playing baseball, Ray."

At an early age, though, he got hooked on heroin. More than half a dozen times when he was in his teens he had been arrested for stealing and selling drugs. I remembered when I was about nine or ten and Hector was in his early twenties, my mother would answer the telephone. She'd let out a scream. *"Mi Dios, siempre problemas.* My God, always problems." She would hang up the phone and lecture me, "Never become like Uncle Hector."

Helplessly, I watched as my mother sobbed uncontrollably when he went to jail. "He could have been anything he wanted, *pero mira, mira,* look at him!" my mother would say.

Fourteen years later he would be found dead, floating facedown in the dark, churning rapids of the East River. My beloved Uncle Hector. No one ever knew if he was murdered or if it was an accident, but I was told he was found with a massive bruise on his face. For years after that, my mother would try to muffle a sob when anyone mentioned Hector.

Sitting now in the stinking cell, I finally understood how my uncle suffered after he had been busted all those times. He must have felt like shit. A hunted animal, sitting in a dirty jail cell, surrounded by drunks, waiting for someone to bail him out.

Where had my cousins and brothers run to? Why had they abandoned me? How come they were so fast? Where was God on this day in June? The guards continued to laugh and crack jokes, all at my expense, I was sure, outside the cell. Nobody was going to put my cousins and brothers in jail. I was there to take the heat for every last one of them. Any minute the real cops would come and haul me to the precinct. Mom, tired and shaking, pleading to God and the officers in her Spanglish mix, would meet me there. Then she would proceed to whack me on my ass and slap my face while shouting, "I'm gonna kill you," as I trembled, knowing that I couldn't hit her back.

"Please, Mom, try not to kill me," I'd plead.

How many times, how many mornings before school, how many nights before she watched the Carson show, had she warned me not to go to the Bronx after school? *Damn, that's why we moved to Queens, to avoid this kind of thing.*

Again I thought of Hector floating lifeless in the river. I knew he had been arrested for shoplifting when he was only ten years old. It had been told to me repeatedly, as a way to stop me from getting into trouble. My mother had spent what seemed like lifetimes trying to save her little brother. Once he had stolen from my parents' dresser drawer. He was probably twenty-eight or twenty-nine at the time and I was in my early teens. "Don't say a word to your parents about what you just saw, okay, Ray? Please promise me that. I'll make it up to you." He had slipped me a buck, thinking that would placate me. In reality, the reason I didn't breathe a word to anyone was because I felt sorry for Hector.

As I sat in that cell, these images surged back to me—my mother standing at her kitchen sink, sobbing, unable to speak, each time Hector was arrested and thrown into jail. *"La vida puede convertirse en una moneda de diez centavos, just like that."* Life can turn on a dime. She cried it over and over.

When my parents came and got me, Pop would be forced to leave the store early, giving up the income from the evening papers, and Mom would have to leave my sisters all alone. And then an even worse thought came to mind: maybe my parents wouldn't even bother to come and get me, as they were so often forced to do after Hector's arrests.

Suddenly I heard the distinct sound of footsteps. I was sure it was the cops as the click of footsteps heading in my direction grew louder. I began hyperventilating. *They're gonna shackle me in handcuffs, shove me into a cop car, book me at the precinct, call me a dirty spic, dump me in a cell full of drunks and addicts. Doomed. I'm gonna get beaten up.*

I looked up. The man wearing the white shirt and navy blazer, the one who grabbed my neck, had now returned. He was standing outside the holding cell with the security guard who picked up the spray paint can. The guard wore a name tag that I still remember to this day: FRANK WILSON, SECURITY.

"Okay, you can let him out now. He's coming with me," the man said forcefully.

"It's no-good hoodlums like him who keep the Bronx—" Mr. Wilson shouted. The big man stopped him.

"Enough, Frank. I said let him out. I'm going to handle this myself. He's coming directly with me. I'm in charge, understand?"

Still shaking, I inhaled a deep, long breath when the guards finally opened the cell door. What did the man mean, that he would handle it himself? Maybe the cops were already waiting for me. Or maybe my parents were coming. Either way, it would probably be a long time before I would see another game at Yankee Stadium.

"Follow me," he commanded.

This time he took me not by the scruff but by the arm. There was still a force to his grip, except this time it felt different.

"You piece of crap. You'll pay for this," Mr. Wilson yelled, trailing behind.

The man paid no heed to Mr. Wilson. He seemed in control. Instead, he tugged on my arm again so that I would keep up with him as we walked through what seemed like an endless maze of long, dark winding corridors. We approached a heavy steel door. He released me and rapped on the door three times. Abruptly a short, thin man with a shock of white hair opened the door.

The next thing I knew, and I'll remember this moment to my dying hours, I was standing in the clubhouse. The heavens had turned, it seemed in a flash. The darkness that had thrown me into the lowest depths of despair had instantaneously lifted. I gasped, looking around the Yankees clubhouse in wonder—as though I had just arrived in the Land of Oz.

Bright, freshly laundered Yankee uniforms hung just so in each player's locker: number 15, Thurman Munson; number 9, Graig Nettles; number 12, Ron Blomberg; number 20, Horace Clarke. I had memorized which player wore which number—and now I was staring at twenty-five neatly pressed pin-striped uniforms. Dazzling white and blue.

I just couldn't tear my eyes off them. This was, after all, the place where my superheroes, guys like Mickey Mantle and Bobby Murcer, got ready for games.

The man introduced me to the older fellow who had opened the clubhouse door. He was now sitting in the middle of the room at a picnic table, writing numbers with a thick black marker on pairs of white underpants and undershirts.

"This is Pete Sheehy. He's the clubhouse manager," the man said. "He's been around here forever; well, almost before I was born, you know, since Babe Ruth played in the stadium. Pete's in charge around here. I want you to do everything he tells you to do. Understand?"

Pete looked up from his pile of jerseys and smiled. He was missing some teeth. With his watery blue eyes and white hair, he looked like a grandfather.

As he carefully went back and forth and up and down several times over each number with his marker, I watched him using the same deliberate strokes that we used when we were tagging. That's when I understood: Mr. Sheehy was applying his talents to do some good; my brothers, my cousins, and I had just been wasting our time.

"Pete," the man bellowed as he handed me back my wallet, "this is Ray Negron. I caught him spray-painting on the stadium. I know you understand. Get him a uniform and give him something to do. He's going to work here in the clubhouse so he can repay the cost of getting the wall repainted. Put him to work, Pete."

Then the man who brought me there pulled out a comb from his blazer pocket. He ran it through his already neatly combed hair, a gesture I would soon come to know well. Abruptly he and Mr. Wilson turned and left. I could hear them arguing in the hallway.

"Look, George, you can't just pick up scum off the streets. You make us look bad by bringing that slime into the clubhouse," Mr. Wilson said loudly. "The Yankees can't help juvenile delinquents like him. We can't change these punks, George. Once they go bad, they stay bad. We're not running a goddamned reform school."

"Frank, this is my decision. I say the kid stays. Maybe I can't help every kid that's out there. But maybe I can help one, just one, Frank. I have no idea if this will work out or not, but I'm going to give it a try. And if it doesn't work, you can blame me. But I say he stays and that's that."

After a moment of silence he shouted, "And who the *fuck* said you could call me George?" He really hollered. I stood there in silence. Mr. Sheehy dropped his marker, his hands at his sides. I looked over and saw Sparky Lyle, the left-handed relief pitcher I had seen so often on television. Sparky had just entered the room and stood by the door, the sides of his handlebar mustache drooping into his wide-open mouth, just like in the pictures.

The only uniform Pete Sheehy could find for me on such short notice belonged to former third baseman Jerry Kenney. The number 2 had been ripped off so you could only see the outline of it. I was a skinny kid, as was Kenney, so the uniform didn't fit too badly. It was just a little big. But I didn't care how it fit. I was wearing the cool New York Yankees pinstripes—the honest-to-goodness real thing, the perfect uniform that never changed, and the uniform that the Iron Horse and the Babe had worn. I felt another surge of excitement far more intense than anything I had ever experienced. Who needed spray paint? I rubbed my hands up and down the sleeves of my uniform.

"Hey, kid, do you have any idea who brought you here?" Mr. Sheehy asked as he folded the underwear he had just marked. I automatically knew that he was a good guy, not like Mr. Wilson, who wanted nothing more than to see me thrown in jail.

"No, I don't," I said meekly.

"That's George Steinbrenner, Mr. Steinbrenner. He's the Boss. He owns the joint." He laughed, a low hearty chuckle, one I would grow to love. "It looks like you're working for him now, kid. No more spray-painting for you."

Mr. Sheehy didn't just end by giving me a uniform. He also found a glove that belonged to designated hitter Jimmy Ray Hart and tossed it to me. He must have thought I could even play the game. The glove had never been used. "Here, kid. When you get out on the field, work this glove in for Hart, will you?" he asked.

In a dream state, I slowly nodded my head. I finished dressing and sat by myself in a corner, waiting to hear what the clubhouse manager wanted me to do. Two players—real New York Yankees—were sitting in the middle of the room signing baseballs. The first was unmistakably Horace Clarke, quiet and muscular, the second baseman who hailed from the Virgin Islands. He cut me one of his famous sly smiles.

"Hey, I'm here if you need anything," he said. It was classic Clarke; he was a humble man.

Bobby Murcer, sporting those longish brown locks so popular the years before Elvis's death, was sitting there, too. He had the kind of sweet smile that revealed he wasn't raised in New York. He was my favorite Yankee at the time. I knew these guys from watching the games, but this was not Channel 11. I had sometimes caught a glimpse of them when they left the stadium, but this was no glimpse. I had dozens of their baseball cards taped to every inch of my bedroom wall. A scrapbook filled with their pictures sat on my dresser.

Speechless, I tried to become invisible. But I couldn't help gawking. Bobby, fit and handsome, was quietly signing baseballs. Then he glanced over at me, a funny grin on his face. Later I learned that he had overheard the story about why I was there. At the time I had the feeling he was sizing me up, almost like he was saying, *I've got my eye on you, Ray Negron. I'm going to be watching your every move.* That was okay by me.

Thurman Munson, heavyset, his shirt untucked and his sneakers untied, sauntered in. He tapped Bobby on the back. "Hey, what's going on, Lemon?" I later learned that many of the players called Bobby by his nickname, Lemon. Fritz Peterson, a southpaw pitcher, had conferred it on him seven years earlier, in 1966, because he thought Bobby's face was shaped like a lemon and sometimes he would have a sour look to him. Bobby flashed Thurman a friendly smile, and I could see that Bobby had a little dip in the side of his mouth.

Peterson himself, six feet tall and probably topping 200 pounds, then strolled into the clubhouse, as did lefty pitcher Mike Kekich, who was about the same size. The newspapers had been full of reports that the two guys had recently swapped wives. I remembered laughing to myself when I read the headline, YANKEE PANKY, in one of the tabloids a while back. But the two looked and acted just like the other guys. No hanky-panky here. In fact, Fritz went out of his way to greet me. "Hey, how ya doin'?" He walked over and shook my hand. It made me wonder if the stories written about them were even true. I tried, as best I could, not to stare at them, either.

Finally Gene Michael walked over to his locker. Stick looked at me and said, "Welcome." He was just as skinny as his pictures.

I wanted to run over and say, "I love the way you dive for a line drive, how you always reach back with your right arm and nail players at first base." I wanted to hug the guy and confess that I had been writing his name in tribute with graffiti all over the Bronx, but it would be a year later before I could get the nerve to tell him that.

The quiet, humid clubhouse then began to grow noisy, a little raucous, as more players arrived. The guys belched, some of the loudest damn burps I had ever heard. My mother would not have approved. But this was baseball as it really was. I listened spellbound as they bantered. "Hey, how 'bout that chick you met last night?" "You'd better watch how much you eat or they're gonna have to use a crane to put you out on the field." "Man, you don't know your ass from your elbow." Blasting the radio, they howled along with "Pillow Talk," Sylvia Robinson's sexually charged hit song. I felt I had entered the inner sanctum of a man's world.

Standing in the center, I watched as the team began to get ready to go out on the field. Bobby Murcer rocked back and forth in his—yes, I could hardly believe it—rocking chair, right in front of his locker. Ron Blomberg, the powerful six-foot two-inch 200-pound designated hitter—the first DH in Major League Baseball—sat eating bagels and lox from a brown paper bag. I later discovered that his many Jewish fans paid tribute to a shared religion, so rare in baseball, by showering him with bagels, then pretty much a New York specialty.

Then I spotted Roy White, a left fielder and switch hitter. He was known for his strong hitting, but he also had a reputation for being one of the classiest guys in baseball. Yet he had the strangest way of getting ready for games that I had ever seen. Right near Roy's locker was a soda machine, but I was a little afraid to go over there because Roy was doing some bizarre karate moves, complete with war cries. Nobody else was paying any attention to him. When the song "Kung Fu Fighting" was released the following year, Roy's karate moves would become even more intense as he, steady Roy White, gyrated to the beat of the song.

The locker room was getting hotter by the minute, so I finally got my nerve up to go over and buy a soda. As soon as I got close to Roy, he let out another huge yelp—which seemed to contrast with his quiet demeanor—and threw a karate punch, missing me by inches. Terrified, I grabbed the soda and ran back to the corner where I was sitting while a couple of guys, including Kung Fu himself, chortled. This behavior was something I had never seen on television. But it would be mild compared to what I would witness in years to come, perhaps the most outrageous being Luis Tiant, the unsinkable Cuban pitcher, who would routinely throw on a Roller Derby costume, with knee pads and elbow and shin guards, and roller-skate around the locker room, carrying a hockey stick while puffing on one of those big-daddy Cuban cigars.

Later in the afternoon, Mr. Sheehy introduced me to Dick Howser, the third base coach. Mr. Howser had a striking resemblance to the comedic actor Bob Newhart, whose hair was always perfectly combed. In fact, Mr. Howser looked more like a pro golfer than a baseball coach in his neatly pressed khakis and loafers.

"You know how to play baseball, don't you?" he asked me.

"Yes." I nodded sheepishly.

"Okay, I'm in charge of batting practice, so I want you to go out to right field and shag balls there. Ray, that's your name, right, when you get 'em, throw to the batboy behind the second base screen. He'll then take the full bucket of balls to the pitcher."

It wouldn't be long before I found out that nobody wanted the job of standing behind the protective screen at second base—that screen was there so line drives wouldn't hit you. Most thought it was boring tossing the balls into the bucket, but I didn't. The pitchers were also supposed to perform that job at batting practice, but they usually slipped a batboy five bucks to do it for them.

I dutifully followed Mr. Howser onto the field, so nervous that I was shaking. I'd snuck onto the field many times before, but never wearing the Yankee pinstripes. The early bird fans—the ones who used to show up early with their own sandwiches—were already in the stands, waiting to watch the batting practice drills.

"Let's play catch!" Ron Blomberg called over to me, after he posed for a group of fans who were taking his picture. I was so tense I couldn't move my fingers. When I threw the ball it bounced on the ground and then flew up and hit the Boomer in the face.

"Hey, man, what the hell was that?" Ron was surprised.

I ran over to him. "Oh, I'm sorry, Mr. Blomberg. I'm just so, you know, so nervous . . ."

"First of all, kid, don't you ever call me Mr. Blomberg. I'm Ron. Now, listen, don't worry, you'll be okay," he said, giving me a hammerlock hug.

AT THAT MOMENT I heard a shout from that anonymous sea of faces in the stands. "Hey, Kiki. Kiki!"

I peered into the seats, into a blur of faces, past first base and spotted my brothers and cousins.

"Kiki, Kiki!" Their voices grew even louder as they continued to call to me.

"What the fuck you doin' down there?" my cousin Ed yelled. "What you doin' in a Yankee uniform?"

"Workin'," I yelled back. "I got a job . . . can't talk now."

"What you mean you got a job?" My cousin Christopher called down to me. Tough beyond his years, but always sweet with me, Christopher looked confused. "They didn't arrest you?"

Ron Blomberg, my new throwing partner, gave me a couple of quizzical looks, like he didn't understand the part about my being arrested. After hours of wanting nothing more than to see my cousins, I prayed that they would now just disappear.

As the hot Bronx sun cooled a bit and late afternoon brought relief from the heat of the day, I went out to shag flies in right field, still not convinced that I wasn't dreaming. *I'm really a Yankee, playing in a real live game. It's gotta be the bottom of the ninth in the final game of the World Series.* I caught a pop-up fly. *The crowd is clapping, whistling, shouting, and going wild. Ray Negron! Ray Negron! They're cheering—cheering for me.*

Mr. Sheehy's assistant, Nick Priore, a man then about forty years old, ran over and said, "Go clean up the Yankees' bats from the batting cage so the Indians can take their turn at batting practice." I began to walk toward home plate, staring up at the stands. "Hurry up. Do what you're told," he snapped. Nick was rude, but he could have told me to shovel shit and then stand on my head for the rest of the night and I would have said, "Yes, sir, more shit, please."

As I was lugging the bats over to the dugout, just an hour before the game, I felt a hand on my shoulder. The anxiety was returning, and I tensed up and whirled around, thinking it might be that security guard or some cop. But the hand on my shoulder belonged to Rusty

Torres. Rusty, who had an Afro like mine, was a well-built young guy, born in Puerto Rico. Like me, he had grown up in Queens, and everybody in the neighborhood knew him because he played sandlot ball there. When the Yankees drafted him in 1966, all the kids I eventually played ball with wanted to grow up and be just like Rusty. He'd been traded to the Indians after the '72 season, the team we were playing that day.

"What you doin' here?" Rusty said, checking out my new uniform. "You workin' with the Yankees now? Batboy? How'd you get this job?" I felt some connection to the past, proud and relieved that one person, Rusty Torres, recognized me from the neighborhood.

By now it was already a familiar litany. I told him about cutting school and spray-painting the Yankee logo on the stadium. His eyes bugged out when I told him about the man who caught me, and how he put me in the holding cell.

"Hey, Charlie," Rusty called to his teammate Charlie Spikes, a hulking former Yankee outfielder who'd gone to the Indians in the same trade.

Rusty had me repeat the whole story to Charlie yet again, as if this had already become some famous Yankee yarn on the very first day.

"God damn!" They cracked up.

Just then, Bobby Murcer, in his best Oklahoma strut, picked up his bat and helmet. He looked up at me and joked, "So, you just got here and you have a fan club already?"

Right then and there, I learned my first lesson as a batboy. Take care of your own players first—especially the stars. They don't expect to be lugging their own stuff around while their batboy shoots the shit with other players, much less members of the opposing team.

"Okay, Ray, you're going to be stationed on the right field line during the game." Mr. Howser came over to me and handed me a small aluminum stool. "Here, take this out there before we start and put it on the tarpaulin."

"Yes, sir," I said and started to head out to the field. But Bobby Murcer called to me.

"Hey, kid, come over here." I dutifully jogged over to Bobby, stool in hand. "You know what would be fun? The game's gonna start in about ten minutes. When you hear Eddie Layton, he's the organist, start playing 'Here Come the Yankees,' I want you to stand beside me and run out on the field with the team."

Too flabbergasted to reply, I just stood there, staring at Bobby, like a complete idiot.

"Now, go on, Ray, take your stool out to right field and then come back here and get ready to run out on the field with us."

I tore out to right field, placed the stool carefully next to the tarpaulin, and sprinted back to where Bobby was standing. He stared straight ahead, his mouth moving as he rapidly chomped on dip. Thurman spit several times and rubbed his hands up and down on his thighs. I held my breath. The organ blasted. I could hear some of the fans by the dugout singing to the lively, familiar beat *Y! A! N! K! E! E S! Here come the Yankees! Let's get behind and cheer the Yankees*, as we—from that night on I always said *we*—trotted out to the field. How many times when my brothers and cousins and I snuck into the stadium had I pretended that there was a crowd cheering for me? Now, when I heard their roar, I wanted to take a bow. Thurman assumed his position behind home plate. Bobby peeled off from me and ran to center field. I took my position in right field, behind number 25, Johnny Callison, looking fit and graceful in his Yankee pinstripes. Finally I let my breath out.

That night we beat the Indians 7–2. I've tried, but I don't remember many details about that game. I was completely focused catching foul balls on the right field line that we later used for batting practice. I was also studying how my gods swung their bats, leapt high in the air to catch the ball, and psyched out the opposing players.

I hope the game gets tied so we have to play extra innings. I'll probably never be out here again. I don't want this night to end.

When the last out was made I ran back to the clubhouse, looking dutifully for Mr. Sheehy. The players had already started laughing, turning the radio up to full volume, hugging and slapping each other on the back in the crowded clubhouse. Mr. Steinbrenner, too, was in fine spirits.

"You think I didn't notice. Listen, I watched you, watched what you were doing out there, way to go!" he said as he went from locker to locker personally congratulating each of his players. "Let's see more of that tomorrow." I heard Thurman say that Mr. Steinbrenner was especially over the moon because we had beaten Cleveland, the Boss's hometown team.

The players devoured salami, ham, and turkey sandwiches on white bread slathered with mustard and mayonnaise, all from a wooden table with a white cloth in the center of the room. Many of the guys appeared to be friends with the reporters calling out to them. Maury Allen, a writer for the *New York Post,* sidled up to Bobby and started joking with him. Allen had a funny way of speaking, high-pitched and fast with a classic New York accent. The man with the great mane of white hair was the legendary Dick Young, the brash reporter and writer of no-bullshit columns for the *Daily News.* There he was, too—pad and pencil in hand—asking Ron Blomberg questions.

The players continued yelling congratulations and slapping each other's backs. They were like kids, and I wanted to be part of their fun forever. I was told to collect the players' dirty uniforms and give them to Mr. Sheehy. He showed me how to clean the mud and dirt off of the spikes, by banging them against the wall or on the ground and then using a wire brush to finish the job. I learned how to wipe off the helmets with a wet towel and how to arrange the players' socks, jocks, and other stuff neatly in each locker. Finally Nick told me I could go and take a shower. I changed into my jeans and T-shirt and traded my cleats in for my old sneakers.

"See you tomorrow, Ray," Mr. Sheehy walked over to me and said. "Tomorrow is a day game, so be here ready to work at 8:30 A.M."

"Yes, sir."

I left the clubhouse singing the Yankee theme song to myself. *Here come the Yankees. Shout it out loud.* As I hummed I walked down the dim gray corridor. I ran right into the duo of Mr. Steinbrenner and Mr. Wilson, whose combined presence somehow brought the strangest symmetry to this weirdest of days.

"We've called your parents, and they are coming to pick you up," Mr. Wilson said, treating me again like the criminal he took me for. A setup. Of course it was. It had all been way too good to be true.

I looked at Mr. Steinbrenner. Our eyes met, and in the gray shadows of Yankee Stadium's corridor, I thought I could detect by his smile and soft expression that it hurt him to hear the way Mr. Wilson was speaking to me.

"Don't worry, Frank," Mr. Steinbrenner said. His voice had grown a little testy. "I'm going to speak to Ray's parents myself and let them know what Ray is going to be doing this summer. I'll take care of this."

Mr. Wilson shrugged, the kind of shrug that every employee

shows when confronted with an owner one must defer to. He took a step behind Mr. Steinbrenner, out of both fear and respect.

Only a few minutes later I watched my parents entering the stadium near the entrance to the executive offices. Pop mopped his brow with his handkerchief. His lower lip quivered, like he might cry any minute. Mom's face was furious. She pursed her lips. *She's gonna smack me with that big old black pocketbook of hers.* I hung my head in shame, as if I were three years old again.

"This is my mom and my dad," I blurted out to Mr. Steinbrenner.

"Are you sure it was *mi hijo*, my son, who was doing the painting?" my mother asked, her Puerto Rican accent sounding even more pronounced to me than it normally did. She had no idea Mr. Steinbrenner owned the Yankees.

"Yes, Mrs. Negron, the head security guard here and I caught him with the can of paint," Mr. Steinbrenner answered, ever so courteously.

"Oh, Jesus, help my son, *Dios*, help *mi hijo*," my mother cried.

"Now then, Mrs. Negron, I want your son to come here every day all summer and then after school for a while and work off the damages. Your son promises me this will never happen again. I want to make sure he's keeping up with his schoolwork this coming fall, too. If he wants to stay here, I'll be checking his next report card." Mr. Steinbrenner's tone was reassuring.

I had trouble believing what I was hearing. At the same time, I knew that my mother couldn't wait to get me alone. But I was all set to trade an ass whipping for a Yankee uniform.

"*Gracias*," my mother said softly. She dug her nails into my arm. "Tuck your shirt in." She spat out the words. Just before I headed to the parking lot to get into Pop's white Chevrolet Impala and go home with my parents, Mr. Steinbrenner took me aside right outside the clubhouse. He was so gentle, I recall, all the gruffness of the morning replaced by a kindheartedness that I won't ever forget.

"Do you know some of the kids who were with you today?" he asked.

"Yes, yes sir, I do," I said.

"Okay, Ray, don't tell me who they are." He put his hand on my shoulder. *He's saying it like he doesn't want me to get hurt on the streets for turning people in.* "Just do me a favor and get them to stop. That would be helping me out a great deal."

"Yes, sir, I will, Mr. Steinbrenner."

"Okay, now, Ray, Mr. and Mrs. Negron, get on home. Here's carfare for the weekend." He handed me a ten-dollar bill. *Ten bucks! Holy shit!* That's how he would pay me that first season. During each home stand he would hand me money, one time a fifty-dollar bill, another time a hundred-dollar bill. Considering that the batboys were paid eleven dollars per game, I felt extraordinarily rich.

The next evening, as instructed, I called my cousins and brothers and told them I was working off the damages at the stadium.

"Hey, talk to some of the guys and do me a favor? Tell them to cool it at the stadium," I said, sounding in only a day, well, a little like Mr. Steinbrenner. After that, other people painted the stadium, but Miguel, Marco, Christopher, and Ed never took a paint can there again. They didn't stop tagging on *other* buildings in the Bronx, though.

I HAVE OFTEN WONDERED what happened during those twenty minutes that I was sitting in that holding cell. In the years that followed, the Boss and I never talked about it. I never asked, and he never brought it up. He had a brusque way of talking. He was not a man to waste words. He could use language as a weapon, but he often preferred silence.

Frequently I would tell Mr. Steinbrenner that I credited him with saving my life.

"That just isn't true. Your story was already written the day that I caught you outside the stadium," he would counter, vehemently disagreeing with me.

For a long time I thought back to his words. I guessed he meant that in spite of the fact that I wasted time and sometimes hung out with the wrong kids as a teenager, spray-painting, cutting school, and not caring about myself or others enough, I always returned to my passion: baseball. Even when I painted the stadium, he would point out, I hadn't written curse words or scrawled some other stupid stuff that other kids did. He would say he believed that I was showing my love for baseball, and the Yankees, by painting their logo. Out of pure affection, he would rationalize an act of vandalism that I could never justify.

After that June day in 1973, a date that soon became more important to me than my birthday, I'd overhear people ask Mr. Steinbrenner about the time he caught me. "Why did you give him a chance?" they would ask.

"There was just something about Ray that made me like him." Mr. Steinbrenner's voice would trail off. That's all he would ever say.

That summer, as June turned into the fireworks of July and then those beastly days of August, I started working at the stadium every day. In fact, there was absolutely nothing that would keep me away from it. No job or errand was beneath me—from emptying the trash to getting the players their favorite food and drink or mopping the clubhouse floor, washing the players' socks and underwear in just the way Mr. Sheehy had prescribed, or cleaning the clubhouse latrines. The stadium became the home I always longed for, a place I wanted to be connected with until my dying day. After a night game I'd collect the players' uniforms and give them to Mr. Sheehy and Nick—who had mellowed just a bit. They laundered the shirts and pants in the clubhouse washing machine in the laundry room. Exactingly instructed, I would make sure the uniforms were carefully hanging in the players' lockers by the next morning.

On those nights, I didn't finish until well past midnight. Since I would have to return the next day by 8:30 A.M. for an afternoon game, I would roll up a couple of towels and sleep on the clubhouse floor. As the moon glowed high above the bleachers, I felt that the stadium was all mine. A few times I woke up at three o'clock in the morning and walked, barefoot, out onto the field, the short soft grass tickling my feet. All was quiet, except for a number 4 train rumbling behind the scoreboard. The feelings of awe and wonder that I experienced the very first time I set foot in Yankee Stadium would never leave me.

The Legend of Billy the Kid
and a Sister Named Adele

"Never stop chasing your dream, never stop believing
in miracles," Billy advised me.

I LOVED MY job more than anything in the world—polishing shin guards, running out to get the guys hamburgers and hot dogs, picking up bats and equipment. There wasn't a single thing I wouldn't do for the team. But I still desperately wanted to be a professional baseball player in the summer of 1973. Afraid I would jinx my dream if I told anyone, I had mostly kept this longing to myself.

The other Yankee batboys weren't particularly interested in taking part in the game. More fans than players, they didn't seem to mind when I'd go out to the field early and take a few swings. Sometimes I'd take infield with the guys I worshiped—Thurman Munson, Gene Michael, and Bobby Murcer.

Back in Queens, I was the second baseman for the Springfield Gardens Eagles. Our tough, no-nonsense high school coach, Chuck Feinstein, became an enthusiastic kid when I told him about different Yankee players: what Roy White liked to eat before and after games or how Thurman Munson joked with some of the guys in the clubhouse.

A few times when I had to work at the stadium Chuck allowed me to miss practices. He asked me not to talk about my Yankee job with the other players, especially two of my friends, outfielder Jim Madorma and first baseman Raul Lopez, the only other Puerto Rican on the team. They were die-hard Yankee fans, and Chuck was worried that my teammates might be jealous. He also didn't want the other players to think I was receiving any kind of special treatment. (Ironically, Raul's son, Christian, would be the one to catch Derek Jeter's 3,000th hit, a home run to the left field stands, thirty-eight years later on July 9, 2011.)

That summer the Boss paid regular visits to the clubhouse to check on his players. "Where's the kid?" he'd ask Pete Sheehy.

Then the Boss would find me and say, "How ya doin'? Doin' all right? How they treatin' ya?"

Every so often he studied me while I took ground balls with the infielders. One day I overheard one of the coaches say, "Your protégé there, that kid, Ray—you know, he's not a bad shortstop, Mr. Steinbrenner."

The Boss pulled me aside. "So, kid, do you really want to become a pro ballplayer?"

"Yes, sir. I do."

"Well, go out there and do your thing. Don't be content just being a batboy," Mr. Steinbrenner said. "Maybe you'll play with us one day. Maybe you'll be our shortstop."

A couple of months after I started as a batboy, on a humid August day, I was so busy taking ground balls and focusing while the stars stepped up to the plate that I didn't realize I was being watched. The Detroit Tigers' manager, a former second baseman, was standing in front of the visiting team's dugout, watching as I leapt in the air to catch a high line drive and as I went deep into the hole to dig up a ground ball. When we finished batting practice I headed toward the Yankee dugout. As I was walking, Thurman shouted out, "Hey, Ray, stop starving yourself and go get something to eat." Then Thurman pointed to my Afro. "Oh, and if I ever get up the nerve to grow one of those, you're gonna have to find me a pick."

I smiled to myself. The guys were always teasing me about something. As I continued to walk across the field I came face-to-face with a hunched-over, wiry middle-aged guy. He had an unusually long giraffe-like neck, which made him look taller than he actually was.

"Hey, kid, I'm Billy Martin," he said in a high-pitched whisper.

Visiting managers weren't in the habit of introducing themselves to me. Now I stood in front of one of the greatest managers in baseball.

"I'm Ray, the batboy." I shook his hand.

"I see you've got pretty good hands." Billy smiled. "Are you familiar with our scout, Emil Gall?"

"Yes, sir. I've seen Mr. Gall at my PAL games."

"Why don't you go out to short and let me hit some to you?"

I glanced around at the Yankee bench. Guys were chewing tobacco and bubble gum, spitting, laughing, and swearing, not paying any attention to me or anything else that was going on out in the field. Yet I could tell that this was a highly unusual scenario: a Yankee batboy working with the opposing manager? I had to sweep the clubhouse floor, polish the cleats, and take the helmets, towels, and bats to the dugout for the game that would be played in a few hours. However, I knew Billy's reputation, not only as a rabble-rouser bad boy who was often irrational and hot-headed but also as a brilliant manager who had been one of the best infielders in baseball, earning him an MVP in the 1953 World Series.

Once I set myself up, he tossed a ball in the air and cracked a hard grounder while I played shortstop. Billy kept this up for a while, pausing every so often. "Let me show you how to handle a ball that's gonna handcuff you." He put his arm around my shoulder and shared his knowledge of the game. I was in a world of my own.

"So, kid, why are you playing second base on your high school team?" Billy asked.

"Because our shortstop, Calvin Bruton, is an All-City player," I said.

"Well, I don't know why you can't be a major league shortstop. You got the goods."

When we were finished, I started to hurry off the field, a little worried that the other batboys might say, "We know you like to play, Ray, but c'mon, we got work to do."

Billy called out, "We'll talk later, kid. I'll be checking you out," as I ran toward the dugout. I glanced back at Billy, that once combative player, leaning on his fungo bat, one hand on his hip. He was staring at me.

"Damn," I said to myself, "that's Billy the Kid."

ALMOST EXACTLY ONE YEAR later, I saw Billy again at Shea Stadium, where our team had moved while Yankee Stadium was being renovated. Wearing brown cowboy boots and jeans, and looking happy and confident, just like the Billy Martin I first met, he had become the manager of the Texas Rangers.

He greeted me warmly. "Hey, kid, good to see you again!"

I was working at Old-Timers' Day, which most people don't know actually began in 1939 to honor the Iron Horse, Lou Gehrig. I was nervous and excited about meeting many of the big stars like "Joltin' Joe" DiMaggio, the immortal slugger and fielder, who spent his whole career with the Yankees, and Casey Stengel, a former Mets manager, and the only Yankees manager to lead the team to five consecutive World Championships, from 1949 to 1953.

The main reason I hadn't slept in a week was the possibility that I'd be meeting Mickey Mantle. The thought crossed my mind that maybe, just maybe, he might recognize me from when I saw him up close, my very first time at Yankee Stadium in 1968. I still carried a Mickey Mantle baseball card in my wallet.

I wanted to look great for the Mick. So before I left my house for the stadium that morning, I made sure I put on a clean button-down shirt, carefully tucking it into a brand new pair of dungarees. The security guards smiled and waved as I walked into Shea Stadium through the executive office gate. I greeted a few of them by name and then checked my watch: 7:30 A.M. I was the first one from the Yankees to arrive. All was quiet as I entered the clubhouse and began to work. Pete Sheehy walked in a half hour later with his assistant, Nick.

"Well, Ray, what a surprise. You beat me here, and I see you've already set up the tables and chairs." Mr. Sheehy surveyed the room. "And the floor is so clean I could eat off of it."

I handed him a cup of coffee. Mr. Sheehy smiled at me and took a few sips. "Great coffee, Ray. Looks like you've taken care of almost everything."

As I put the clean uniforms that I had just taken out of the dryer into the players' lockers, I kept an eye out for old-timers arriving. Balding players with paunches, guys who hadn't seen each other since they were traded or, worse, sent down to the minors, began swapping stories and exchanging addresses. The clubhouse quickly became crowded and noisy, but I kept my focus on looking out for the Mick.

Mr. Sheehy handed me a couple of baseballs. "Casey's in the manager's office. Why don't you go in there and ask him to sign these balls for you?"

"Are you sure?" I asked.

"Yes, Ray. Go on," Mr. Sheehy said.

Nervously, I took the balls and ran into the manager's office. Mr. Stengel's back was to me. He was pulling up his pants. "Can you sign my balls?" I blurted out.

"You mind if I put mine away first?" he answered without turning around.

I hesitated, and then laughed nervously while the old man, whose nickname was "the Old Professor," tucked in his shirt and then signed the baseballs.

I darted back to the clubhouse. Mr. Sheehy stood there laughing. "How'd it go, Ray?"

I should have known that Pete Sheehy, one of the great practical jokers in the clubhouse, had just set me up. One of his favorite pranks was to quietly plant a coat hanger in the back of a player's pants while he was dressing.

"You're sick," I said, trying to hide my smile.

I went back to my chores, still waiting for my hero. Then I spotted him. He had arrived later than the others and was standing in the middle of the room, chatting with none other than "Chairman of the Board" Whitey Ford, that legendary Yankee southpaw, who was now our pitching coach. Mickey looked a little older than I remembered. His pale blond hair was just beginning to turn a little gray at the temples, but he still had that boyish smile, thick neck, and strapping build. He sat down and started shooting the breeze with Billy Martin, his old friend and Yankee teammate from the 1950s. I sat there in complete awe, staring as they laughed together.

"C'mon, I got more sleep than you did last night, for chrissakes. You only went to bed a few goddamned hours ago," Billy chided Mickey. I took a deep breath while working up the nerve to introduce myself to the Mick.

As I tentatively walked over to him, two current players, Tippy Martinez and Dave Pagan, rookie pitchers, asked if I would have Mickey sign their baseballs. I took those balls, plus my own, and waited for a slow point in the conversation, studying Mickey's lamb chop sideburns, so fashionable at the time, listening to him tell baseball stories in his Oklahoma drawl, and thinking how good he still looked in the Yankee pinstripes. Billy, noticing me out of the corner of his eye, smiled and shook my hand. Then I turned to Mickey and introduced myself.

"Well, how ya doin' today, kid?" He flashed me that famous smile. I wondered if he would be as funny as Mr. Stengel.

"Fine, sir." I smiled back and handed him two baseballs. Players first. *I'm actually standing here talking to Mickey Mantle!* After staring at the Mick for a minute, I dashed over to the players and presented them with their signed balls. Another rookie pitcher, Mike Wallace, asked me if I would get a ball signed for him. Back I went to Mickey.

This time he didn't look up at me but turned and spoke directly to Billy. "I'll tell ya, if I'da had a say in this, we'd be quittin' about now so I could take a nap." Mickey scrawled his signature on that ball, too, and I took it back to Mike.

Two more players approached me with balls, asking if I would get them signed. I hesitated because I still hadn't gotten around to asking Mickey to sign my own baseball, but I walked over to Mickey and stood in front of him.

"Get the fuck out of here with these fuckin' balls!" Mickey Mantle, *the* Mickey Mantle who was more of a hero to me than John Wayne or Gary Cooper, now glared at me. He slammed the balls onto the floor. They rolled under the table. Quickly I bent down to pick them up. I

wanted to hide under that table for the rest of my days. Since I couldn't, I scooped up the balls and stood in front of Mickey, frozen with fear.

"Go away! I toldja to get the fuck outta here!"

A hush seized the room. I felt like everyone was staring directly at me. They weren't used to seeing Mickey Mantle, amiable Mickey Mantle, angry, much less watching him holler. Squeezing my hands together and taking long, deep breaths, I was doing everything I could to keep from crying. This was my big moment in life. Mickey was supposed to be putting his arm around me and saying, "Sure, kid, anything for you."

Burning with shame, I stood there, motionless. Then I took off as fast as I could for the back room. Once I was inside, I started sobbing. Not just anyone, but Mickey Mantle, had cursed me out. I never even got a baseball signed for myself. I was livid with the players for sending me to Mickey three times. Couldn't they just get their baseballs signed themselves?

A few minutes later, I heard the door open. I expected it was someone from the team, coming in to calm me down. Too humiliated to turn around, I just stood there crying, me, an eighteen-year-old kid, bawling my eyes out.

Then I heard somebody laughing.

"I'm sorry, kid. You just look so funny back here weeping in front of that goddamned coffin." I looked up and saw Billy Martin, smiling broadly, his Yankee cap pushed back over his unruly hair, his hands thrust in his back pockets. I then realized that I was standing directly in front of a dark-colored wooden coffin, right there in Shea Stadium.

Billy, known for his gruffness, put his hand on my shoulder. "Talk to me, kid," he said. "I saw what happened out there. Look, kid, Mickey can be that way sometimes."

It wasn't until later that year that I learned, to my surprise, that Billy and Mickey had been drinking buddies for a long time, often getting into barroom brawls together. One of the players would eventually pull me aside and tell me that the two were bound by three common passions: booze, baseball, and broads.

"You gotta understand that a lot of people bother him," Billy went on. "Hey, I know those balls weren't for you. It happens every year. Players take advantage of the kids like you in the clubhouse, and they make you guys get their goddamned baseballs signed for them."

I wiped my eyes with the back of my sleeve. He continued, "But you gotta be a man. C'mon, shake it off and come back out. Okay? And, Ray, one more thing, ya gotta apologize to Mickey for disturbing him."

"Me apologize? But *I* didn't yell."

"I don't think you get it, Ray. Come on, kid. That's what a man would do. Now, go on. Wash up in the men's room and get your shit together. Come on, I'll take you back there. Be a man."

Billy looped his skinny arm around mine, and we walked back to where Mickey was sitting.

"Hey, Mick, look who I found. This is Ray, you know, the kid you just screamed at. Hey, he didn't mean it. He has something he wants to say to you." Billy gave me a gentle nudge toward Mickey.

I took a deep breath. "I'm, I'm sorry, Mr. Mantle. I didn't mean to bother you," I managed to blurt out. Just uttering those words made me feel better. I sure didn't want this lifelong hero to be mad at me.

"God damn, kid." Mickey broke into that stadium-wide grin. "Just how many fuckin' baseballs didja want me to sign?"

Billy stepped forward. "He's a good kid, Mickey." Then he mussed up my Afro. "I sure am glad I can't grow one of these," he said, and Mickey laughed.

I smiled as Billy said, "Now go on back to work, son."

Later, after Billy and I had become good friends, the film *A Bronx Tale* would be released and I would see myself as the young boy, Calogero, who idolized an older man named Sonny, who reminded me of Billy. Whenever Billy was at the stadium, he went out of his way to find me. Our deep love of baseball and our knowledge of the game brought us together. I would have been a batboy for free, just as Billy would have managed for no pay, that's how much we both cherished the game. We often laughed about that day with Mickey and the balls and how I never was able to get my own Mickey Mantle–autographed baseball. Eventually I learned that the coffin belonged to shortstop Fred Stanley, who had been storing it in the back room—who knows how he got it in there—so he could send it to his house and have a bar made from the wood.

We talked about how much I wanted to be drafted, too. Billy started regularly checking on my progress. "It's no bed of roses out there, but, kid, you're as talented as anyone. Ya gotta work your ass off and do your best." Billy urged me to get into the best shape I could and suggested that I box in the Golden Gloves, the tournament sponsored by the *New York Daily News* that my Uncle Hector had been in. Former heavyweight champion of the world Joe Louis was a Golden Gloves champion, as were Muhammad Ali and Sugar Ray Leonard. Boxing a few days a week helped me get in great shape. My hitting and fielding continued to improve. During my senior year the Springfield Gardens Eagles won the division championship, our first in years.

Billy and I soon discovered another common bond: both of our fathers had abandoned us when we were little, and both could get brutal after one drink too many. Jose Valdez, my father, an air force officer, immigrated to New York from Cuba in the 1940s when he was a kid. He was handsome, charismatic, and a good artist—he painted landscapes in oils—but he drank too much and carried on with women. When the song "Papa Was a Rolling Stone" was released by the Temptations in 1972, my mother often teased me, "This song reminds me of your biological father. I hope you don't turn out like him." She didn't realize how much it hurt me when she said that.

When I was little, my mother, Ventura Perez, or "Jenny" as everyone called her, had a job as a garment factory seamstress. She worked side by side with my grandmother Ramona and my great-grandmother, whom everyone called Mama, stitching clothing for fancy Fifth Avenue department stores. According to the family stories, my mother had returned home early from work one warm spring night in 1959, when I was three and a half, and caught my father messing around with another woman. I had been watching television when I heard my mother screaming and cursing. I crouched behind a chair and watched as she ran into the bedroom of our small Bronx apartment. She found his gun stashed in his bedside table drawer and charged him with it. "You're not getting away with this again!" she shrieked.

"*Puñeta*, you bitch!" He ran toward her, his gait uneven. Relatives told me he was drunk, just like he was on so many other evenings. I covered my eyes and ears, but I could tell that his words were slurred. I heard him slap her, and then I heard her muffled cries. I watched as he dragged her limp body into the front hall closet. He slammed the door.

Then he spotted me hiding behind the chair. "We're gettin' outta here." He grabbed me and led me into the bedroom, hauled a suitcase from under his bed, threw in some clothes from his drawer and mine, and carried me out the door.

"Quit your cryin', for chrissakes! She's okay, she's okay."

My father squeezed my hand so hard it hurt. He hailed a car that took us to the airport. On the way I fell into a deep sleep in the back-seat. When I woke up I was sitting in an airplane next to my father. *Where are we going? Will I ever see my mama again?*

"Your mother's no damn good," my father repeated over and over.

"That's not true." I shook my head. I wanted my mother. I wished I was sitting in her lap, listening to her sing Spanish songs before she tucked me into bed.

The propeller plane took us over the Atlantic Ocean until, six hours later, we landed in Cuba. My father took me to his relatives' home, a small house on a dirt lane in the country, an hour's drive from the airport. He briefly spoke in Spanish to the elderly couple that lived there, handed them a wad of cash, set my suitcase on the floor, and disappeared. During the following days there were no children in the house or in the neighborhood to play with, and at night I had a hard time falling asleep as the constant rain beat down on the tin roof.

"*Juega afuera.* Go play outside." The tired old woman pushed me out the back door. There, I'd sit in the dirt watching chickens pecking at each other. I soon discovered that pigs take the longest pees in the world and roll around in their own excrement. There was nothing else to do except think how much I missed my mother.

One morning, six months after my father had abandoned me, I heard knocking on the screen door. On the doorstep stood a woman wearing white shorts and a bright pink top.

I gasped.

Petite, with a short, stylish haircut, my mother had never looked more beautiful. I ran to her crying so hard I could barely breathe. My mother had finally saved enough money to come to Cuba and rescue me. If she had waited just a few months longer, when Castro took over, I might never have been able to leave. Even as a four-year-old boy, I knew it was a miracle.

I always thought that I had one of the roughest childhoods of anyone I knew. That's until I met Billy. He was named after his father, Alfred Manuel Martin, a Portuguese man from Hawaii, who had left the family when Billy was a baby. Billy didn't see his father again until he was fifteen years old. His dad, whom Billy looked exactly like, told him he wanted nothing to do with him. Billy never used Jr. after his name. In fact, until he entered grade school, he thought Billy was actually his given name. From the time he was a baby his Italian maternal grandmother called him "Bellissimo" (most beautiful), which became shortened to "Belli" and then transformed to Billy by his playmates.

I found myself telling Billy that I, too, had been born with a name I no longer went by. Roman Raymond Valdez, my given name, was changed to Roman Raymond Negron when I was eight years old and legally adopted by my stepfather. When my family moved from the violent streets of Brooklyn to the quiet middle-class neighborhood of Springfield Gardens, I reinvented myself with yet another new name: Ray, which sounded more like the Mikes, Eds, and Jimmys, kids from Irish or Italian backgrounds, that I was now going to school with.

Ironically, both Billy's mother and my mother were named Jenny. But Billy's mother wasn't as loving and kind as my mother was. Although they were both hardworking, strong, domineering mothers,

Billy's mother grew angry and bitter. Because Billy's likeness to his father was a constant reminder to her of the man who abandoned his family, she took her frustrations out on Billy.

"She was ridiculously hard on him," Billy's son, Billy Joe, once told me. In fact, Billy Joe said that his father never felt loved in his own home.

Billy became my soul mate, a father figure, even though he was all too maligned in the press. Eventually, after a couple of years, we became so close that we knew we spoke the same language. I was becoming his sounding board, almost like his psychiatrist. I listened as he let off steam.

Because of the encouragement from both Billy (who was still managing the Texas Rangers) and Mr. Steinbrenner, I slowly began to accept that I was becoming one of the best amateur players in New York in 1974. I was playing the position I had always yearned for, shortstop, on four different teams, Catholic Youth Organization, Police Athletic League, and two sandlots. When I wasn't working at the stadium or hanging out with my steady girlfriend, Barbara, I was practically living on the subway, traveling from Manhattan to Queens to Long Island to play baseball. Eventually several scouts started coming to my games, and my teammates were noticing.

"I don't know why you're so sure you're going to get drafted," one of the guys said. "You're too skinny and you've got a ways to go with your hitting."

"Hey, man, you aren't strong enough to be a pro," another said.

When I told Yankee outfielder Walt "No Neck" Williams about my teammates' comments, he started laughing. "Hell, I'm five foot six." Billy empathized, "People always told me the same thing, Ray. But I've got ten years in the major leagues. Don't let anybody say something like that without putting up a fight. Believe that you are the best. Believe you can make it."

His words were a huge boost. He helped me become more confident and hopeful that I might some day become a pro ballplayer. A few weeks into the 1974 season, the Boss had his scouting director, Pat Gillick, who would later become one of the great general managers in Toronto, Baltimore, Seattle, and Philadelphia and would be inducted into the Hall of Fame, take me into Flushing Meadows Park, the fields in back of Shea, and privately work with me on two different occasions.

"Mr. Steinbrenner asked me to give you a workout. He's got this illusion—I don't know because I've never seen you play—that you could become a professional ballplayer. I'm gonna throw batting practice to you, Ray, and see if you can play shortstop like he says."

Pat hit a bunch of ground balls, watching me carefully, repositioning me and telling me where my game was weak and strong. An Andy Griffith–type guy, down-to-earth, friendly, and outgoing, Pat later watched me work out with the team and left me with a confidence that I could most likely play pro ball.

"Having a powerful man like George Steinbrenner advocating for you is pretty great," Mr. Gillick said. "And even if you don't make it as a player, Mr. Steinbrenner will be there for you. I'm not sure of your relationship, but I can see he's taken a strong liking to you."

That season I was working out with the team, taking batting practice (BP). By mid-September the Yankees were in first place.

During a home game against the Baltimore Orioles I was playing shortstop during BP. Boog Powell, an Orioles first baseman, whacked a hard shot up the middle. I extended my glove, knowing I had no chance of getting it. But the ball took a bad hop and—as it often happens with many plays in baseball—it somehow landed in my glove. I followed through on the play the whole time. The Orioles' great defensive shortstop, Mark Belanger, was standing next to me.

"Wow!" he said. I smiled at him and triumphantly jogged off the field.

"Hey, batboy! What's your name?" a short, stubby, white-haired man wearing a plaid shirt called out to me. He was standing at the railing by the dugout, talking to a distinguished-looking man wearing khakis and a blazer.

"Ray, Ray Negron," I said. I walked over to him, unaware that he was the Pittsburgh Pirates' super scout, Howie Haak.

"You interested in playing baseball?" the other man asked. He was Pete Peterson, director of player development for the Pirates. They were at Shea Stadium that day because they were checking on the Yankees in case the two teams were to meet up in the World Series later.

"Okay, Ray, give me your number and we'll have our New York scout, Dutch Deutsch, call to give you a workout," Pete said. Dutch had signed Willie Randolph a couple of years before.

As I walked back to the clubhouse I said to myself, *This is my lucky day.*

Two days later Dutch called. "Meet me tomorrow at Alley Pond Park in Queens at 10:00 A.M."

When I arrived the next day Dutch introduced me to Fred Cambria, a major leaguer whose claim to fame was that he had beaten future Hall of Famer Tom Seaver of the Mets in a 2–1 pitchers' duel in 1970, Cambria's rookie season.

Dutch asked me to run a 60-yard dash, which I did in a good time, 6.8 seconds. Then he asked me to hit while Fred threw batting practice to me for an hour. I felt confident and comfortable as I smacked line drives all over the park.

After I fielded, Dutch walked over to me and said, "Your graceful style reminds me of Gene Michael's. I see you've patterned yourself after him." Indeed I had!

"I'm going to recommend that they draft you as high as possible." Dutch shook my hand. Another lucky day.

"YOU GOT DRAFTED in the second round!" It took me a moment to realize that the jubilant voice on the other end of the phone was my baseball coach, Chuck Feinstein. It was a cold day in that January of 1975 when New York City seemed as if it would slide into the ocean. I was still living in Queens, at my parents' house, after graduating from high school.

"Drafted?" I asked.

"Listen, Ray, I just found out that you were drafted by the Pittsburgh Pirates," he said. "The scouts have been in touch with me. So let me hang up now. I know Pittsburgh will be trying to call you any minute."

The Minnesota Twins' scout, Herb Stein, had called me the night before asking if I was interested in signing if I was drafted. Sure, I had replied, happy that the interest in me had reached this level. Now I hardly had time to process what Coach Feinstein had said before the phone rang again.

"Ray Negron? This is Murray Cook. I'm in player development with the Pittsburgh Pirates." This time the voice on the other end was quieter, more businesslike. "We want to congratulate you. You've been chosen in our second round of the draft. In a few days we'll be back in touch with more details."

The plan had always been that the Yankees would wait to select me, because they didn't expect me to go until the twentieth round or so. Although I was elated to be drafted by a major league team in the second round, I knew that Mr. Steinbrenner would be disappointed that it was another team that had drafted me. For a few minutes I also worried about leaving my girlfriend, as any teenager would.

My hesitations quickly disappeared after a day or so. All I could focus on was that my dreams of getting drafted had finally been realized. The same people who said I would never make it—those kids I played on sandlot teams with—were now slapping me on the back saying, "Yeah, Ray, I knew you could do it!" If I couldn't play with the Yankees, then why not wear the same uniform that Puerto Rico's greatest player and one of my heroes, Roberto Clemente, wore? The next day the title of a sports story in the *Long Island Press* read, YAN-KEE BATBOY PIRATED.

A few months after I was drafted, I was at Yankee spring training, getting ready to leave for the Pirates' training camp. I drove out of the parking lot just as Mr. Steinbrenner was pulling in.

"You didn't see me," he said as I got out of my car and went over to talk to him. Mr. Steinbrenner had recently been suspended for making illegal contributions to Richard Nixon's reelection campaign.

"We didn't evaluate you properly," Mr. Steinbrenner continued. "If the Pirates chose you in the second round, we didn't do our job, Ray." I didn't like disappointing the Boss, but I felt proud that Mr. Steinbrenner had wanted me to play with the Yankees so badly.

Billy called me from Texas. "Great news, kid." He told me that although he was sure the Yankees were sad to see me go, he thought that I would perform well. "Keep doing what you've been doing in batting practice," he said. "You'll be big."

In the spring my parents drove me to the airport. A car weighed down with my sisters, my grandparents, and my girlfriend, Barbara, followed us. You would have thought I was going off to war. My parents fought to carry my bags through the airport.

When we arrived at the gate everyone started crying. Barbara hugged me. The romantic hit song that year was "My Eyes Adore You." I could feel every word to that song as Barbara kissed me and told me that she loved me for the very first time. I was full of high hopes as I headed to Bradenton, Florida, to play for the Pirates.

In a matter of days I soon realized that being in the Rookie League was similar to going to summer camp. In Bradenton, I was just one of a bunch of nondescript guys, the Bradenton Pirates, playing in a small complex, traveling to cities that seemed to suit their own minor league status. I had expected large crowds at the stadium, reporters chasing after me, and pictured myself dining in fancy restaurants, not Burger King or Denny's. The fan base in Bradenton was nonexistent—a hundred fans tops. Florida was so hot and humid that it made me long for August in the Bronx. In between practices and games my teammates and I hung out at the nearby mall and checked out the teenage girls, who were probably playing hooky from school. Sometimes after a game we would sit in the players' lounge and watch the Yankees game. Inevitably one of the guys would turn to me and ask, "Is Murcer really a good guy? How does Munson treat you?" At Yankee Stadium, the superstars had treated me just like a player.

My God, I'd say to myself, *I wish I was back in New York*.

In mid-August, after we had just finished playing the Texas Rangers' farm team, I was changing in the locker room when Woody Huyke, our manager, tapped me on the shoulder.

"Come into my office," he said. I followed him into a small, cluttered room at the end of the clubhouse.

"Sit down, Ray." Woody closed the door. "Things just haven't worked out," he stammered. "Unfortunately, uh, I'm going to have to, um, give you your unconditional release." I felt dizzy as I stood there taking in his words. I thought back to how I had clutched almost from the moment I arrived in Bradenton. The scouting report on me was fairly simple: great glove, no bat.

I just couldn't hit. In fact, my batting average was a pathetic .143. Every time I saw a curve ball, I realized I wasn't going to be a major league star. Perhaps it was my youthful optimism, but despite my poor performance, I didn't expect to be released so soon.

Feeling numb, I packed up my bags and headed back to Queens. As I sat on the plane waiting to take off, I reflected on the life of a ballplayer. Certainly it was a million-to-one shot to make it to the pros. The bottom line was I had my shot and I just didn't do it. I wasn't sure that I had the strength it took to keep pursuing my dream. This time there was no fanfare at the airport as I collected my suitcase at the baggage claim and hailed a cab to my parents' house. A few days later I passed a newsstand on the corner. I picked up the *Long Island Press*. This time the small headline of an article read, YANKS BATBOY THROWN OVERBOARD.

A letter was waiting for me, inviting me to play for the Texas Rangers' A club. I knew Billy must have put in a good word to the Rangers about me. He had come back to the Yankees as their manager in early August 1975 and been following my progress. Instead of being happy, I was jittery and apathetic and couldn't sleep. I didn't want to embarrass Billy, Mr. Steinbrenner, my parents, or myself any further. I didn't leave the house or take any phone calls for a few days. Everyone, especially the Boss, had had such high expectations for me.

I was too humiliated to show my face. But Yankees second baseman Sandy Alomar somehow managed to get my phone number for Billy.

"Get your ass down here first thing tomorrow, Ray," Billy said when he called me. "I've got something for you to do." He asked me to come back and finish the season as a batting practice pitcher and all-around fill-in guy.

I knew I had to make a choice: go to the Rangers' farm team as a player or stay with the Yankees. I was afraid to gamble, so I chose the Yankees. At that point, as a soon-to-be twenty-year-old, I wanted something steady in my life. Billy and I sat in his office for hour-long stretches while he explained the many ways for me to use my talents within the organization.

In the process he revealed something more about himself: how after he graduated from high school he had hoped to be signed by a Pacific Coast League team. "I was just too small and thin. No one wanted me," he said, twirling slowly around in his office chair, his eyes fixed on his hands.

"Then when an Oakland Oaks farm team finally hired me they sent me three hundred bucks to buy good clothes and a suitcase. A few weeks later I was playin' in the Arizona-Texas League at Phoenix." I later found out that Billy had hit .392 and batted in 174 runs in 130 games while he was in Phoenix. At third base he led the league in the fewest errors and the most putouts and assists. This won him a spot with the Oaks, where he played for Casey Stengel, who immediately loved Billy for his direct way and toughness.

"Casey and I were made for each other," Billy told me.

Whenever I expressed doubts about myself and where I was going, Billy would say, "Don't worry, Ray, I would have gone back and lived with my mother, too. Hell, you're a nicer kid than I ever was. Just don't go getting into the kind of goddamned trouble I was in as a kid. Even if I'm not with the Yankees, you can always go wherever I go. Remember you're a baseball man."

When Billy said things like that, I wished we were related. I really envied his eleven-year-old son, Billy Joe, who often came to home games. Like his dad, Billy Joe wore the number 1 and also played second base on his Little League team. Sometimes when we were on the road, Billy would bring him along and talk to him about the players. He was soft and sweet with Billy Joe, and the two could watch baseball together for hours. Nothing meant more to Billy than his son. Watching them laugh together made me wish that my loving stepfather wasn't so busy running the bodega. But I was comforted that Billy seemed to have all the time in the world for me. Here was a man who truly understood me. I made my decision: I was staying with Billy and Mr. Steinbrenner.

As I mentioned, Billy and I had a private language that defied everyone else. His dark, penetrating eyes always revealed his deepest feelings. He'd shoot me a look and I'd know exactly what he was thinking. While he and I walked around the clubhouse we'd sometimes impersonate stadium workers, players, batboys—even Mr. Steinbrenner wasn't off-limits for Billy.

"I'm the boss here, Billy. If I want to call you when you're in the dugout, well, that's just what I'm going to do. I can do whatever I goddamned please." Billy's imitation of Mr. Steinbrenner was not only pitch-perfect but also taboo, of course.

When I looked surprised, Billy would say sarcastically, "Oh, Ray, I'm so sorry I forgot that the Boss is your big buddy."

An excellent storyteller, Billy liked to entertain me with baseball history and wild tales of the times he and Mickey played and traveled together. Billy was infatuated by the Wild West and loved recounting stories of the Civil War, Jesse James, and the real Billy the Kid. We had that in common, too, since Westerns were my favorite shows on television.

In fact, Billy was the first person to educate me about the injustices committed against the American Indian. "Nah, kid, you got it all wrong. The cowboys weren't always the good guys. Some of them were shitheads, too. Understand, son, they stole the land from the Indians."

Billy seemed to know something about almost every subject, but mostly he knew the game of baseball inside and out. He had developed a reputation as a genius, one who could turn any team he managed into a winning ball club. The players and I would watch Billy during games. Looking like he was miles away, Billy would get an intense, almost crazy look in his eyes when he whispered to us that a player was ready to steal.

"Look how weak that outfielder is. Watch how he throws the ball back from the outfield," he would whisper to me. "Now, check out that manager in the dugout over there. I can see he's giving his signs." Billy could pick off signs better than anyone else, mostly because he learned the nuances of the game from the grand master of them all, Casey Stengel. During a game he was always three innings ahead of the rest of us. He was a card shark, only with baseball.

The following year, 1976, when I was twenty, I came back to the

Yankees as a full-time batting practice pitcher, still hoping—yes, some dreams never die—that I might get another chance at playing for the team. Even if I didn't, I was in high spirits as long as I was around Billy and the Boss.

After a two-year absence, the team was happy to be home in our newly renovated stadium. I never felt I belonged more to the Yankees than I did that season. We started off strong and were 10–3 in April. By mid-June we had a 7-game lead, and by the end of July our lead in the division swelled to 14½ games. Guys like Nettles, Mickey Rivers, and Munson, who was voted MVP at the end of the season, had become a new Murderers' Row. Billy was in complete control of our coaching staff. Three of our coaches—Bob Lemon, Dick Howser, and Gene Michael—would later become managers, a tribute to Billy himself.

Two other coaches on Billy's staff especially influenced me that year and for many years to come. Elston Howard, the first black Yankee and first black coach in the American League, didn't let that security manager, Frank Wilson, push me around. Once when the Boss was away, Wilson made me go over to the visitors' locker room, where the work was harder and you weren't allowed on the field with the players.

"Where's Ray?" Elston asked Pete Sheehy.

"Wilson took him over to the other side," Pete said.

Elston marched over to the visitors' locker room and saw me standing with Wilson.

"He's supposed to be on our side," Elston said.

"No, I need him over here," Mr. Wilson said with a smirk.

"Come back with me, " Elston said and then turned to Wilson. "If I have to place a call to Mr. Steinbrenner and let him know what's going on, I will."

Mr. Wilson stared straight at me as Elston and I walked back to the Yankee clubhouse.

"From now on, you let me know when the big guy isn't around," Elston said. "I'll try and look out for you that much more. There's not a whole lot of difference between what I see you've gone through with some people around here and what I've had to go through over the years. I hope you learn from this. You gotta stand up for what's right, Ray."

I liked watching Yogi Berra, one of the best and smartest people I've ever known in baseball, tease Elston, whose locker was next to his.

Yogi, quick with his quips, would crack Elston up. "You can observe a lot by just watching," he'd say. Or, "If you don't know where you're going you'll wind up somewhere else." The two were such good friends that it was hard for me to believe that Elston once took the catcher's position over from Yogi. Their solidarity taught me how friends were supposed to treat each other.

The whole season was, despite the best efforts of the press, smooth. No static. Mr. Steinbrenner even arranged for the legendary film star James Cagney, whose role in *Yankee Doodle Dandy* was a Boss favorite, to sit in his wheelchair by the clubhouse door to meet the players and give some of them pep talks. Mickey Rivers, our amusing center fielder, danced in front of Mr. Cagney, saying how much he liked his footwork in the film.

"Good job, Thurman. I like how you get the job done. You're a fine example to us all." Mr. Cagney shook Thurman's hand after a game.

Looking back, it may have been the most noncontroversial team I was ever a part of. We cruised toward the division title that sweltering August, and as the chill of autumn set in on October 14, our usually well-ordered stadium turned into an unruly and wild carnival ground during Game 5 of the playoffs.

Around midnight during the bottom of the ninth, Chris Chambliss, our twenty-seven-year-old first baseman, smacked the first pitch from the Kansas City Royals reliever, Mark Littell, just over the right center field fence. Somehow Chris managed to reach second base as he tore through the masses of fans who were pouring out onto the field. At third base the frenzied crowd knocked him down. He managed to pick himself up and plow through the throngs toward home plate, but he was swarmed by so many fans in that area that he ran straight to the dugout and into the clubhouse, where corks were popping and champagne was spraying. Word started spreading in the clubhouse that Chris had never touched home plate. He quickly found two cops and asked them to walk him back there. Flanked by the officers, Chris walked back onto the field, which was now littered with beer bottles, and stood in a three-foot hole where the fans had dug up the plate. Now that nightmare, those twelve long years since our last pennant win, when we were anything but triumphant, was behind us.

The Boss, in the middle of the rowdy clubhouse celebration, must have hugged me half a dozen times that night. Earlier in the evening I watched as he stepped into his office, took off his signature navy blue sport jacket and gray pleated slacks, and traded them for a cheap plaid polyester suit, knowing his clothes were going to be soaked in the merriment. Only hours later he was as boisterous and giddy as a kid who had just hit his first home run. This was the Boss's first great Yankee win. He paraded Billy around the clubhouse like a show dog.

"We're gonna fill this goddamned ballpark with fans next year!" he shouted and mussed up Billy's hair. Then the Boss disappeared for an instant, returning to the clubhouse arm in arm with one of the biggest movie stars of all time, Cary Grant. I watched as the Boss led the most glamorous male star of his era—a man tall, dark, and even more handsome in person than on the screen—to the back lounge, off-limits to the press. The players jumped up and down and sprayed each other with champagne. As if on cue they chanted, "Juday, Juday, Juday!"—an expression then widely associated with the movie star. Although I've asked people over the years, I can't find anyone who is completely sure why those words are still attributed to Cary Grant. Some think it is a reference to his friend Judy Garland.

Rejoining the team in the lounge, I reached out and touched Cary's back, just to see if he was indeed real.

"This is one of your biggest fans," Mr. Steinbrenner said, introducing me to the film star. I handed Mr. Grant a towel to mop off the champagne that soaked his shirt and elegant silk tie.

"Thank you," the star said, just as graciously as he had in my favorite Cary Grant movie, *That Touch of Mink*. In that film he and Doris Day watch a Yankees game while sitting in the dugout next to Mickey Mantle, Roger Maris, and Yogi Berra, all playing themselves. He thanked me again before walking over to embrace Billy.

Everyone in the packed chaotic clubhouse was in love with Billy that night, from Mayor Abraham Beame, who helped drench Billy in champagne, to Governor Hugh Carey, who posed for pictures with our manager. Billy, in fine spirits, would say in between beer and champagne drenchings, "This is our first. Oh, what a win!"

Mr. Steinbrenner chimed in, "Yep, it's our biggie, Billy, this win is our biggie." They were like two little kids.

Then the Boss turned to me and said, "Ray, you were a big part of this."

"Hey, buddy," Billy said, "even if you were Italian, I couldn't love you any more."

This was the Boss and Billy the Kid that I had come to love. I wanted them to stay that way forever.

"I NEED THAT ONE spark plug to get us to the Promised Land," I heard the Boss say a few days after we were swept in the World Series by the Cincinnati Reds. He had been going after Reggie Jackson for months and had been almost magnetically drawn to him as to no other player. He was ecstatic in late November to announce to the New York press that he had finally signed the superstar.

This was in the first few years after the Curt Flood decision, the beginning of free agents—players whose contracts with a team had expired were now eligible to sign with another team—and the media was covering Reggie's every move, from the fancy restaurants he frequented to the cars he drove to the women he squired around. The Boss, not a man used to losing, desperately wanted to win a World Championship. It had been far too long a drought—our last World Series win was in 1962—and he believed that Reggie was our ticket to victory. Mr. Steinbrenner and several players were overjoyed about Reggie's presence.

As excited as everyone was with Reggie's arrival from the Baltimore Orioles, however, it seemed that there was going to be serious trouble between him and Billy. When Billy managed the Tigers in 1972, Reggie's A's beat them in the playoffs. Reggie was once quoted in the press as saying, "I hate Billy, but if I played for him, I'd probably love him." From the time Reggie arrived, it was impossible for the two men to be in the same room without some kind of sparring going on. Billy was becoming more volatile by the minute.

One night after a spring training game in 1977, some of the players and I went to the bar to celebrate a win over the Mets at the Bay Harbor Inn, a large hotel in Tampa where the team was staying. Mr. Steinbrenner had purchased the hotel earlier that year. Although I didn't drink, I was always there when the guys asked me to go out with them. We were sitting at the bar, looking out to the heated swimming pool, when Billy walked in. It was about 1:00 A.M. He seemed happy that we had won the game that night. He and I spoke about how even though it was spring training, Mr. Steinbrenner was always psyched when we beat the Mets. Then Dock Ellis, a popular right-handed pitcher, grabbed Billy's sleeve. "Hey, Billy, this bartender won't serve us any more drinks."

With lightning speed Billy leaned over the bar, grabbed the hapless guy by the collar, and screamed, "What the hell is wrong with you? Why aren't you taking care of my men?"

Dock and I instinctively grabbed Billy's arms, wanting him to stop.

"You son of a bitch," Billy continued, cursing the bartender, wrestling from our grip. At that moment, I realized that despite his small stature, he was powerfully strong.

During our talks, Billy often brought up his childhood, and for a second, as he unleashed his anger, I saw a glimpse of him as a poor, scrappy kid, fending off street gangs in his tough, racially mixed, Depression-era West Berkeley neighborhood. I finally stood up and left the bar. I wandered out to the reception area, where tourists were checking in. "Welcome to sunny Florida," I heard the man behind the desk say. I could still faintly make out Billy cursing as I walked back to my room at the inn.

A few weeks later, when the team had returned to New York, Dick

Howser said, "Ray, Billy hasn't shown up for batting practice yet." I left the field to find him and was surprised to see him sitting in his office, staring at the floor.

"Billy, you okay?"

"Yeah, yeah, I'll be all right, kid." He stood up and walked slowly toward the field. I could smell booze on his breath. I didn't know what to do or what to say to him. We got through batting practice that day without an incident, but I was sweating the whole time, worried that Billy would explode.

Something had dramatically changed from one year to the next. I doubted it was Reggie's presence, but by the end of the season, no one was surprised if Billy didn't show up for batting practices. At that point some of the players were talking about his past problems with alcohol. Everybody knew about the time at the Copacabana nightclub in May 1957 when Billy celebrated his infamous twenty-ninth birthday with Yogi, Hank Bauer, and Mickey, among many others. They were all sitting at a table in the middle of the room, drinking and carrying on, when some rowdy guys came in and started insulting the performer and their friend, Sammy Davis Jr., with slurs you wouldn't dare say in polite company. When punches started flying, the media was all over the story. The Yankee general manager, George Weiss, traded Billy, who had been trying to defend Sammy, to Kansas City a month later. From what I was told by people who were there, it seemed that Billy was unfairly blamed for starting the brawl. It sounded as if Hank Bauer had started that fight, but Billy took the fall because the general manager wasn't a fan of his.

Then there was the time when Billy was playing for the Reds in 1960 and got into a fight with Chicago Cubs pitcher Jim Brewer. Billy was up at bat and thought that Jim pitched too close to his body. So he charged the mound, punched Jim, and broke his jaw.

The fights and tantrums had continued well into that decade. I tried not to listen to the players' stories of Billy's past rampages. Sometimes I even refused to believe them. Billy had always been decent, so good to me and to many others.

He had a swagger that black and Latino players especially liked. I felt proud that the 1977 Yankee team was diverse, a luxury that Elston Howard hadn't experienced. One June afternoon a sportscaster Billy knew from the Texas Rangers strolled into the clubhouse and walked into Billy's office without knocking. I was sitting on the floor, polishing helmets while chatting with Billy, when the man burst into the office.

"You know, Billy, I never thought I'd see the day when the New York Yankees would have so many coons and spics on it," the guy hollered.

Billy, his glasses halfway down his nose, sat quietly at his desk without flinching and studied that night's lineup card. After a minute or so Billy looked up and stared at his old acquaintance. "Give me a team with twenty-five coons and spics on it, as you call them," he shouted. "If they can play baseball, then they're gonna play for me. Now, get the hell out of my office!"

"C'mon, Billy, don't you be that way."

"No, don't *you* be that way." Billy stood up and moved toward the guy.

I sat, I thought inconspicuously, on the floor in silence, hoping the man wouldn't notice me, a scrawny kid with a big bad Afro. But I didn't have to worry—the guy bolted out of Billy's office so fast, he didn't so much as glance at me.

Billy looked down at me and said, "It's 1977 and that shit is still going on. I'm sorry, kid." Then he picked up his lineup card and kept working on it, as if nothing had happened.

After that incident I decided to reach out to Billy. I simply tried to listen as he confided his frustrations with the Boss and some of the players. I was honored that Billy would talk to me about his deepest feelings.

Once, feeling somewhat brave, I said, "Why'd you pick that fight with Brewer?"

"The motherfucker deserved an ass whipping. So I gave him one."

"Well, when you argue with Mr. Steinbrenner, I get nervous," I told him.

"Why?"

"I don't want you to turn around and hit him, Billy."

"Hey, kid, some guys deserve ass whippings, but the Boss ain't one of 'em. You never know, Ray, maybe he could whip *my* ass."

We both laughed. Billy had his ups and downs, but I wanted nothing more than to be able to help him.

One incident from the 1976 season had always stuck in my mind. During that summer, I was pitching a round of batting practice when Rick Dempsey suddenly threw a bat at me. "You can't pitch and you're throwing off everyone's timing! You should never be out here pitching again," he shouted. Dempsey went straight to the dugout and cursed me out to Billy.

The next day when I went into the clubhouse, Pete Sheehy, acting as the messenger, said, "Ray, don't put on that uniform. You gotta go see Billy."

I walked into Billy's office. Dressed in his pinstripes, he was sitting there with the Boss, who was wearing his usual jacket and tie. When Billy looked at me, it was the first time I couldn't fully read his expression. I guessed I was about to be fired.

"I told Mr. Steinbrenner that you can't throw batting practice," he said. "In fact, you are horse shit. Take over, George."

Mr. Steinbrenner looked me up and down. "If Billy says you're horse shit, then you're horse shit. So you won't be pitching batting practice anymore." I turned to leave, deeply distraught, but knowing that Billy and the Boss were probably right.

Billy stopped me and pointed to a pile of boxes in the corner. His tone softened. "Hey, Ray, Mr. Steinbrenner and I talked, and we want you to learn to use this video equipment. You can start taking films of the pitchers and hitters. It's an old football trick from when the Boss was coaching football. You film the guys and then you show it to them. That way they can see what they're doing right and what they're doing wrong."

I was ambivalent at first, but with Billy and the Boss's encouragement, I taught myself how to use the equipment and quickly began approaching players who were slumping. I filmed their playing and then showed them the tapes the next day. Lou Piniella, one of the better hitters on the team and my number-one student, loved watching himself on tape.

"So, Ray, shouldn't my hands go back more on the bat? Should I be standing further away from the plate?" Even though Lou knew the answers to his questions after watching the video, I appreciated that he would still ask my opinion. I was always grateful that Lou took my job seriously, because he got the other guys to take notice of what I was doing, too. If I couldn't pitch batting practice, at least I could help the players get better. I felt useful again as the Yankees became the videotape innovators in Major League Baseball.

I SURE WISHED I had been the one behind that camera on June 18, 1977, when the feud between Billy and Reggie erupted in a nationally televised game at Fenway Park. The day before, we had headed for Boston to play a three-game series. A few weeks earlier we had been tied with the Red Sox for second place. Now we were in first, but that particular night we lost.

On the next night, Jim Rice, Boston's awesome slugger, hit a fly ball, which landed right in front of Reggie. Jim hustled and made it to second base. But Reggie had appeared to be in no hurry to make the play.

"Shit, what's he doing out there?" I heard Billy yell. He thought that Reggie's throw back to the infield appeared to be halfhearted. "I'm gonna get that son of a bitch," Billy said to Yogi.

The next thing I knew, Billy sent out Paul Blair to replace Reggie in right field.

As Paul jogged out to the field, Reggie looked at him quizzically. He then pointed to himself and said, "Me?"

Taking a player out in the middle of an inning is almost unheard of.

"You'll have to talk to Billy about it," Paul said, taking Reggie's position on the field.

Reggie ran back to the dugout and stood on the top step as he screamed to Billy, "What the fuck did I do?"

"Hey, you don't hustle, you don't play for me," Billy, the ultimate of baseball hustlers, responded. I had been sitting next to Billy, but when

Reggie took his glasses off and tossed them onto the bench I was sure a fistfight was going to break out. I scrambled to the other side of the dugout, wanting nothing to do with their conflict.

"What are you, crazy—humiliating me on television—in front of fifty million people?" Reggie continued down the steps to the dugout.

"I don't give a shit." Billy turned around to walk away. "When you decide you want to play right field, I'll put you back in. Not until then. I treat every player the same and you know it."

Billy whirled around and charged Reggie. "I ought to kick your ass!" Elston Howard, now our first base coach, tried to separate the two.

"Who do you think you are talking to, old man? Don't you ever show me up again, motherfucka!" Reggie screamed.

"*Old man?*" Billy was eighteen years older, a few inches shorter, and about forty pounds lighter than Reggie. Still, he could be ferocious.

"I'm gonna show you an old man! I'm gonna break your fuckin' ass." He lunged at Reggie but was held back once again by Elston and Yogi.

Like a rocket coming at us at rapid speed, I could see a television camera zooming into the dugout. I grabbed a towel from the bench, plunked myself in front of the camera, and threw it over the lens as fast as I could.

"I'll crack you in the head if you keep on shooting!" I yelled to the cameraman. I wasn't sure if Billy and Reggie were going to come to blows, but if they were, I sure as hell didn't want this to go on nationwide television. Most of all I didn't want the Boss to see what was happening.

Elston grabbed me. "No, no, no, you're gonna get in trouble." He pushed me down to the bench.

What I didn't notice was another camera, this one in center field. The cameraman was recording the whole damn confrontation, yes, just as Reggie had said, in front of fifty million people. Later I would learn that broadcaster Joe Garagiola's voice, as if taking the mantle from Phil Rizzuto, had been blasting over the airwaves—"There they go!"

Reggie yelled, "Billy, I can never please you. You don't like me. You don't think I can play ball. You never have."

Billy was constantly reminding Reggie that his playing had yet to match his bravado. "So far you've only hit twelve home runs and you've struck out forty-seven times this year," I had heard him say to Reggie in mid-June.

"You gotta get outta the dugout," I shouted over to Reggie, worried that there might be more fighting. He quickly got up and left. The rest of the game was a complete blur. All I remember is that when the game was over the players ran off the field, dejected. We lost 10–4.

"What the hell is going to happen next?" I heard Thurman say. Catcher Fran Healy, pitcher Mike Torrez, and I ran ahead to the clubhouse. Reggie was holed up in the trainer's room, off-limits to the media. He motioned for us to come in.

"Come on, Reggie," I said. "Let's go back to the players' parking lot. There'll be a cop there and he'll get you a cab." Reggie left by himself and walked a couple of miles back to the hotel.

I felt particularly strange. One of them was my mentor; the other was becoming a close friend. No one on the team was caught more in the middle. The next day, a Sunday, I woke up at eight and headed for the ballpark. Billy arrived shortly after I did, around nine thirty. "Let's take a walk," he said. Billy looked like he had slept in his clothes. We left the clubhouse and walked to the dugout.

"This thing really turned crazy last night," Billy said. "What do you think happened, Ray?"

"Reggie did *not* see that ball. He wasn't loafing on that ball like you thought." Billy listened to me but didn't respond.

At that time, I think, Billy was looking for any reason he could find to take Reggie out. The *Boston Globe*'s front-page story that morning read, "Neither man backed down." Beside the article was a picture of Reggie and Billy going at it while I covered the television camera with a towel. The headlines in the papers screamed YANKEE COVERUP and BILLY JAX CLASH. The extensive television coverage chronicling the incident didn't help matters either. The relationship between Reggie and Billy seemed to be permanently poisoned.

The antagonism would continue into the next year. In July 1978, Reggie bunted a foul on the third strike for an automatic out. This was against Billy's orders. Outraged, Billy grabbed a radio and then a beer bottle and smashed them against his office wall. He suspended Reggie indefinitely. When Reggie returned to the team five days later, he didn't express one bit of remorse about defying Billy's orders.

Infuriated, Billy told reporters, "They deserve each other. One's a born liar [Reggie] and the other is convicted." He was referring to the Boss's illegal donations to Nixon's 1972 campaign.

The tension was so thick that it couldn't possibly last. The fans had become more obsessed with the Billy-Reggie row than with the game itself. On July 24, 1978, Billy finally resigned under pressure from Mr. Steinbrenner. Highly emotional, Billy read from a prepared statement apologizing to the fans and stating that he had to resign due to health issues. Who knew that Mr. Steinbrenner would secretly call Billy the next morning and rehire him for the 1980 season. In the meantime, Bob Lemon, a mild-mannered guy, who had been the Chicago White Sox manager, was named the Yankees manager. But five days later at Old-Timers' Day, Mr. Steinbrenner, fond of surprises, snuck Billy into

Yankee Stadium through a tunnel near the batting cage. I was surprised when I saw Billy standing there in uniform, flanked by a couple of New York City police officers.

Famed announcer Bob Sheppard's distinguished voice reverberated throughout the stadium during the afternoon of July 29. "The manager for 1980, and hopefully for many years to come . . . number one . . . Billy Martin." The 46,711 fans were stunned at first, but then the ovation was so loud for Billy that even Joe DiMaggio felt upstaged. Billy was elated with his reception.

But to backtrack a bit. The day after Billy had resigned I was driving over the 59th Street Bridge toward Queens. At the end of the bridge I impulsively made a U-turn and drove back over the bridge and south on the FDR toward New Jersey, where I knew Billy was staying. I just had to check up on him and make sure he was okay. Billy greeted me at the front door.

"Come on in," he said. He looked drained. I walked into the living room of his rented town house and sat with him for almost three hours. The Yankees were playing the Kansas City Royals, but we switched the television to a National Geographic show. Billy cried the whole time, saying over and over, "I don't hate Reggie." I knew the two of them would never be friends, but I was hoping that someday they might be able to at least get along.

"You know, you, Reggie, and Mr. Steinbrenner are a lot more alike than you think," I told Billy.

"How so?"

"Well, you all have big egos." I chuckled. "You guys are compassionate, especially where kids are concerned. And you three are all great to me." I put my arm around Billy.

Reggie respected Billy's talents on the field. He was in awe of Billy's ability to be three innings ahead of the game. I tried to tell Billy that. But I knew there was a much bigger problem: Billy was at war with himself, and he was losing the battle. In his heart, I think, he knew that, too. While Billy was great at managing players, he couldn't manage his own life. As I drove home that night, everything began to make sense: *Billy may have serious drinking problems, and I need to help him out.*

A FEW DAYS AFTER the Yankees defeated the Los Angeles Dodgers in six games to win the World Series in 1978, I received a phone call. I recognized the raspy whisper immediately. "Hey, Ray. Long time," he said. Hearing Billy's voice, I found myself wishing that he had been there to receive the World Series trophy instead of Bob Lemon. I started to tell Billy that, but he cut me off.

"I'm going to open a Western wear shop on Madison Avenue. How'd you like to work for me part-time?" Billy asked. I hesitated because I only wanted to work at the store if Billy was going to be there, working alongside me. I told him that.

"Of course, kid, it's my store," Billy replied. "Come on over the week before Christmas and I'll put you to work." I had deeply missed Billy. Now I was excited to be around him again. I thought the store would be good for him. He had always loved his Western wear and his cowboy boots—I don't think I ever saw him in anything other than cowboy boots—and that style was all the rage. In fact, the store would be a good way to keep Billy out of trouble and lift his spirits. I was sure that if Billy was there at the store the fans would come by in droves.

When I showed up the first day, an elderly man greeted me, introducing himself as the store manager. "I'm supposed to show you what to do around here," he said.

"Is Billy coming in?" I asked him.

"He might stop in later on." He shrugged. The manager led me to the basement, where I listened to pop versions of "Jingle Bells" and "Santa Claus Is Coming to Town" blasting from the store's stereo system while I stuck price tags on boots. I waited all afternoon for Billy, but he never showed up.

The next day, the manager taught me how to take inventory. Again I asked if Billy was coming to the store, and again he said, "Maybe later this afternoon." But by 6:00 P.M. Billy had not arrived. The same thing happened on the third day, and I finally went to the manager and quit. If Billy didn't care, why should I?

"I need to talk to Billy," I said to the manager. He called Billy at the Westbury Hotel, right across the street from the store, where he was staying at the time.

"What, you're quitting?" Billy asked. His voice had a cheerful ring.

"I wanted to work with you," I told him. "Billy, I don't care about the money. I just wanted to be there with you." In the perfect world I imagined, Billy and I would spend that winter sticking price tags on the bottom of boots. We'd become salespeople together, helping the customers and having some fun.

No, we don't have the blue lizard boots in stock, ma'am, but I'll be happy to order them, and the pink ones for your husband, too. In my mind, Billy and I would continue the close relationship, mimicking those fancy people on the very best stretch of Madison Avenue, having the great time that we had had at the Yankees.

"Meet me outside my hotel in fifteen minutes," Billy barked. "We'll go get something to eat together." We hailed a taxi and headed for

Patsy's, a famous Italian joint in the West 50s. Billy turned to me in the taxi and said, "I'm going to be traveling a lot, and I won't be at the store much." Staring out the window, I sat next to him in silence, trying to hold back tears.

The restaurant was crowded and noisy. We stood in the doorway while several waiters dressed in white jackets and black bow ties bustled about taking orders and chatting with the customers.

"Wait here a minute," Billy whispered to me. He disappeared into a private room in the back. A few minutes later, the maître d' told me to follow him. We walked through the busy restaurant all the way to the back and then up a flight of stairs. I spotted a big table with a white linen tablecloth where a group of people were sitting around, talking and smoking. It took a few minutes for my eyes to adjust to the light. Sammy Davis Jr.! He was dressed in a plaid sport coat, white shirt, and crisp linen pants. I instantly recognized him.

"So, you're Ray." Sammy stood up and shook my hand. "Billy talks about you incessantly." Although I towered over Sammy, he seemed to loom over me. "So, how long have you been with the Yankees? What do they have you doing at the stadium? Ever see Steinbrenner? I love that guy's energy." To my surprise, Sammy spoke a little Spanish to me. "*Amigo, mi abuela*, my grandmother, you know, she's Spanish," he said. "She lives in Harlem."

I glanced around the room, and Frank Sinatra—he was the man—stood there chatting with Billy. Frank wasn't very tall, but he had a stately presence. I noticed how he gestured with his hands when he talked to Billy; his movements, fluid and polished, seemed almost choreographed.

"Hey, you're Billy's boy." Frank shook my hand, his blue eyes, just as they said in the press, were twinkling. No wonder he was nicknamed "Ol' Blue Eyes." How could such an icon know about me, Ray Negron, a Yankee batboy? The aura of Sammy and Frank, part of the famous Rat Pack—the press and the general public's name for that bunch of famous actors known for their heavy drinking and womanizing—made me giddy. I had followed their exploits on television. By the time I arrived at the Yankees I could recite every Frank Sinatra film. I had dreamed of meeting him one day, especially since I knew that he was at all the '76 playoff games, sitting in the owner's suite with the Boss.

"Please, Ray, have a seat." Sammy pulled out a chair for me at the table.

I sat down between Sammy and Billy, trying not to make myself too obvious. I wanted to take it all in—to memorize every last detail. It was mind-blowing, right out of the movies, with Frank Sinatra holding court. Billy was in the middle of it all.

"So, if I ever make another film, Billy, I'd like to have you in it," Frank said, smiling and turning to Billy.

"Shit, I don't know," Billy said. *One in a Million: The Ron LeFlore Story*, a CBS film starring LeVar Burton and Billy as himself, had just aired on television.

"C'mon, you gotta consider working with me, Billy." Frank laughed. "Hey, I'll even throw in a coupla good-looking dames if you do."

Everybody at the table began joking and telling stories. Sammy, chain-smoking, never seemed to stop laughing while he sat tapping his feet, like a tap dancer on speed.

Billy, even though he was laughing along with Frank, was still that urchin of a boy from West Berkeley. He was in as much awe of Frank as I was. The scene was a window into a world of Billy's that I had never known existed.

"We just got out of bed," I heard a few of them say to Billy. "To our first meal of the day!" They raised their glasses.

Afterward Billy dropped me off at a friend's apartment. He once again said to me, "In my lifetime you're going to do some great things." Somehow he saw something in me. Mr. Steinbrenner, too, had seen it. It was something that I had never been able to see in myself. Billy, drunk or not, had a wisdom others could never match.

"I'm going to Dallas. I'll call you when I get back," Billy said that night. The harsh winter of '78–'79 went by and there was not a single word from Billy. He didn't call again, but it didn't matter.

During the off-season that year I visited my cousins Ed and Christopher in East New York a few times. They noticed how serious I had become over the last few years; my work at the Yankees now took top priority over connecting with my family members. Always glad to see me, my cousins treated me with respect, without a hint of jealousy. Sometimes we sat together on their front stoop. They knew all the guys in the neighborhood who stopped by to talk. I tried not to notice when they talked about buying or selling drugs. My cousins were my brothers, and I was happy to spend time with them. Sometimes we'd drive around the neighborhood with one of their friends. Ed would brag about me. "Hey, man, this cousin of mine is a big shot with the New York Yankees."

The guys especially wanted to hear stories about Billy Martin. There was never another white man who could speak their language as well as Billy. "Tell me what happened when he had that fight with Reggie. Does he ever punch you out, Ray?" Ed asked and laughed. Leaving East New York one snowy winter afternoon, I shivered as I passed a young man who was sprawled on the sidewalk, a block from my cousins' home. As I briskly walked to the subway, I wondered if that was what would become of Ed and Christopher.

B y mid-June 1979, in response to our uneven playing because of injuries on the team, Mr. Steinbrenner announced that he and Billy had resolved their differences. Always impatient, never afraid to cut his losses early, the Boss sped up his plan to rehire Billy Martin. On June 18, 1979, he moved Bob Lemon up to the front offices. Bob's twenty-six-year-old son had been killed in a dune buggy accident at the beach in the early spring. Bob, as it turned out, would never be the same. Billy was to take over the team for the rest of the year. The reinstatement started out happily—36,211 fans showed up that day to welcome the returning Billy, who was seemingly on his best behavior and getting along well with the players.

At one point in the season, I stood by Reggie's locker changing into my street clothes. Shortstop Fred Stanley, known as "Chicken" because of the way he ran out on the field, came over to me. "Ray, would you do me a favor and run up to the PR office? I need a couple of pictures of myself to send out to some fans."

"Sure," I said. I quickly dressed and ran upstairs to the public relations office. The door was open, but the lights were off. "Hello?" I called out. No one answered. I walked in the room and called out again. Still no answer. I knew that they kept black-and-white pictures of players in the metal file cabinet by the wall. I opened the drawer, looked under STANLEY, and grabbed a few pictures of Chicken.

A semi-high-ranking Yankee official greeted me as I walked out of the office. "What are you stealing?" the overweight man asked.

"I'm not stealing. Fred Stanley asked me to get some pictures—"

"Bullshit! You're in deep shit for this. Mr. Wilson's going to love this. We finally got you. Now, come with me."

"Go fuck yourself." I surprised myself by the words that flew out of my mouth. Then I tore down the hallway and took the stairs three at a time back to the locker room. I was sweating and out of breath as I handed Fred the photos.

"What happened?" he asked.

I told him what had just occurred upstairs.

"Oh, I gotta go tell Billy about this," Fred said.

"No, please don't tell him," I said.

"Yeah, don't tell Billy," another player yelled from across the room. "He's capable of shooting the motherfucka."

"Okay, then, I'm telling Reggie." Fred ran into the trainer's room. Reggie was sitting on the table with his pants on, no shirt.

"Where's the cocksucker?" Reggie came out of the room with Fred.

"He's probably freeloading in the pressroom," Fred said. Team officials and managers often went there for a beer after the game.

Reggie returned to his locker and put on his shirt, and then he and Fred left the locker room together. I followed quietly behind them. They stopped in front of the pressroom, and Reggie walked in.

"This is going to be good." Fred looked at me and winked.

I wasn't sure where this was leading. I was scared shitless.

A minute or two later Reggie came out of the pressroom, holding on to my accuser's lapels.

"He was stealing," the beefy man said.

"You're going to make some stink over Fred Stanley's pictures?"

Reggie said. "If anything like this ever happens again, we're going to have some problems."

The man took off back to the pressroom. Reggie looked at me, just as Billy was coming down the hall.

"What's going on?" Billy called to us.

"I took care of it. I took care of it," Reggie answered, smiling. He turned to me. "Don't say anything to Billy, Ray. It will only make the situation worse."

How I wished Reggie could have helped Billy, too, before he was arrested a month later in October in Minneapolis on assault charges. He was no longer the Billy I once knew so well.

Mr. Steinbrenner had no choice but to fire Billy once again.

Sadly, I never worked with Billy again after that. He went on his own way, as he always would, heading to the Oakland A's while I spent another season with the Yankees. The following year I began pursuing another dream, that of acting in films. Reggie had introduced me to his own agent, who made sure I was cast in a few commercials, which eventually led to some film work. Unfortunately, I usually had difficulty remembering my lines. Not certain that I could make ends meet being an actor, I became an adviser with the Tokyo Yomiuri Giants, traveling back and forth to Japan several times a year. My job was to sign American players and take them to Japan. Because the owner knew that I had worked with George Steinbrenner, he wanted me to work for him in Japan so that he'd have something in common with the great Yankee boss.

I would meet up with Billy now and then when our paths crossed. He would look the same, maybe somewhat sadder, yet we always fell into easy conversation. During the 1980s it was impossible for any baseball fan, much less me, to understand how he could get into more highly publicized scuffles. He was restrained by umps from attacking a fan. His arm was broken during a heated argument with a Yankee pitcher, Ed Whitson, while they were in Baltimore. Yet none of this would stop Billy from being fired and rehired by Mr. Steinbrenner three more times during the next ten years, creating a drama for baseball like nothing else during that decade.

IT WAS WELL KNOWN in our family that my cousins Christopher and Ed, who were still living in Brooklyn, and my half-brothers, Marco and Miguel, who were living in the Bronx, were going through a tumultuous time, too. Marco and then later Miguel were sentenced on drug charges in the 1980s and sent to Rikers Island. It took them many long hard years before they straightened themselves out and started, much to everyone's relief, leading respectable lives.

Christopher was using and dealing drugs. He wasn't able to resist the lure of the street gangs. When he began using the drugs that he was supposed to sell, he fell further and further into the world of addiction. On a scorching summer day during that brutally hot summer of 1988, when Christopher didn't have the money to turn over to the dealers, he was dragged into an alleyway. The dealers beat him up, tortured him with razor blades, and shot and killed him. I remember the fury and anguish in my uncle's voice when he called me at my mother's home in Queens around noon.

"*Mi Dios! Mi Dios!* How can this be?" My mother collapsed on her bed. I thought back to Uncle Hector. I tried to comfort her, but my own pain was too great. A few days later, Phil, one of Christopher's brothers, was brought to the funeral home in shackles. He was in jail for manslaughter. This was almost as horrifying to me as Christopher's death. As a teenager, when he had lived with us, Phil looked like Smokey Robinson. My cousin Ed, haggard and drawn, sat next to his mother during the service. I later found out that he was suffering from AIDS that he contracted from using a dirty needle. I looked over at Aunt Olga. She had tried so hard to get her boys into rehabilitation programs, but there was never enough money in the family to pay for them.

My own fortunes provided the family some hope. In the winter of 1989 I began running a Senior Professional Baseball Association team, the St. Lucie Legends, in Port St. Lucie, Florida. I was having a great time hanging around guys like Graig Nettles, Bucky Dent, and Luis Tiant, players I had known during my earlier years with the Yankees. It felt like old times, and the tragedies of my own family seemed a long way away.

On Christmas night I was sitting on the sofa with my young son, Jon-Erik, listening to carols on the radio, when Mort Fleishner, a writer/producer for ABC News, called around 8:00 P.M.

"Have you heard?" Mort asked.

"Heard what?"

I instinctively knew that this was not someone calling with more Christmas cheer. After a long silence Mort said softly, "Billy Martin was killed."

It felt as though my father suddenly collapsed and died. Billy was only sixty-one years old—too young and way too tough. It couldn't be true. Billy and Mr. Steinbrenner had been together in Tampa just the week before. There were rumors that Billy was going to return for a sixth time as manager of the Yankees, until Mr. Steinbrenner released a statement that he had offered Billy a position as special adviser and Billy had just accepted.

The ABC writer told me that Billy's truck had skidded on an icy road and slid three hundred feet down an embankment in upstate New York, near his home. Billy and his friend William Reedy had spent the afternoon at a local bar. Neither was wearing a seat belt. At 6:56 P.M. on Christmas, Billy Martin was pronounced dead. His friend survived but was seriously injured.

I remembered the last conversation I had with Billy, a year before in Anaheim. "Never stop chasing your dream, never stop believing in miracles," Billy advised me. "Someday, Ray, you are going to know exactly what your dream is." I thought about the various jobs I had had since I left the Yankees, how I had enjoyed acting and traveling back and forth to Japan as an agent. I still had big plans for myself, and now Billy wouldn't be there to see me living my dream. I cried all night long. Four days later, Billy finally got in death a New York tribute that often eluded him in real life.

I tried to go to Billy's funeral at St. Patrick's Cathedral on December 29, but when I arrived at the West Palm Beach airport, I started hyperventilating, something I had never done before. I walked into the airport, turned around, and took a taxi back home. I couldn't step on that plane because I refused to believe that Billy Martin, the man I thought of as my father, was really dead.

Instead I went home and turned on the television. Every channel was filled with news reports: over 6,500 people, a crowd befitting a movie star like Cary Grant or Frank Sinatra, attended the funeral, half of them standing outside in zero-degree temperatures. The mourners ranged from Mickey Mantle, his stalwart buddy and teammate, to Mr. Steinbrenner and even former president Nixon, whose embattled position seemed to mirror Billy's. I would never forget the sight of what seemed like a street army of young boys, all wearing Yankee caps.

The headlines in the papers the next day said, BILLY COMES HOME. I sat in my house, tears streaming down my face, and read that the casket lay under a four-foot Yankee logo made of tulips. To the right of the body was a stand with a Yankee cap and his uniform, number 1. Billy, never one to shy from publicity, would have loved every minute of his own service, I thought.

The new decade of the 1990s began in gloom. For months after the New Year I kept asking myself over and over how I could have helped Billy. My thoughts would turn to Ed and Christopher. I had failed them, too. I wasn't sleeping or eating much. I would drive from my suburban town house in Port St. Lucie to the ballpark, where once again I was caught up with baseball, my escape from the world.

As the general manager of the team, responsible for signing and releasing players, working on improving the team, and acting as public relations manager, I was busier than I had ever been. Yet at night when I came home from the ballpark I was tortured by thoughts of how I could have prevented Billy's and Christopher's deaths.

Then in March an angel landed on my shoulder. Adele Smithers, the president of the Christopher D. Smithers Foundation, the nation's oldest private philanthropy devoted to treating alcoholism, reached out to me. She knew of my close relationship with Billy. Adele and I had met a few years back when someone in the world of baseball introduced us. Addiction was becoming epidemic in sports, and many ballplayers had consulted her. She set up a meeting with me to talk about the nature of addiction.

"You were working for an alcoholic, Ray." Adele spoke to me like a cool Brooklyn girl or a sister from the Bronx. No bullshit. "I'm sympathetic to what you've gone through. It's so frustrating to see someone you love with addiction issues. You've got to understand the role of an enabler before you can start helping others." Adele gave me an armload of books and introduced me to leading doctors in the field.

I started getting in touch with my cousin Ed regularly to see how he was feeling. One afternoon I called his hospital room. Aunt Olga answered the phone. "Thanks for calling, Ray, but Ed isn't able to speak." She was sobbing.

Then I heard Ed's familiar voice, only softer. "Ray . . . is that . . . ?"

His mother put the phone to his ear. "You know that day that you were caught at the stadium, Ray?" His voice trailed off and there was a long silence.

"Come on, Ed, keep talking, let me hear you," I said.

"I thought I was the lucky one because I got away," Ed whispered. "But you, my man, you were the lucky one in the end." I listened quietly.

"Always make it work, Ray," Ed was able to say, still only in a whisper, before hanging up the phone. He died a few hours later. I sat in silence, crying off and on for the rest of the day. But finally, after a few weeks with Adele's support, I knew that I had no choice: I had to honor my cousin. I never wanted to forget Ed's last words.

I became closer to Adele during that time. She prepared me to reach out to others, especially struggling baseball players. I learned how to identify players who might be addicts. "You are doing God's work," she would often say. In the middle of the 1990s, I went to Mr. Steinbrenner and told him that I had learned that addiction was a disease.

"That's bullshit," the Boss said. "Why can't these guys just stop using drugs? I just don't understand."

"Well, you know, Boss, that my cousin died from AIDS not too long ago. I don't think he could just stop."

"Was he a homosexual, Ray?"

"No, he wasn't. He was involved with drugs and he was using a dirty needle," I said. "Boss, I think you'd better talk to Adele." After a few weeks Mr. Steinbrenner agreed to meet with her. Shortly after their meeting he approached me.

"So, should we think about Darryl?" the Boss asked me in June 1995 after Darryl Strawberry was suspended from the San Francisco Giants for drug use.

"Yes, I think that Darryl could be a productive ballplayer," I said.

"Okay, maybe I'll start negotiating with his lawyer," the Boss said. "And, Ray, you know you and Adele just may be right about this disease thing." Six months later the Boss also signed Dwight Gooden, who had been struggling with addiction for years. I took Dwight to AA meetings, got a trainer for him so that he could work out every day, and spent time with him sharing my understanding of the disease. Darryl and Dwight were eventually able to turn their lives around enough to help the Yankees win the 1996 World Series. Today, they are still working to stay clean, one day at a time.

This was the beginning of a long relationship with Adele, who ultimately became the second most influential person in my life, after the Boss. Today she is Golda Meir, Eleanor Roosevelt, and a female George Steinbrenner rolled into one. You just don't mess with Adele. Her vast knowledge continually straightens out my thinking. I didn't want to fall into the traps that Mickey Mantle, Billy Martin, and my half-brother, cousins, and uncle had been caught in. I'm not certain if I would have heard Adele's valuable and lifesaving messages—if you work the program, it works for you—were it not for those experiences with Billy and so many of my family members.

One afternoon, when I received a letter from a player thanking me for getting him into AA, I called Adele. Proud of her Italian heritage, her maiden name being Croci, she said, "You are something, Ray Negron. Even if you were Italian, I couldn't love you any more."

There was no doubt; Billy was speaking to me through an angel.

3

The Birth of Mr. October

At one point in the evening Thurman walked over to
Reggie. "I was proud of you tonight. You sure put on some
show, Mr. October."

ONLY A COUPLE of months after the Yankees hammered the Dodgers in the 1977 World Series, Reggie and I were jogging around Central Park. Passing the parking lot of Tavern on the Green, we came upon a yellow school bus, its rear wheels spinning in a deep, dirty snowbank. When Reggie heard kids' squeals, he stopped, turned around, and ran over to the bus.

"Look, it's, it's . . . Reggie Jackson!" cried a young boy.

"I'm stuck," I heard the driver tell Reggie.

"Okay, kids, let's go. Gotta get off the bus, please!" Reggie called. "Ray, c'mon over here and stay with the kids. I'm gonna rock the bus, I'm gonna rock it." Reggie got behind the bus, leaning his 210-pound frame into the vehicle, jumping up and down, swaying and pushing with all his might while the kids screamed, *"Reg-gie! Reg-gie!"* Finally the bus lurched forward. *"Reg-gie!"* The kids cheered as I led them back onto the bus. They looked out of the window and waved, still chanting, *"Reg-gie! Reg-gie!"* Their mantra seemed to practically levitate the massive yellow school bus.

We yelled, "Good-bye," and continued jogging through the park. Approaching 59th Street, we came upon a familiar-looking couple. She, a small Asian woman, wore big dark glasses. He was thin with longish hair, a scarf looped around his neck.

"Hey, there!" he called to Reggie, clearly star-struck. "Way to go, chap—congratulations on winning the ball game. Impressive performance." His accent was unmistakably English.

"Thanks, thanks very much," Reggie responded, equally in awe, having recognized the often-elusive celebrity and his wife, Yoko Ono. We stopped jogging, and they talked a few more minutes. John Lennon and Reggie Jackson, two of the most celebrated men in America, were having a heartfelt exchange.

Afterward, I sat quietly in Reggie's apartment, awed by the series of events I had just witnessed. Thirty years later, when Paul McCartney came to a Yankees game, I was able to tell him about Reggie's chance encounter with John that day.

In only six months Reggie had gone from one of the lowest points in his career to the highest. I thought back to a little over a year earlier, in the late fall of 1976, when Mr. Steinbrenner had aggressively pursued Reggie for weeks. The Boss flew the superstar, who had hit forty-seven homers in 1969 and had earned an MVP trophy in 1973, to New York, sending his personal limo to pick him up at the airport, even telling him, "You can own the town, Reggie. There will be so many business opportunities for you in New York, you'll be able to pick and choose like you're at a long buffet table."

At a Hyatt Hotel in Chicago he met with Reggie and wrote the deal on a hotel napkin. On the bottom of it Reggie scribbled,

I won't let you down. —Reginald M. Jackson.

Three days later, Reggie triumphantly arrived in New York. He was wearing a fur coat and three consecutive World Series rings on his fingers. "I'm not coming to New York to be a star, I'm bringing my star with me," he told the press. A burgundy and silver Rolls-Royce with black leather interior was included in his $2.96 million five-year contract—way above the average $50,000-a-year salary that most Major League Baseball players were making back then. Reggie cruised around the city, sometimes with a beautiful blonde beside him, which at the time raised a few eyebrows.

Each man brought a sense of glamour to the other. The Boss was well aware of the excitement and celebrity appeal that Reggie would give to the New York fans. So was the press. On December 6, 1976, the *New York Times* editorial page wrote, "By choosing New York Jackson has become the Yankees' first black superstar, not to mention their first black millionaire." Reggie, the opposite of the self-effacing Elston Howard, in turn, recognized and gravitated toward the Boss's genius at promotion, strongly aware that Mr. Steinbrenner, too, wanted nothing more than to win. The Boss and Reggie, two huge personalities, became the yin and yang of the Yankees.

Billy Martin scoffed at Reggie, dismissing him as a West Coast celebrity. It was true, Reggie all but turned into a debonair black Clark Gable, strolling onto a movie set, whenever he stepped into the clubhouse. Billy, who was earning around $75,000 at the time, was more like a combination of a modern-day Bat Masterson and cowboy. He resented not only the money that Mr. Steinbrenner was lavishing on our new teammate but also the attention he was giving him.

Reggie instinctively knew how to get along with the Boss, who demanded respect without ever asking for it. Billy, on the other hand, read a newspaper article quoting Reggie as saying, "It's going to be great with the Yankees because George and I are going to get along real good, and that's very important." Billy had desperately wanted Oakland A's left fielder Joe Rudi, calling him the best player of his generation. He became determined to show Reggie who was really in charge of the team.

While Reggie waited for his first spring training with the Yankees, he also expected the customary welcoming phone call from his new manager. Yet Billy never called. Spring training hadn't even started yet, and already Billy and Reggie were in a standoff.

On the first day of spring training in Fort Lauderdale, in February of 1977, a huge number of fans and reporters lined up outside of the ballpark. Reggie chatted and smiled, posed for photographs, and signed at least 150 autographs before Billy called him inside the clubhouse. That same day, Billy told sportswriters that Reggie wouldn't be in the cleanup position—the fourth place in the batting order, reserved for the most powerful hitter on the team. Reggie overheard the interviews and said, "What are you talking about? I've got three rings here." I thought that Billy's refusal to put Reggie in the fourth position was probably because our first baseman, Chris Chambliss, had been our big slugger for the last couple of years.

At first, Fran Healy, our six-foot-four backup catcher, was the only player who reached out to Reggie. Fran, a quiet, unassuming guy, sensed that players like Sparky Lyle and Graig Nettles—down-to-earth guys who had been on the team for a long time when the Yankees weren't winning—were giving Reggie the cold shoulder. Like Fran, I didn't worry about what the others thought. We admired Reggie's work ethic during spring training. He ran laps longer, did double the sit-ups, and lifted more weights than anyone else on the team. I had never seen a player with such confidence. Yet Reggie was self-deprecating and almost deferential when he was around the Boss, treating him like a father.

Three days into spring training, Reggie came up to me while I was sitting on a bench in the clubhouse, polishing helmets. We had been shorthanded the last few days, and I was working longer hours than usual.

"You know, there's something about you that I really relate to." I was surprised that a player of his stature would sit down next to me. "I've been watching you. You're about twenty-one, aren't you, Ray?" He asked me a few more questions, and I found myself telling him how, spray paint and all, I came to the Yankees. We discovered we both spoke Spanish. Reggie's paternal grandmother had hailed from Puerto Rico. On long bus trips Reggie and I would lapse into Spanish when we wanted to have a private conversation.

Yet I confess, I had been wary of Reggie in the very beginning. Back in 1974, I went over to the visitor side of the stadium when the Yankees were playing Oakland and tried to find him. I really wanted to meet the great slugger. While Reggie was something like Babe Ruth to me, he was at the same time a huge personality I was uneasy about meeting, especially since my unsettling encounter with Mickey Mantle had occurred just a month earlier. Unlike many of the other batboys, who came to work, collected their paychecks, and went home, I was usually deeply impressed by many of the players. I often made a fool out of myself so I could meet my heroes, waiting outside the stadium for autographs, almost like a groupie, finding out what time a certain player might show up at the clubhouse.

When I finally found Reggie that day, I stuck my hand out and introduced myself. "I'm Ray, the batboy."

"Good," Reggie said matter-of-factly, "go get me some socks."

I found him a pair of socks and quickly left. I figured if this guy was going to be anything like Mickey when I asked him to sign balls for the players, I wanted nothing to do with him.

Now Reggie had already created a wide gulf between himself and the rest of the team, one that only widened after Robert Ward, a writer on assignment with *Sport* magazine, sat down and interviewed him at a local bar during the first week of spring training.

"It all flows from me," Reggie was quoted as saying. "I'm the straw that stirs the drink. Munson thinks that he can be the straw that stirs the drink, but he can only stir it bad." Those words became notorious among Yankee fans and would dog Reggie for years. Once an advocate for bringing Reggie into the Yankee fold, Thurman turned his back on him when he found out that Reggie had a much better contract, complete with incentives. Thurman, whose salary was $250,000 that year, had an unwritten agreement with the Boss that he would always be the highest-paid Yankee.

Some of the guys heard about the interview even before it ran. They weren't too happy about it, especially since we had just come off the great 1976 season. Thurman had been such a revered Yankee during the mid-'70s that the guys couldn't believe what Reggie had said to the reporter.

We won our opening game in 1977 against Milwaukee 3–0 in front of the biggest crowd in five years, almost forty-four thousand fans. For a moment I thought that the team might just forget our differences and pull together. Yet we lost the next eight out of nine games, suddenly finding ourselves in last place in the Eastern Division by April 19. During that period Billy benched Reggie because he went against Billy's rules and spoke to the press about an elbow injury. Billy rarely talked about medical matters and felt that if anyone should speak to the press about injuries, it should be the manager, not the players.

The morale in the clubhouse quickly sank lower than a .100 batting average. Some of the players complained to the press not only about their salaries but also about the management and their schedules. The guys were especially hostile to Reggie. Normally when a big star, someone of Reggie's stature, takes batting practice, the other players stop what they are doing and watch. Now the area around the batting cage was often empty when Reggie was batting. Most of the team ignored him whenever he tried to start up a conversation.

"These guys don't like me, Ray."

"I think you're wrong, Reggie," I said. "I really think you're dead wrong." How I wanted to believe my own words.

The fans were equally tough on Reggie, expecting him to hit a home run every time he stepped up to the plate and make a diving catch each time he took to the field. When he struck out or made an error, they booed him. "Look, Ray, the fans don't boo nobodies," Reggie told me defensively a few times after games while he was changing in the clubhouse.

The New York press, even more judgmental than the New York fans, wrote that Reggie's career was dying, that his best years were behind him. During a game in mid-April Reggie hit a homer and then walked off the field, hunched over and limping, his way of sticking it to the press. "They think I'm finished, that I'm old and tired. I'll show 'em," he said. Fran Healy, who was becoming closer to Reggie and often stayed at his apartment, listened to Reggie's problems. Both of us tried to cheer him up.

"Hang in there," I'd say.

Reggie began inviting me to eat with him at Oren & Aretsky, where a Reggie-signed bat hung over the mirror at the bar. One of the owners, Ken Aretsky, who today owns the upscale New York restaurant Patroon, watched out for Reggie on many nights, because a lot of hockey fans who frequented the place could get a bit rowdy, sometimes hostile. Or we'd go to Jim McMullen's, another of his favorite Upper East Side celebrity hangouts. When Reggie and I walked into a restaurant, the patrons would start clapping if Reggie had had a good night. Or I'd hear people whisper, "Look, look over there, that's Reggie Jackson."

All eyes were on New York's new star. The maître d' always had a reserved table in the corner for him. Reggie and I would inevitably spend the evening talking about two of his favorite subjects, cars and acting—Reggie had done analysis on ABC with Keith Jackson and Howard Cosell the night we won the pennant in 1976.

To this day most people don't know that Reggie has a huge vocabulary. He peppered conversations with words I'd never heard before—"chastise," "obsequious," "retractable." I listened in amazement as he went from discussing baseball and other players to quoting from the Bible and weighing in on current affairs. He had the uncanny ability to go from sounding like Richard Pryor to Einstein—maybe even a little like Shakespeare—in less than a minute.

By early May, the team had rallied and we were in first place because guys like Munson, Rivers, Chambliss, and Nettles were producing. But in mid-May Reggie slumped. Earlier in the season on a road trip to Oakland, Billy had benched him against power left-handed pitcher Vida Blue. Anxious to face off against his old teammate, Reggie was offended.

"I'm worried about our struggles against southpaws," Billy told him. When the game went for fifteen innings and Billy didn't call upon Reggie once, it seemed to have a disturbing effect on Reggie's psyche.

"I'm not that great of a ballplayer," Reggie told me sarcastically back in the clubhouse. "I'm probably overpaid, too."

On May 23, the same day we were playing our first game against the Boston Red Sox, *Sport* magazine with Reggie's quote about being the straw that stirs the drink hit the newsstands. Early that afternoon some of the guys brought copies into the Yankee clubhouse. Groups of players huddled over the magazine before the game.

"That prick," a player said, after reading Reggie's quote.

"Dirty son of a bitch," another yelled, hurling the magazine into the middle of the room.

"Hey, I was misquoted," Reggie mumbled. I looked over and watched how he dressed quickly, his head bowed. After he left the clubhouse a few guys went over and kicked Reggie's locker.

"C'mon, Thurman, you know what writers are like." Fran Healy sat down next to Thurman. "Some of Reggie's quotes are out of context."

"Yeah, for three fucking pages?" Thurman countered.

The tension in the clubhouse, however, didn't hurt Reggie's playing. In fact, I noticed how often it didn't matter what was happening off the field with Reggie; once he was out on the field he usually had no problem getting into his "zone."

That afternoon, in the second inning, his second time at bat, he hit another double. In the seventh inning, with the Red Sox ahead 2–1, he blasted a deep homer, tying the score. Reggie stood there for a few seconds, watching the ball sink into the stands. Then he rounded the bases, and as he crossed the plate, the team ran out to shake his hand. Reggie ran right up to them and did the strangest thing—he turned away and headed for the back of the dugout.

When the inning was over, the players, running out to the field, looked shaken by Reggie's snub. This time Reggie, too, had lost his groove. He overran a ball, playing a Red Sox single into a double. Willie Randolph forgot to cover first on a bunt that turned into a single. Both runners eventually scored. We lost the game 4–3. As the players retreated into the clubhouse with the press following close behind, the players talked about Reggie, "If that's the way he wants it, fuck him," a player said.

"Hey, Reggie! Why didn't you shake hands?" a reporter called out.

"Bad hand, I had a bad hand," he said, looking like he wanted to disappear.

"He's a fuckin' liar," a player said. "How's that for a quote?"

Once again I had to endure a painful scene, Reggie sitting alone in the clubhouse in dejected silence.

The press turned to Billy. "Maybe Reggie was mad at me because I didn't play him a couple of games against left-handers. Go ask him. I'm sure he'll have some answers for you. Ask him about the ball that got away from him at the start of the eighth. He probably forgets about those things," Billy said.

Later I ran into the Boss in the hallway.

"I wish Reggie hadn't done that interview," Mr. Steinbrenner said.

"Reggie told me he was misquoted," I said. "I really don't think he said that, Mr. Steinbrenner."

"I don't know if I can believe you, Ray," the Boss said. "You're like Mother Teresa around here. You believe everybody. Hell, Reggie and Billy can do no wrong in your eyes—and that's just not the way it always is, Ray."

We had six more days at the stadium before we went to Boston: a game against the Red Sox the next day, a twi-night doubleheader against Texas, and three games against Chicago. Many of the players weren't speaking to Reggie. I found Reggie sitting in the clubhouse, once again staring into space. I sat down next to him and tried to make small talk.

"You okay?" I asked. His face was broken out in a red rash. I thought he might have the measles.

Reggie stood up and shrugged. "I'm gonna ask Billy to call a team meeting so I can apologize." He went to find Billy.

Billy, however, refused to call any such meeting. "Hey, if you really want to apologize, you're gonna have to go to each goddamned player," he told Reggie. When the press was barred from the clubhouse a half hour before the game against Chicago, Reggie went from locker to locker saying he was sorry.

"Okay, don't worry about it," Lou Piniella said.

"Let's just get it together," Fred Stanley said.

Most of the guys just stood there, said nothing, and then turned their backs to Reggie.

During the next few weeks Reggie, as if powered by controversy, actually raised his batting average forty-four points in the span of twenty-three days. Yet his relationship with Billy was as rocky as ever. Billy still refused to put him in as cleanup hitter, and Reggie complained to anyone who would listen, including the press.

I thought back to how Reggie had handled the media after that June 18 incident in Boston when Reggie and Billy almost came to blows. Returning to the Boston Sheraton that night, I had headed straight for Reggie's room. He had invited in some members of the New York press, the ones who had written flattering pieces about him. He told them how he was constantly mistreated and how the only one who treated him fairly was the Boss.

"Everyone else treats me like dirt," he said.

I stayed in Reggie's room with him for another hour while the phone rang incessantly.

"Hi, is this Reggie Jackson?" The voice on the other end was someone from the media, just as it had been every time the phone rang.

"No, this is Ray Negron," Reggie said. "Reggie's not here." After that night many of the Yankees started using aliases whenever they traveled to avoid being tracked down by fans and the media. That's actually still true today, and I've since known popular players who check into hotels using monikers like James Bond or Al Capone.

That night one of the players knocked on Reggie's hotel door and said that Billy wanted to see me. I went down the hall to his room. Billy sat on his bed, holding his head in his hands. "Damn, I'm sure Steinbrenner's gonna can me for going after Reggie."

A few minutes later, after I had returned to my room, my phone rang. "Ray, I don't understand your friend Billy," the Boss said. "Why can't he try to get along with Reggie? Don't you talk to these guys, Ray? Aren't they supposed to be your friends?"

I was worn out and drained. I couldn't help feeling that I was in the middle of a big family feud. I didn't want anyone to get hurt.

"I don't know what I'm gonna do, Ray. I might have to let Billy go." Mr. Steinbrenner rambled on.

On an especially sticky July night I remember feeling like I was back in grade school, trying to settle disputes in the schoolyard—I found myself in the both lucky and unlucky position where I loved Billy, the Boss, and Reggie. I was worried that Reggie, who rarely smiled now, was becoming more and more withdrawn. Some days I would find him alone in the clubhouse. Instead of poring over his fan mail he was reading the Bible. I started helping Reggie, running errands for him and opening and answering his mail.

A few weeks later the Boss called me into his office. "Have you been helping Mr. Jackson?"

"Yes," I said. "Are you mad?"

"No. Stay on. Help him. I'm going to talk to Billy and tell him you're helping Reggie."

"I'm doing it because I like Reggie," I said.

"Just shut up and do a good job." The Boss walked out.

A few days later I saw Billy. "So, George told me what's going on with you and Reggie. Are you doing it because he asked you to do it or because you're friends?"

"I'm his friend," I told Billy.

"Well, keep it up." Billy said. "It will help me, too."

I was relieved. If Billy was like my long-lost uncle, Reggie was becoming the big brother I never had. I was trying to gain the respect of each of them, desperately wanting everyone to get along.

By the middle of the season, I became Reggie's right-hand man, with the Boss's blessing, attending to his personal needs as I traveled with him and the team. I was the only one in the clubhouse to be some-one's first assistant at the time. Even though I soon became known as "Reggie's guy," I never stopped helping all the players, because I genu-inely cared about each and every one of them. They were, after all, the Yankees.

Pete Sheehy, the clubhouse manager, would say to me, "You're to Reggie Jackson what I used to be to Lou Gehrig." He told me how he used to mail Lou's love letters when he was courting his soon-to-be wife, Eleanor, and how he always liked helping Lou with special chores. Pete was also close to Babe Ruth.

"I see you're going through a similar kind of stress that I went through with the Babe and Lou," Pete confided one day. "They'd been real close in the very beginning when they first started playing together. In fact, Babe was like Lou's big brother. But over time they stopped getting along. I found myself right there in the middle. My advice, Ray, is to just be yourself. Stay right there and never show one that you care more about him than the other."

Pete's words gave me a renewed confidence that not only could I help Reggie and Billy get along, but maybe I could smooth things out with the rest of the team, too.

Eʋᴇʀʏᴏɴᴇ ɪɴ ᴛʜᴇ ᴄʟᴜʙʜᴏᴜsᴇ knew that I idolized Elvis Presley. When he died unexpectedly on August 16, 1977, I was in mourning. The next day I arrived early at Reggie's apartment.

"Hey, why so quiet?" Reggie asked as I opened his fan mail. Reggie received hundreds of letters, some positive, others not so glowing, every week.

"The king is dead," I said.

"Yeah, and . . ."

"I'm a big Elvis fan."

"So, do you think I'm like the Elvis of baseball now?" He put his arm around my shoulders.

"No, not really," I said.

"Why not?"

"Well, whenever Elvis worked on one of his films he always included his 'boys,'" I said. A few times Reggie had taken me to midtown to do a Getty commercial shoot. It was fun watching Reggie work. I couldn't believe how comfortable he seemed in front of the camera and how he learned his lines so easily. I saw a whole other side of Reggie.

Without hesitating, he walked over to his phone and called his agent, Matt Merola. "Hey, when are we working again as far as a commercial is concerned, Matt?" he asked. "After this season? This coming winter? Okay, make sure that Ray Negron is in that commercial." Through Reggie, I ended up filming three commercials with him that winter for Volkswagen, Old Spice, and Panasonic.

Because of Reggie's endorsement of Volkswagen, they had given him a four-door tan VW Rabbit. Reggie sure as hell wasn't going to drive that car, so he let me use it. Every time he hit a home run Getty would send him a package of gas coupons, which he then gave to me. Reggie took care of me, and I, in turn, took care of him. Working in his spacious Fifth Avenue apartment, I answered his phones, watered his plants, made his dinner reservations, and kept his cars clean and filled with gas. Once, he and I came out of his building and he spotted my car, which was parked on the sidewalk in front of his building. Because I worked for Reggie, the building let me park there. "Fuck it, let's just take your car today," he said.

"Ray, this car is filthy," he sighed as he climbed in the passenger side. "If you want me to ride in this motherfucka you'd better learn how to keep it clean." At first I was a little defensive, but soon I realized that Reggie was only trying to teach me how to care for my possessions.

A few days later I arrived at Reggie's apartment. "We've got some important work to do. Put your coat back on." He hailed a cab, and we pulled up in front of a Madison Avenue clothing store. At first, I didn't realize what he was doing. Reggie carefully chose Yves St. Laurent dress shirts, fine linen pants, and alligator belts. I tried on Bill Blass leather jackets and raincoats. As I modeled the clothes, Reggie gave his opinion. "I like the pants, Ray, but not with that shirt," or "Why don't you try on a deeper blue jacket with that one?"

Reggie had always been a stylish dresser. He knew just how to pair the right sport jacket with the perfect tie, always careful that his clothes were pressed and clean. He thought it was important that I, too, dress the way a Yankee should.

"You see the way the Boss puts himself together, Ray? He always looks sharp," Reggie said to me. I was excited that Reggie wanted to make sure that I was part of the team. "If you want to be a Yankee, Ray, you gotta dress the part, man."

He bought an entire wardrobe for me that day. No one had ever taken me shopping in my life, and I just didn't make the kind of money that allowed me to look half as sharp as Reggie. Usually I threw on a pair of worn dungarees and a T-shirt, and if I needed to dress up, I'd wear a polyester leisure suit. I left the store wearing a pressed pair of designer jeans, a crisp cotton button-down shirt, and tan loafers.

"Damn, you look like a little Reggie," he said, looking at me as we walked up Madison Avenue together, carrying colorful shopping bags. Although I went to Reggie's Fifth Avenue apartment almost daily, I always performed my duties and went straight back to the stadium or home to Queens. As we passed trendy boutiques, hotels with door-men, and people who looked as if they had just stepped out of the fashion pages of a magazine, I often felt like I was in a foreign city.

"If I'm the king of New York," Reggie joked with me, "then you gotta be the prince of the city, Ray."

Reggie lived across the street from the Metropolitan Museum of Art, on the twentieth floor of a high-rise with spectacular views of Central Park. He had exquisite taste and owned only the best linens, china, and furniture. Eventually Reggie trusted me so much that he gave me a set of keys to his apartment.

During the middle of the '77 season, while Reggie was away, I planned a small party in his apartment. I invited a girlfriend and her friends over. I confess, I wasn't completely comfortable doing this, but I wanted to show off for my friends. I led my girl into Reggie's bed-room, and her friends went into the guest room.

Just as I was about to shut the door, Ramon, the doorman on duty, called up from downstairs. I ran out of the bedroom to answer. "Reee-gie is here. Reee-gie is back and he is unloading his car. He'll be up shortly."

"Oh, damn it, Ramon, do me a favor. Delay him any way you can. Delay him. I gotta get everything fixed up." I happened to be friends with most of the doormen in Reggie's building. We spoke Spanish together, and sometimes Reggie and I got them Yankees tickets. The doormen, in turn, were loyal to both Reggie and me.

"Go out through the service entrance," Ramon said. "I'll have the elevator there waiting for you."

"Oh, shit!" I yelled as I gathered our clothes, threw away the food and bottles, turned the stereo off, and shouted, "Let's go!" It was something out of a Marx Brothers movie. My friends and I dashed into the service elevator just as I heard Reggie putting the key in the lock.

As we were driving over the 59th Street Bridge toward Queens, one of my friends yelled, "My rings! I left my rings on the nightstand in the guest room."

The next morning I felt a bit sick to my stomach as I put my key in Reggie's lock. I walked into the living room. Reggie was on the phone, lost in conversation, smiling. I hurried by him and searched the guest room. No rings. I went back into the living room, where Reggie was still talking on the phone.

"Yes, baby, I'll see you later tonight," Reggie was saying. "Oh, hold on a second, hon." Reggie put the receiver down, motioned for me to sit on the sofa, and held up his hand. "Hey, these yours, Ray?"

Reggie wriggled his fingers. The morning light bounced off the three gold rings resting high on his pinkie.

I sat there, frozen. Finally I nodded my head. Reggie picked up the receiver. "Oh, so we'll meet up a little later, then . . ."

For at least ten minutes he kept on talking while I sat there, pretending to read the newspaper. Then he hung up, slipped the rings off of his pinkie, and silently handed them to me.

"Reggie, I'm so sorry. My friends and I were in your apartment . . ." I started babbling.

"Oh, okay, you and your girl were in my bedroom?" Reggie asked.

I nodded.

"Go get your things. Let's go to the stadium now." Reggie drove in silence.

When we arrived at Yankee Stadium we spotted Thurman sitting on the trainer's table. Reggie went over and sat down next to him while I started to do some chores around the clubhouse, thinking how in May or June these two guys never would have sat down together. "Hey, come on over here, Ray," Reggie said.

He scooted over on the table, and I found myself in the middle of Thurman and Reggie. "So, Thurman, Ray here had a little party at my apartment the other night and he took some chick into my room. They were on my bed. And I found some rings in the guest room."

I held my breath.

"What would you do, Thurman, in a situation like this?"

Thurman laughed and put his arm around Reggie. "Reggie, what would you have done if you were Ray's age?"

"Hey, man, but look what he was doing!" Reggie said. "Thurman, I really need your help. You've known Ray a lot longer than I have. What do you think? I think he should be suspended for one month, don't you?"

"Oh, c'mon, Reggie." Thurman gave him a gentle nudge. "How about making it a week?"

"Ray, give me the keys." Reggie held out his hand. "You're suspended for one week."

I was saved, but seeing these two guys joking with their arms around each other was perhaps sweeter than keeping my job. That day I had learned my lesson: I made sure I was never *caught* again when I had a party at Reggie's apartment.

In mid-September the team was in Boston for two games. After an inconsistent start we were working our way to the playoffs. Miraculously we had come together like a well-oiled machine. Despite resisting for months, Billy had also put Reggie in the cleanup position in mid-August, after the Boss finally said, "Bat him fourth."

The upshot? Reggie walloped thirteen homers and batted in forty-nine runs over the next fifty games of the '77 season. He began smiling more, joking with the other players and asking them to go out and eat with him. I realized that when Reggie was confident and happy, I was, too. In fact, I felt the same way about the Boss and Billy. My mood was directly tied to theirs.

I drove my VW Rabbit with my friend Hector Pagan, a quiet, reserved batboy, up to Boston for those two games. We lost the first night 6–3, but the team was still confident. We were on a roll. How different it felt to be in the Boston clubhouse this time, compared to two months earlier when Reggie and Billy almost came to blows.

"Hey, Hector, where's the Volkswagen?" Reggie asked in the clubhouse after the game.

"In the parking lot."

"Ray, Hector and I are going to wait in the VW. You round up the boys, you know, Thurman, Guidry, and Gullet and the rest. We'll just crowd in—it's only two or three blocks to get drinks."

Reggie, sitting in the passenger seat, couldn't stop laughing when I brought the guys out to the VW. Thurman and pitchers Ron Guidry and Don Gullet piled in the back of the car, sitting on top of each other. I jumped in the middle of the front seat, crammed between the gear-shift and Reggie. The car was so packed that the upper half of Hector's body hung out of the side window as he drove the car through the side streets of downtown Boston. He honked the horn as we screamed, "Yankees, number one!" out the window.

"Turn here, prick!" Reggie suddenly yelled. I glanced over at Hector. At first he looked a little perplexed, but when the guys started laughing, he grinned.

"We sure have come a long way in a short time," Hector said to me between honks.

A few weeks later we managed to get into the playoffs, pushing our way through to get back into the World Series. Despite Reggie's phenomenal playing in the regular season, Billy decided to bench him in Game 5 against Royals left-hander Paul Splittorff, who had been tough on Reggie in the past. Reggie had had a horrendous playoff series, 1-for-15 and no RBIs. Even though there was only one goal in mind, to win the championship, Billy and Reggie were still barely speaking. I watched the game from home on my little black-and-white television, a coat hanger serving as an antenna. I had no idea what was going on behind the scenes in Kansas City.

Back at the clubhouse a few days later, I heard the story: Billy had called Fran Healy into his office.

"I need you to do me a favor. Tell Reggie he's not playing," Billy had said.

"You're the manager. You fuckin' tell him," Fran had replied.

"Please, you'll help the team. I don't want a big scene," Billy had countered.

"Oh, all right." Fran then went over to Reggie's locker and told him the news. Reggie had slammed down his cleats, but left it at that.

In the top of the eighth, Billy had motioned to Reggie, "Grab a bat." The Royals had a 3–1 lead. I sat on the edge of my sofa as I watched Reggie slap a single, bringing Willie Randolph on third into home. That was the only run that inning, but I knew it was an important one. Reggie had cut the deficit. The score was 3–2. But by the end of the ninth inning we had scored three more runs and had won our second straight American League pennant.

Everyone was nervous that there would be a repeat of the previous year, when we were swept by the Reds. That turned out not to be the case. We split the first two games at Yankee Stadium and won two out of three against the Dodgers in Los Angeles. New York was ecstatic when we came back with a 3–2 lead in the Series and the chance to take it all in the sixth game. Fans slept at the stadium in order to line up the next day for tickets. On street corners, in stores, on subways, I felt like the entire city was talking about Reggie Jackson and the New York Yankees.

Standing in the outfield on that cool, windless Tuesday night, shagging balls with the players before the game, I shivered as I watched Reggie take the last five minutes of batting practice. I listened to the sharp crack of his bat and saw him blasting one ball after another high over the fence. The fans sitting in the right field seats were cheering as if Game 6 had already begun. I could tell that Reggie felt a tremendous sense of urgency to get the Series over with and prove his critics and fans wrong. I hoped that after he put his all into batting practice that he still had enough stamina left for the game.

Burt Hooton walked Reggie his first time at bat. Then, during the bottom of the second inning, Reggie connected on his first swing with Burt's fastball. His line drive missile landed in the right field stands, bringing the score to a 4–3 Yankees lead.

"Go ahead, Reggie, please take a curtain call," I said as the crowd cheered wildly.

"No." Reggie was adamant. I think he was still hurting from the boos and the constant criticism throughout the season.

The Dodgers then sent Elias Sosa in to pitch. With a runner on first, Reggie smacked an even more vicious line drive to the right field seats. "Man, if anyone had been in the way, that ball would have gone right through their chest," Fred Stanley yelled. I glanced up at the scoreboard. We were leading 7–3. Now I wasn't the only one insisting he take a curtain call. The fans, in between chants of *"Reg-gie, Reg-gie,"* were wailing for him to come out of the dugout.

"Go out and take a curtain call, please," I pleaded with him. "Come on, Reggie, you gotta go out there this time.

"No," he said. Then he turned to the television cameras, smiled, held up two fingers, and mouthed, "Hi, Mom!" It was getting colder on the field by the minute as the wind picked up, but it felt warm in the dugout. Billy strolled over and patted Reggie on the cheek.

"Okay, Reggie, if you hit a third homer, you gotta go out there and face the crowd," I said. He was onstage, and it was time the whole world began to appreciate him.

Reggie laughed. "You know, Ray, you're crazy. But I'll tell you what, if I hit a third home run, I'll do it."

The next time Reggie came up to bat, in the bottom of the eighth, I dashed into the bathroom, thinking I'd be gone less than a minute. But I raced out of the men's room when I heard *THWACK!* The crowd was roaring. I couldn't believe that I had missed seeing Reggie up against pitcher Charlie Hough. With one swing, he launched a knuckleball 475 feet deep into the black of center field. The crowd went crazy, chanting *"Reg-gie, Reg-gie"* for what seemed like an eternity while the scoreboard flashed the picture of that hit over and over. Miraculously, Reggie had hit each homer on the very first pitch from three different pitchers. Batboy Joe D'Ambrosio and the players mobbed Reggie after he touched home plate. Now they weren't just slapping him on the back, they were hugging him, too. He finally took a seat on the far end of the bench. Players surrounded him, waiting to shake his hand. I could see he was elated. Reggie came toward me from the other side of the dugout. While the crowd chanted *"Reg-gie! Reg-gie!"* he smiled and sat down next to me.

"You promised, Reggie," I whispered in his ear.

He slowly stood up and walked out onto the field. I watched him as he tipped his cap to the frenzied crowd. In the thirty seconds that he stood there I saw the tension ease out of his frame. He had finally come to grips with his mistakes as well as the bad feelings in the clubhouse. Relaxed and on top of the world, Reggie at last took his proper curtain call.

Billy greeted him as he walked back to the dugout. "You really did a number on 'em tonight, didn't ya?" He hugged Reggie.

Thurman shook Reggie's hand.

Then Fran slapped him on the back. "Amazing, three home runs, each one on the first pitch." Actually, considering that Reggie had also homered during his final at-bat in Game 5, Fran was wrong: Reggie had belted four home runs on his last four swings.

"All is forgiven," I said to myself as the players congratulated Reggie.

In the top of the ninth, Reggie came out to the field wearing a batter's helmet to protect him from the coins that the fans were throwing. I had never seen quarters, even a few half dollars, being tossed on the field like confetti. The Dodgers put a run across in the ninth, but that would hardly matter. The game was over.

We had won, 8–4. Triumph! Jubilation! Sweet victory!

The New York Yankees had won the World Series, the first time since 1962. The stadium was out of control as the frenzied fans climbed over the wall, out onto the field. Reggie, looking like a football quarterback, took off his protective helmet and sprinted in from his position at right field, body-checking hordes of fans who were blocking him from getting to the dugout, while cops, nightsticks in hand, followed closely behind.

Ecstatic players mobbed the locker room, spraying and drinking champagne, water, and beer with gusto. Soaked! Everyone was drenched. We were hugging, dancing, shouting, and singing. Mr. Steinbrenner, dressed in his crisp white shirt and blue tie, wet from head to toe, was right there in the middle of it all.

"We'll be back next year," he told Bill White, a Yankee announcer who was doing locker-room coverage for ABC that night. When Bill asked about changes for the next season, the Boss replied, "Changes? We don't need any changes. We're World Champs and we'll be back next year." As I walked by him, he tousled my hair and gave me a big wink. He took a swig of champagne.

At one point in the evening Thurman walked over to Reggie. "I was proud of you tonight. You sure put on some show, Mr. October."

I watched them and smiled. "That's a cool name," I said to Thurman.

Later, when I looked around the clubhouse for Reggie, I couldn't find him. After checking everywhere I finally tracked him down, sitting on the couch in the manager's office, sipping champagne, his arm around Billy. The two motioned for me to come in. We shook hands and hugged.

As I was leaving the office, I glanced up at one of the television monitors in the clubhouse. ABC was replaying Reggie's third homer. I watched as Howard Cosell said, *"Oh, what a blow!* Way to top it off! Forget about who the Most Valuable Player is in the World Series. How this man has responded to pressure! Oh, what a beam on his face. How can you blame him? He's answered the whole *world!* After all the furor, all the hassling, it comes down to this."

I walked out to the dugout. The October moon lent a glow to the field while the familiar number 4 trains rumbled by in the distance. The last of the rowdy fans were leaving the ripped-up field, wading through a sea of paper. My dungarees, sneakers, and black leather jacket were in the locker next to Reggie's. I changed and waited for him. The cleaning crew had already started sweeping and mopping up.

J<small>UST FOUR YEARS BEFORE</small>, I had been on the outside, waiting to get the players' autographs, sneaking into the stadium, pretending to be a Yankee. Now, I was on the inside. We had just won the World Series, the first Yankee win for Mr. Steinbrenner, Billy, and Reggie. I thought back to the chaotic, soap-opera beginning of the season, and

I hoped that maybe, just maybe, with the help of Mr. Steinbrenner, I had played a little part in how far we had all come together. I had dreamed about a night like this for most of my life, and now I never wanted the evening to end.

I felt someone tap me on my shoulder. "Come on, Ray, let's get out of here. We've got a parade to get ready for, and you're going to be right there with me," Reggie said.

FEW WORDS CAN describe the feelings that I had that night. I was proud of Mr. October, not only for his three home runs, but also for his personal behavior. Reggie would never completely forgive Billy Martin for the way he felt Billy treated him that year. Yet, for that one miraculous night, I can say that they were friends. When my first son, Jon-Erik, was born in 1985, I decided that Reggie should be his godfather. It was truly the only way that I could fully honor our friendship.

4

Two Cheesies: What I Learned from Thurman Munson

First and foremost, however, Thurman was a team
player, and even after he became captain, his personality
never changed.

THREE YEARS INTO my life with the Yankees, Mr. Steinbrenner decided that he wanted his team to have a captain. He turned to Thurman Munson, who had been named Rookie of the Year as starting catcher in 1970. Thurman, as most fans know, was a sensational player and natural-born leader. The Yankees hadn't had a captain since the great Lou Gehrig retired in 1939. Out of respect to the legend of Lou, Joe McCarthy, the manager back then, declared that there would never be another Yankee captain. His statement held true until Mr. Steinbrenner turned to Thurman. But the Yankee catcher wasn't one for the spotlight. Thurman immediately told Mr. Steinbrenner that he didn't want the job.

"I'll be a terrible captain," he said. "I cuss and swear at people. I yell at umpires, and I don't like signing autographs or talking to reporters."

"Well, that's too bad. We need a leader, and you're my man." Case closed. George Michael Steinbrenner was in the habit of getting exactly what he wanted. That's why he was called the Boss.

If there was a regular kind of guy, Thurman was it. Rain or shine, he showed up at the ballpark every day, put on his uniform and his catcher's equipment, crouched down behind the plate, and played baseball. Like Lou Gehrig, he was humble and modest and always played hard and true.

A great defensive catcher, Thurman was trusted by the pitchers.

He also knew each hitter's strengths and weaknesses. When Thurman was injured and in pain, he made up for it by pushing himself, being extra quick behind the plate. His shoulder sometimes bothered him, but he would compensate by throwing sidearm as opposed to over the top. Thurman was never once on the disabled list, despite his physically demanding position. A terrific hitter, one of the best number-three batters in baseball, he had exceptional concentration and could hit to all fields. He could also hit in the clutch, just as good as anybody.

First and foremost, however, Thurman was a team player, and even after he became captain, his personality never changed. He treated everyone the same—from George Steinbrenner to a lowly batboy, like me. Of course, being the captain of the New York Yankees was a tremendous honor, and although Thurman knew it, he didn't like to be called "Captain" by the other players. He just wanted to be one of the guys. He never wore a *C* on his uniform as they do on other teams. With Thurman, it was just something you knew.

I remember one time when our huge designated hitter, Cliff Johnson, began fooling around with Thurman, referring to him as "Captain."

"What's with this 'Captain' shit?" Thurman said. He walked over to his six-foot four-inch, 225-pound teammate and pushed him onto a nearby couch. Cliff never called him "Captain" again.

Once, I, too, made the mistake of saying, "Hi, Captain."

Thurman said, "Come on. Ray. You know my name."

The less Thurman acted like the captain, the more his teammates respected him. Thurman was a great guy to be around. When I first met him in 1973, I was in awe of his confidence. Yet he had a certain reserve, too, that many people often mistook for grumpiness or moodiness.

You could always tell if he liked you because if he did, he would goof around and tell jokes, showing off his midwestern and blue-collar roots. Toward the end of 1973, he started including me when he got a little rowdy. He had a slapstick, off-the-wall kind of humor. He loved the television show *The Three Stooges* and did one of the best impersonations of Curly's famous laugh, "nyuk, nyuk, nyuk," that I have ever heard.

You never knew what Thurman might do next. The Boss had a large wood-paneled office, filled with framed autographed pictures of celebrities like Kirk Douglas and Cary Grant. An oversized chair in the shape of a baseball mitt sat in the corner. The Boss was meticulous, and every piece of paper was in its place. Walking in there, I sometimes thought, *This is what it must be like to be in the Oval Office of the White House.* I was standing in the office once, chitchatting with the Boss, when Thurman burst through the door, wearing shower shoes. He parked himself in Mr. Steinbrenner's chair and plopped his feet right up on the center of Mr. Steinbrenner's desk. Thurman stared at me, I looked over at the Boss, and we sort of chuckled as Thurman talked about an upcoming game. The Boss never told Thurman to take his feet off the desk during our conversation.

When Thurman felt like growing a beard during a road trip in August 1977, he did so to defy the Boss's no-facial-hair rule. He could just be that way sometimes. Maybe that had something to do with his relationship with his physically abusive truck-driver father. I had heard that Thurman's father was competitive with him and often belittled his playing. His father had abandoned the family when Thurman was in grade school. While we were on the road that summer, hanging out in Thurman's room one night after a game, I shared with him that my father, too, had taken off when I was young.

"How do you feel about that?" he asked.

"I don't think about it too much these days," I said. "I've got a step-father who's a good guy. Plus, I've always buried myself in baseball."

"Yeah, Ray, that's a good thing to do. I've always lost myself in sports, too," Thurman said. "You know, you're more fortunate than I was when I was your age because you've got Billy, the Boss, and Reggie caring about you. I didn't have anyone looking after me when I was young, like you do, Ray."

A couple of guys asked Thurman if he was worried about what the Boss would say about his facial hair. "Hell, no!" he replied. After three or four days on the road Thurman's beard attracted more and more attention and questions from the press. His face, like his body, was heavy, his hairline was receding, and his small brown eyes were deep-set. I thought he looked kind of like a walrus with that beard, but I never said anything. Finally the Boss yelled at Billy Martin, for supposedly losing control of Thurman. So after eleven days with a beard, Thurman decided to shave it off in a motel room in Syracuse, where the team was playing an exhibition game.

After a loss, some of the players would come into the clubhouse and start kicking and throwing stuff. Thurman was never like that. His philosophy was, if we lost today, we would win tomorrow. He didn't see losing a ball game as a reason to lose your cool. He just didn't dwell on things. It was one of the reasons why he was a good captain.

Thurman was always doing things for other people. I remember when we were playing against the Detroit Tigers in 1979. Lynn Jones, a young black rookie outfielder for the Tigers, was up at bat. As Thurman crouched behind him, sizing him up before he gave the pitcher the sign, he could see that Lynn's shoes were old and ragged. "Hey, kid, what size shoe do you wear?" Thurman asked. Lynn looked at Thurman quizzically as if to say, "Why would you care?"

After the game, while we were in the clubhouse, Thurman called me over. "Ray, do me a favor, go to the visitors' clubhouse and give these shoes to Lynn Jones. Let him know that it's a gift."

When I brought over the spikes, Lynn could hardly believe that a star from an opposing team would care enough to notice his shoes. "Thurman said he was going to get me some new shoes. Tell him I said thank you." Those were the days when players and teams weren't sponsored and didn't receive shoes from the manufacturer by the truckload like they do today.

As a batboy hanging around the clubhouse, I was constantly running errands for the players. In fact, I couldn't wait to help the guys out. There were often some funny requests, too. Right across from Yankee Stadium on 161st and River Avenue was a McDonald's. Thurman loved their cheeseburgers. I would be in the locker room doing my chores when suddenly Thurman would yell, "Ray, two cheesies!" I knew exactly what he wanted. I would tear out of the dugout, taking the shortcut through center field and out the center field gate. I'd sprint under the El, where the rumble of the trains was like music to me, a reminder that I was in my favorite borough, and then I'd return as fast as I could with two still-hot cheeseburgers for Thurman.

While Thurman surely loved his baseball and cheeseburgers, they were second and third in his life. Number one was always his two little girls, his son, and his wife, Diane, a pretty midwesterner with light brown hair and blue eyes. (Thurman always called her Diane, even though her given name was actually Diana, so we called her Diane, too.) She had been his childhood sweetheart in Canton, Ohio, and they had been together since both were twelve years old. He would often take her with him on his paper route. They were also on the school safety patrol together. Thurman hated being away from her and their young family, so he learned how to fly, and in the winter of 1978 he bought his own single-engine propeller airplane, a Cessna 150. Some guys brought their families to New York for the summer, but Thurman's family stayed in Ohio. Now he was able to fly home to Canton for every off-day during the season.

After games I often drove him in his brown Cadillac to Teterboro, a small airport just west of the city in Bergen County, New Jersey, where he kept his plane. I would drop him off right on the airfield. Then I'd sit in the car and watch him climb into the cockpit, taxi his two-seater plane to the end of the runway, and take off. Hector Pagan, the other batboy, used to come with me so I would have company on the ride back. On the way to the airport we would listen to Thurman's favorite radio station, WHN 1050, playing Tony Orlando and Dawn and Neil Diamond hits—and to Thurman telling funny stories about his kids.

Once I asked him if his son was named Thurman, too. He laughed and said, "Heck no!" Hector, driving, started snickering. Then Thurman looked over his shoulder at Hector and said, "And it ain't Heck-tor either."

After a day off, Thurman would usually fly back from the Akron-Canton Regional Airport in the afternoon to be ready for a night game. Hector and I made sure we arrived at least fifteen minutes before he was scheduled to land. Sitting in the car at the edge of the runway, waiting for his little white plane with the red stripes to slowly materialize in the sky and then touch down, I always marveled at Thurman's courage in flying his own plane. He'd park that plane alongside the others, jump out of the front seat, small suitcase in hand, and saunter over to the car.

"The great Thurman Munson!" I once had the courage to say.

"Shut the hell up." He smiled and pretended to give me a punch in the arm. Even though I was kidding, I really meant what I said. Hector and I were always proud to be riding in the same car with the New York Yankees' captian.

On the drive to Yankee Stadium, Thurman would inevitably say, "Ray, I'm starving. Let's stop at McDonald's. Wouldn't you love a cheesie, Ray?"

One summer day after I picked Thurman up, we found ourselves at the McDonald's across from the stadium. Thurman sat outside waiting while I went in to buy the food. It was a nice day, and the playground next door was full of kids. Thurman watched a boy pushing his little brother on a swing. As I came out with the order, I could see that the boy on the swing had Down syndrome.

Then I heard a commotion on the playground, and when I turned around, Thurman was gone. He was walking quickly toward the playground. That's when I heard two older kids taunting the younger ones. "What's the matter with your brother? He's a dumb-looking guy," they yelled, shoving the boy pushing the swing.

Thurman stopped, put his hands on his hips, and shouted, "Hey, you kids, get out of here. Leave the little guys alone!"

Everyone in the playground stopped what they were doing and watched as Thurman's voice grew louder. The older kids quickly ran off, and Thurman returned to the table, hand in hand with the boy who had Down syndrome and his brother. Their mother, a young African American woman in her twenties, walked beside them.

He handed me some money. "Go buy them some burgers, Ray." The kids and their mother sat down and ate with us, not recognizing Thurman. He asked where they went to school and what their favorite movie was. He talked to both boys exactly the same way I often heard him talking to his teammates.

Mr. Steinbrenner eventually came to realize how I took care of the players. Starting in 1977, he sent me on as many away games as I could attend, to help out and run errands for the team. Detroit was a particularly rough city, and Billy Martin always asked the players to stay close to our hotel, the Pontchartrain, in the middle of downtown. We never ventured far, mostly hanging out in each other's rooms, playing cards and watching television.

While Detroit was known to be a hotbed of racial tension with burnt-out neighborhoods and an abandoned downtown, it was also a city that was famous for its grilled, natural-casing hot dogs, served with chili sauce, mustard, and onions. I usually went around taking orders from the guys and then headed over a few blocks to the Coney Island, a big hot dog stand, just like the ones on the Coney Island boardwalk, where they sold the best hot dogs in town.

One day in late May during the 1979 season, a friend of one of the players came over to me while I was writing down the players' orders and said, "Hey, Ray, before you leave, why don't you roll a couple of joints for me?" The guy handed me a box with some weed in it. I stood there, almost embarrassed. I had no idea how to roll a joint.

Thurman turned to the guy. "Ray doesn't smoke, you jerk. What's wrong with you?" Thurman looked at me. "I'm sorry that he put you in that position, Ray. Go get the hot dogs and pretend this didn't happen."

"Well, he must be the only Puerto Rican in New York who doesn't smoke weed," the guy retorted.

Thurman stared at the guy. "Show some respect! You owe Ray an apology." It didn't matter who you were, if Thurman saw something that was wrong, he was there to stand up for you. That day I realized what made Thurman so respected in the game of baseball. If you want respect, you have to show respect.

The next night after a game, while we were still in Detroit, I was sitting by Reggie at his locker. He was usually the last one to leave the clubhouse, because he got dressed meticulously, making sure he was wearing just the right shirt and pants. The equipment guys were leaving the training room, and Thurman was right behind them.

"Hey, you still here?" Reggie called over to him.

"Yeah, Geno was working on my knees," Thurman said, referring to our trainer, Gene Monahan. "What are you guys doing now?"

"We're going over to that sports bar owned by Gordie Howe," Reggie said. "Wanna come?"

"Yeah, I'll go check it out," Thurman said.

I ran outside and got a cab for the three of us. I sat in the front, and Thurman and Reggie climbed in the back. When we got to the bar the place was packed. A lot of our players were there, and so were friends of the owner. Gordie was the only player to have competed in five different decades, from the 1940s to the 1980s, in the NHL.

Reggie found a seat at the bar. "Hey, over here, Thurman. This place has really great burgers. Want one?" Thurman shrugged and said he didn't think he was that hungry. Reggie laughed because it was rare that Thurman wasn't hungry enough to eat a cheeseburger. "Well, I'm not that hungry either," Reggie said. "But I could eat."

"Okay, so we'll order one burger," Thurman said.

I watched as Reggie scooted over on the bar stool, leaving room for Thurman to sit on the other half of the seat. The two of them sat there, each one taking a little bite, passing the burger back and forth.

"You know something, Reggie?" Thurman said. "This burger doesn't taste too bad even after you've eaten off of it." I wish I could have taken a picture. There they were—two of the biggest stars in Major League Baseball, who had not always been on the best of terms, sharing a bar stool and a cheeseburger.

THE YANKEES HAD slipped to fourth place that first few weeks of the season in April of 1979, and we had been struggling to recover. In early June, though, Reggie injured himself and missed several games. Days later, Billy Martin replaced Bob Lemon as our manager. A month later, Al Rosen, our president and COO, left. On top of that, Thurman was stressed with the severe pain in his knees. I spotted the hurt in his eyes as the trainers iced him down. Thurman was such a gamer, though; you could never tell if he was upset about his injuries. Billy had recognized this and had worked with Thurman, playing him in the outfield on several occasions and putting him in as designated hitter.

On July 26, in the final of a three-game series in New York, we beat the California Angels for the second time, 2–0. Thurman didn't play that night since his knees were really bothering him. After the game, I was busy in the clubhouse helping the team prepare for a six-day road trip, packing bats, balls, and mitts into the big metal chest, which would be flown to Wisconsin.

"Do you need my car when I'm away?" Thurman had let me borrow his car a few times before, when the team was traveling.

At first I didn't hear Thurman because he spoke to me from across the room.

"Hey, I know you don't like to help me because I have a pretty face, Ray," Thurman said, walking over to his locker. "But I guess you don't need my car—you've got Reggie's Rolls," he said as he changed out of his uniform into his street clothes.

"Rolls?" I laughed. "Reggie won't ever let me take that car out unless I'm gonna wash it or get it gassed up." Besides, I had learned my lesson and wouldn't dream of taking out a girlfriend in Reggie's car.

I did love driving Thurman's car around my Queens neighborhood, though. Quickly I discovered that it was a lot easier to pick up girls cruising around in a brand-new Cadillac than in the Volkswagen Rabbit that Reggie had given me. Thurman encouraged me to borrow his car. I always took good care of it, getting it washed and waxed and making sure that the gas tank was full when I returned it.

"Do you really need my car, Ray? I'm a little worried because I don't like you driving back from the airport alone when it's going to be so late," Thurman said. "Don't come with me tonight unless you really need my car."

"Well, I've gotta play some games for my league while you all are gone," I said. At the time I was playing on a sandlot team on Long Island. "If it's okay with you, I won't go with you tonight, Thurman. But thanks for the offer."

I helped him pack up his away uniforms and equipment. We walked out of the clubhouse together.

"See you soon," Thurman said patting my shoulder.

"You know, I just don't understand how you can fly back and forth to Canton all alone in that airplane," I said.

Thurman put his hand back on my shoulder, resting it there. "Well, Ray, if you knew Diane, really knew her, then you'd understand."

I watched him climb in his car and drive out of the parking lot, toward Teterboro Airport and the open sky. In turn, I headed underground for the familiar D train. Passing the graffiti-ridden walls, I spotted a large number 15 sprayed in neon orange bubble letters. I couldn't help thinking of the lyrics to Simon & Garfunkel's "The Sounds of Silence," about prophecies written on subway walls. How eerie that I would meet Paul Simon years later, and that he would turn out to be the voice of Thurman Munson in my animated film, *Henry & Me*.

W E WERE SWEPT three straight games in Milwaukee beginning on July 27. Then the team flew to Chicago for another three-game series, which ended on August 1. This time, the tables turned and we swept the White Sox. The next morning I read about the game in the August 2 early edition of the *Daily News*. I saw that Thurman had uncharacteristically started at first base. He was batting third and went 0–1 with a strikeout and a walk before being replaced by Jim Spencer in the bottom of the third. We won the game that night 9–1, but since Thurman had been taken out I thought he must be in serious pain.

That afternoon, an off-day for the team, I was hanging out in Rockaway, Queens, with my friend Arthur Rubenstein, who had a batting cage in his backyard. We were hitting balls into the cage when Arthur's mother appeared at the door. A small woman with short dark hair, she stood there and wiped her brow with a pale blue handkerchief.

"Ray, come in here." She looked hot and tired.

I walked in the door and saw that *General Hospital* was on the television, but the banner that ran across the bottom of the sscreen caught my eye: "We interrupt this show for a special report." The ABC anchor, Roger Grimsby, said, "New York Yankee All-Star catcher Thurman Munson has been killed in the crash of the plane he was piloting. His plane crashed this afternoon at the Akron-Canton Regional Airport in Ohio, where he was practicing landing and taking off. Thurman Munson was thirty-two years old."

In silence we sat in the living room and watched the news broadcasts—switching from channel to channel to see if we could get more information. It had to be a mistake. Thurman couldn't be dead. He was Superman. My hands starting trembling. I sat there staring at the television set long after the news ended. Finally I turned to my friend. All I could say was, "Life is funny sometimes." Then I broke down in tears—tears that wouldn't stop for the next five days. I went back outside, and Arthur pitched to me. I hit the ball over and over, harder each time.

I woke up early the next morning, and for an instant it seemed like any other Friday morning getting ready to go to the ballpark. Then it all sank in. On the way to the subway, I passed the newsstand where I bought the *Daily News* every day. Out of habit I fumbled in my pocket for change to pay for the paper but when I saw the headlines, AIR CRASH KILLS YANKS' MUNSON, I froze, staring at the photo of the charred wreckage of Thurman's plane. Then I glanced at the boxes at the bottom of the paper. 3 DEPUTY MAYORS GO IN KOCH SHAKEUP; FIRE BOMB ATOP BROOKLYN BRIDGE; NIXON DROPS PLAN TO BUY E. SIDE CO-OP. There to the right was a picture of Thurman, looking like the warrior he was in his Yankees cap. I shoved the coins back in my pocket and slowly walked down the stairs to the subway.

I felt ill and anxious when I arrived at the clubhouse. The first thing I did was remove one of Thurman's bats from the bat bag and hide it in my locker. I knew how important his final bats would be—a way to keep him close.

Pete Sheehy, the clubhouse manager, and I began to get things ready. That morning, Pete had a blank look on his face, and it made him look older than his sixty-nine years. He walked over to me and touched my arm. "You know, Ray, out of habit, I walked out of my house this morning and looked to my left, thinking that Thurman would be there to pick me up today and bring me to the stadium." Pete's voice trailed off. He didn't drive a car, and Thurman, who liked to arrive early at the stadium, often gave him a ride.

I realized that Pete had gone through this intense kind of sadness before during his many long years with the Yankees, starting with the tragic loss of our last captain, Lou Gehrig. I looked at Pete and pictured him listening to Lou's famous farewell speech at Yankee Stadium on that hot July 4, 1939. "Fans, for the past two weeks you have been reading about the bad break I got. Yet today I consider myself the luckiest man on the face of this earth. I have been in ballparks for seventeen years and have never received anything but kindness and encouragement from you fans . . ." Pete had often told me how hard it was to see Lou, in his thirties, suffer from the deadly amyotrophic lateral sclerosis, or ALS, a disease with no cure.

Pete had lost others he was close to over the years, including second baseman Tony Lazzeri, who died from a fall at age forty-two, and Yankee manager Miller Huggins, who passed away at age fifty from a rare illness in 1929, only two years after Pete had started working for the Yankees. To a clubhouse manager, every player and manager who walks through the door is one of your kids and you take care of them all. Another of Pete's kids was now gone.

The clubhouse was strangely silent as the players began to file in one by one. Everybody looked empty. First Lou Piniella came in, white as a ghost, and then Graig Nettles, looking like he had just been punched in the chest. I could tell they hadn't slept all night. Their eyes were red and swollen. These were two of Thurman's closest friends, and I figured they were taking it the hardest.

I tried not to, but I couldn't help staring at Thurman's locker, which was right next to the trainer's room, where everyone passed by as if they were passing a casket lying in state. The team kept a safe in the trainer's room, and everybody was going in and out to put their stuff away or get taped for the game. As I walked by Thurman's locker, I swore I could feel his spirit. I felt sure I could see that number 15 on his back as he bent over to tie his shoelaces, his chest protector hanging loose on him, his hat turned around backwards, ready to go out and catch. It was a strange feeling, but I wasn't the only one who felt it. Everybody was hesitating as they walked by, resisting the urge to reach out and touch the locker. I kept thinking, *Any second now Thurman's going to come bouncing through the clubhouse door, laughing, telling me to buy two cheeseburgers for him across the street.* Thurman couldn't really be dead.

I found Bobby Murcer asleep on a couch. The day before, he had flown from New Jersey to Ohio, spent the night with Thurman's wife and kids, and had just flown back this morning.

Mr. Steinbrenner tried to talk to the team. His shirt was wrinkled and his tie was crooked, something I had never seen. His eyes were so swollen it scared me. I had never witnessed him cry. I thought that now, for the first time, he had found that someone was bigger than he was—and that was God. No matter that he was the Boss. Now God was stepping in.

"There were some cracked ribs and teeth." The Boss spoke slowly and unsteadily. "He was trapped in the plane." Hell, I thought, cracked ribs and teeth weren't so bad. Thurman had certainly gotten hurt worse than that playing ball. It wasn't realistic, but I truly kept saying to myself that maybe Thurman wasn't really dead. He was so god-damned tough. He could get himself out of that plane. My thoughts were running wild, and then I heard Mr. Steinbrenner say something about fire. "He was trapped." Suddenly the reality and the horror of it hit me, and I thought about the pain and how scared Thurman must have been. I hoped it had all gone quickly.

The Boss broke down. Then the whole team started sobbing. Somebody said how everything seemed so small now that Thurman was gone. Mr. Steinbrenner acted as the father figure to us all, maybe for some for the first time since he bought the team.

"If you need time off, money, or just someone to talk to, come to me," he told us.

Then Billy Martin, looking like he'd slept in his clothes, stepped forward to speak. My eyes kept drifting over to Thurman's locker. I could see his personal things in there—photos of Diane and their kids. Clothes. Plaid pants. That ugly blue and orange striped shirt we kidded him about. Those extra pairs of spikes he always had on hand to give away to others. Many of his possessions were there in his locker just like they had been before the team went on the road trip on July 26—waiting for Thurman to come back.

Billy could only get out a few words. This was the only time in my life when I saw that the game wasn't the most important thing in Billy's eyes. Then Bobby Murcer came forward to tell us how Diane Munson and the kids were doing. He said that she was a strong woman but would need all of us to help her through this. I thought of the times Thurman talked about her and his kids. They were so little. I knew it would be very hard on them to lose their father so suddenly. Then the locker room grew so quiet that all you could hear was the sound of sobbing. I had celebrated two World Series wins with these guys in this very same locker room. I remembered the happiness and the spray of champagne that stung our eyes. Now the same guys were there, hardly able to stand, as they shook with tears. It was a family mourning the loss of one of their own, the Yankee family—what had become my family.

For a few minutes, nobody knew what was going to happen next. Thurman had been the captain, and it had been his job to pull the players together when something was wrong. Who could do that for him? Finally Reggie Jackson stepped into the middle of the room. He started reciting verses from the Bible in a soft voice while tears streamed down his face. My mind raced back to that evening when the two of them sat on that bar stool sharing a cheeseburger. Thurman was always there for everyone else. Now it was Reggie's turn to be there for him.

Bobby Murcer told Diane Munson that there was no way we could play the game that night. But Diane told Bobby that we had to play because that is how Thurman would have wanted it. I knew that was true, and so did the other players, but nobody's heart was in it.

"I've got a tough job for you, Ray." Billy Martin, standing next to the Boss, pulled me aside. "Can you go out to Teterboro Airport and pick up Thurman's car?" I looked at Billy, and then I looked at the Boss.

"Ray, we really need you to go out there and pick up Thurman's car," the Boss said.

Naturally I said yes, but I sure as hell wanted to say no. I was much too spooked to go out to the airport and get in Thurman's car without driving him back to the stadium. But when Thurman asked me to do something, I never thought twice about it. I figured the team had a much tougher job, to go out on the field and play the game that night. This was the least I could do.

As Hector drove me out to the airport, he turned to me. "You know, Thurman always was my favorite player. He was so kind to me." Then Hector's voice cracked and he, too, started to sob. We pulled up to the parking lot at Teterboro Airport. Thurman's brown Cadillac was right where he had left it. It took the sight of his car to convince me that Thurman's death was finally real. I walked to the car and then looked back at Hector. We nodded, and then he drove away.

As I slowly opened the door and climbed in, I realized this was the first time that I was coming back from Teterboro without Thurman. I switched on the car radio. It was tuned to WKTU, a disco station. I left it on and listened to Donna Summer belt out "Last Dance." I thought back to a few Saturday mornings in early July when Thurman and I had watched *Soul Train*, a popular show then, in the players' lounge together. Thurman had copied the dancers, mimicking "dancing the line"—where one dancer, flanked by groups of people, swivels his hips, claps, and dances down the line from beginning to end—just exactly like they did on the show. Lou, Bobby, and I urged Thurman on.

"Oh, yeah. Shake it!" Man, Thurman had rhythm! That big hulking walrus of a guy could dance his ass off.

As I drove back to the stadium through heavy traffic, I figured that Thurman must have tuned in to that disco station to stay awake.

It had been late as we walked out of the clubhouse together the last night I saw him.

That night, before the start of our four-game set with the Baltimore Orioles in the Bronx, we paid tribute to our Thurman in a pregame ceremony that Mr. Steinbrenner had carefully orchestrated. The fans wept as a cool, light mist enveloped the stadium. The starters stood at their defensive positions, holding their caps over their hearts, but the catcher's box remained empty. There was no way we could replace our catcher.

"We pause to pay tribute to Thurman, our brother and your baseball son," a priest intoned. Robert Merrill's voice cracked as he sang the national anthem. Then our legendary announcer, Bob Sheppard, asked the crowd of 51,151 for a moment of silence as a tribute. That moment quickly turned into a loud and sustained outpouring of love for Thurman, a standing ovation that seemed to last for twenty minutes. Even the members of the Orioles applauded and stood to pay their respects. Jerry Narron, the Yankees' backup catcher, waited near the dugout.

Everywhere you looked there were signs and banners, many of them made from bedsheets and scrawled with spray paint. WE LOVE YOU, THURMAN and YOU'LL BE A YANKEE FOREVER, THURM 15.

Luis Tiant, our star Cuban pitcher, seemed to be the only one who brought his game to the park. The other players seemed lifeless, like flat ginger ale. Three up, three down. It all seemed rote without energy or spirit. During the game Graig Nettles had to keep running into the clubhouse so that no one would see him cry. Reggie, in right field, was shaking as he placed his mitt over his face several times to hide his emotions. But rookie Jerry Narron had the toughest job of all: stepping into Thurman's impossible-to-fill shoes. He had been the catcher the night before Thurman died, and now he was in that position again, only with much different stakes.

We lost the game, but it didn't mean a thing. We were all like zombies back in the clubhouse. We lost the following night to Baltimore, too. We had lost games before, and I knew how Thurman always reacted. He took a shower, got dressed, and went home. We would win tomorrow. He never dwelled on losses, and we all knew he would want us to feel the same way. The Orioles had beaten us 1–0 the first night and 5–4 the second, and not a single person in that locker room cared.

Following the August 3 game, after some of the players had already gone home, Thurman's bat was beginning to weigh heavily on my mind. Part of me really wanted to keep it forever. I walked into Billy Martin's office. He was talking to the press, so I started to walk out.

"Hey, come here, kid, don't leave." He grabbed me, and we ducked into his closet to get away from the swarming media. I held the bat up. I knew how special it was, and I knew that Billy should have it.

"I hope you're not mad at me," I said to Billy.

"I could never be mad at you, Ray," he said, and then once again he told me, "I couldn't love you any more even if you were Italian." We cried in each other's arms while the press waited outside the closet, trying to get the latest word on Thurman. I was glad, and somewhat relieved, that Billy had the bat. I knew I had made the right decision.

The funeral was scheduled for Monday, August 6. Mr. Steinbrenner chartered a plane and said that every member of the team and their families would go. There was a game that night, but he didn't care about that one either. If we didn't make it back, Mr. Steinbrenner said, we would forfeit. We belonged that day in the heartland, in Canton, Ohio, giving Thurman the respect and love he deserved.

There were so many people at the funeral that they had to move it from the church to the Canton Civic Center. Former teammates and friends flew in from all over the country—I was lost in a sea of faces with red eyes. Lou Piniella and Bobby Murcer spoke in the large room filled with fresh flowers. Their voices were choked and raw from crying. Then a priest spoke. I tried to listen, but it was so hard to focus. I stared at the casket and the framed picture of Thurman in his Yankee hat and pinstripes next to it.

The priest asked the team to stand and be official pallbearers. Dressed in suits, they rose silently from their seats and walked forward, forming a line on each side of the simple wooden casket, covered with white flowers. People slowly went up to the casket to pay their respects and say farewell. I didn't think I was ready to do that.

I waited to talk to Diane Munson, dressed in black from head to toe, holding hands with her children. I tried to listen to what other people were saying to her because I didn't know what to say. When I finally got up there, the only words I could manage were, "I really loved him."

She nodded and hugged me. "I know. You were always a help to him," she whispered.

I returned to my seat in the back of the room, staring at the backs of the team as they stood beside the casket. Then one of Mr. Steinbrenner's aides, a security guard, tapped me on the shoulder and told me that the Boss wanted me to come up to the casket and stand beside him with the team. "Mr. Steinbrenner wants you next to him." I followed him. While I was standing beside the Boss, I felt like I was going to fall apart in front of everyone. I hadn't really slept in days, and I couldn't stop my tears as I looked at the casket and the photo of Thurman beside it.

The Boss, his face puffy and red, put his arm around my shoulders. "Stay strong. It's almost over. You can do it."

As I looked up and down the row of players, I heard Diane's words to me. Thurman always liked for me to be there for him. Even though a lot of the players said I was Reggie's guy, Thurman knew that I was everyone's guy. I thought about the little things that I did for Thurman. He wasn't too particular when I packed his bags for away games, as long as he had the shirts and pants he needed. I always knew just how he liked his coffee—lots of cream and light sugar. I made sure that he had a few Cokes and some snacks in the car whenever we drove to the airport. But I didn't do these things just because it was my job; I did them happily because I loved him.

Though a man of few words, who rarely let others into his private world, Thurman had given me a valuable gift. He taught me how important it was to show a soft side. The message was clear: Thurman wasn't going to be around to look after those two little boys on the playground or help out a rookie player who needed new spikes, but I was.

Through my muffled sobs, I could hear an echo booming across the locker room. "Ray! Two cheesies!" I watched the players pick up the casket and turn to leave. I whispered one last good-bye, thinking what an honor it was to have been a small part of the life of a great man.

Bobby Murcer: Because We Loved Him

There's an old expression, "Once a Yankee, always a Yankee,"
and in Bobby's case nothing could have been truer.

NUMBER 1—THAT'S WHAT Bobby Murcer wore—and he was the number-one attraction from the minute he joined the Yankees for good, after returning from the army in 1969. Most sportswriters dubbed him the next Mickey Mantle and thought he was the ticket to pulling the Yankees out of their slump, but to me, Bobby was just the cat's ass. I imitated the bop in his walk, echoed his Oklahoma twang, and stuck a can of Skoal in my back pants pocket, just as he did. Damn, even the name Bobby Murcer was cool.

By the time I arrived at the Yankee clubhouse that summer in 1973, Bobby and Thurman, who both joined the Yankees in 1969, had become best friends. The two, old-fashioned men from the heartland, gave all they could to the game of baseball. They knew how to play, and they knew how to win.

As a boy growing up in Oklahoma City, Bobby lived and breathed the legends of Ruth, Gehrig, and DiMaggio. Humble and charming, he wore the Yankee uniform with more pride than anyone I had ever known. Bobby went from Clark Kent to a trim Superman when he put on his pinstripes. Thurman's charm, on the other hand, was that he was completely unaware of his image, right down to his clashing polyester plaids. All blue-collar, squatty and brash, he could be cocky. Some guys said, "Man, Thurman's grumpy." If Thurman was John Belushi, then Bobby was John Denver.

In the beginning of the 1974 season Bobby had the courage to ask Pete Sheehy if he could bring his rocking chair into the clubhouse.

"Sure," Mr. Sheehy said.

But a few days later, when Bobby walked through the door carrying a simple, sturdy wooden rocker, Mr. Sheehy said, "Are you really going to sit in that thing?"

Bobby parked himself in that rocking chair, his throne, for hours every day, answering questions from reporters, snoozing a bit, listening to country-western music. Inevitably he'd play the card game Spades with Thurman, who plunked himself down in any old chair he could find. That rocker, part of Bobby's country boy charm, had an ear-piercing squeak, and at one time or another we all gave Bobby grief about it. He didn't pay any attention. He just kept right on rocking.

In early June, Sparky Lyle, our resident practical joker, known for sitting on players' birthday cakes buck naked, entered the clubhouse carrying a saw. You could always tell when Sparky was up to something; he'd raise one of his bushy eyebrows while his handlebar mustache drooped to one side. Then you knew you were in big trouble. That particular day, Bobby was nowhere in sight. I looked over in the direction of Bobby's locker, where some of the players had gathered. Sparky picked up the rocker with one hand and started sawing the legs off.

"Now, don't you guys say a word to Bobby." He laughed, took his tools, and quickly reattached the shortened legs to the rockers. A little while later, Bobby entered the clubhouse, went over to his locker, stepped out of his street clothes and put on the long johns that he always wore underneath his uniform, and sat down in his rocking chair. His knees rose right up to his chest. He looked around at his laughing, cheering teammates, then kept right on rocking. A few minutes later, Thurman ambled over, and the two started playing cards. They talked about their kids and their wives—both of them had married their high school sweethearts—just like they always did. No mention of anything unusual.

I loved when Bobby brought his son, Todd, into the clubhouse. Todd, about eight or nine when I first met him, reminded me of a blond version of Opie on *Andy Griffith*. "Ray, will you watch Todd for me?" Bobby asked when I was doing my chores. I'd take Todd out to the batting cage and pitch to him. He was just as sweet and good-natured as his father. Bobby played hours of catch with Todd. Often, he'd mess up Todd's hair and say, "I love you, son."

I'd watch Bobby with Todd and listen to Thurman talk about his three kids and wonder if my biological father ever talked about me. As a young man this was my first experience watching two guys I admired being good fathers. Later in my life, when I became a dad, I would remember how Bobby and Thurman treated their kids.

When the tall, dark, boisterous Lou Piniella arrived at the clubhouse, in the beginning of the '74 season, it was almost impossible to ignore his penetrating voice, punctuated by hearty guffaws, especially when he was laughing at his own jokes. He'd stand by Thurman's or Bobby's locker, analyzing his swing, from when I recorded it earlier, trying to figure out how he could improve. "What would you think if I put my weight on my left foot instead of my right? Should I hold the bat back here?" Thurman and Bobby laughed at Lou's intensity—"You sound like some sort of goddamned professor," Thurman chided—but the three quickly became friends.

Thurman, on the other hand, had no time at all for dissecting the game of baseball. When I was videotaping the players, he never once looked at the tapes. "You want to analyze me with that camera?" Thurman asked me.

"Yeah," I said.

"Okay, put the camera on," he said. Thurman stuck his thumb in his mouth and started blowing on it. Incredibly, his stomach filled up with air. Laughing, I could hardly hold the camera still as I watched his stomach grow larger and larger. So much for videotaping Thurman.

Bobby's approach to the game, pure energy and sheer joy, was never more apparent than when he ran out to the field to organist Eddie Layton's version of Paul McCartney's "Get Back." Bobby trotted to the beat of the popular Beatles song almost as if he was dancing. It was like watching a Little Leaguer playing ball when he was out in center field.

Conversely, Lou incessantly talked hitting strategies with Bobby and Thurman. They would sit down on a bench in the clubhouse and listen to him ramble. Then they'd chuckle watching him stand in left field, going through his batting stance when there was a lull in the game. Whenever Thurman sauntered into the locker room, Lou was one of the few who could shout, to anyone who would listen in the clubhouse, "Let's give a big hand to Thurman Lee Munson."

"Give me a damn break, Lou!" Thurman would laugh.

Bobby was deeply disappointed when our manager since 1966, Ralph Houk, resigned after the last game of the 1973 season. Ralph, an optimistic John Wayne–like character, had played with Mickey Mantle and Joe DiMaggio. He knew how to treat players and bring out their star power.

"You're our guy, Bobby. You're gonna lead us to the Promised

Land. We're gonna win this year," Ralph told Bobby every season. Despite Ralph's optimistic nature, though, he and the Boss had gotten off to a shaky start. A former major in the army who had won a Purple Heart serving in World War II, Ralph didn't like it when Mr. Steinbrenner presented him with a list of players needing haircuts during the '73 season. Like Billy Martin, Ralph was his own man, unafraid of arguing with umpires in order to protect his players.

Our new manager, Bill Virdon, had the strong physique—big arms, broad shoulders—of a state trooper and the personality to match. A former center fielder for the St. Louis Cardinals and the Pittsburgh Pirates, he had been managing the Pirates when he joined the Yankees. The only time I ever saw him show any kind of passion was when Thurman struck out a few weeks after Bill took over. Frustrated, Thurman hurled his batting helmet. Bill pushed me out of the way so I wouldn't get hit and then turned to Thurman and yelled, "You're not that good!" Bill's attitude was that all the players were the same. I saw Bobby's subtle grimaces whenever Bill barked an order, but part of Bobby's grace was taking things in stride, riding the waves, keeping his cool, trying his hardest.

While Yankee Stadium was being renovated in 1974 and '75, we played at Shea, the other major league stadium in New York. We opened the 1974 season with a 6–1 victory over the Cleveland Indians to a small house, only 20,744 fans. We weren't able to attract a large crowd at Shea, where the Mets logo sat right above the Yankees logo on the scoreboard. We won our next three games as well, starting the season 4–0, but then we only won four of our next eleven games. Bill decided to pull Bobby out of center and put him in right field. On May 28 he replaced Bobby with Elliott Maddox, the twenty-six-year-old speedster who had just come to us from the Texas Rangers.

That night a television on top of one of the lockers was tuned to WPIX, Channel 11, the Yankees station since 1951. Jerry Girard, the sportscaster, announced, "With Elliott Maddox playing center field the Yankees will now have a better shot at winning."

"Well, now that the liability is out of center field we have a chance of measuring our ring sizes," Bobby said, a hint of sarcasm in his voice, as he turned to Elliott. They stood in front of their lockers, laughing together. Bobby, of course, was referring to the championship rings. He was always trying to make someone else feel better. Bobby told Elliott he didn't mind giving up center field to someone of his extraordinary skills.

As the season wore on, Bobby started playing much better in his new position in right field, though he was struggling with his hitting. The right field fence at Shea, thirty to forty feet deeper than the one at Yankee Stadium, with its famously swirling winds, made it a particularly tough arena for Bobby, a left-handed power hitter. Back in the clubhouse, I'd find Bobby sitting calmly, rocking, deep in thought. I knew he was trying to figure out how he could improve his batting. Thurman, on the other hand, was having an excellent season—he made his third All-Star team and won his second straight Gold Glove Award, and was emerging as a slugger, hitting a career high of twenty home runs—but he could feel Bobby's frustration. He usually got Bobby's mind off the situation by asking him about his kids or his wife, Kay.

"C'mon, Bobby, I'm gonna tape two bats together, then you're gonna hit that ball," Lou Piniella would say, laughing loudly. "It's just a question of time, just a matter of time. Remember, you're the great Bobby Murcer."

"You'd better believe it," I said whenever Lou spoke. Sometimes

Lou sang, "Hang on in there, Bobby," slightly altering the lyrics of the 1974 Johnny Bristol song "Hang On in There Baby." I'd join him in the chorus. But Bobby, after averaging twenty-six homers a season between 1969 and 1973, hit only two home runs at Shea that year, one on September 21, the other on September 22.

A few weeks after the end of the season—we had finished with a record of 89–73, two games behind the Baltimore Orioles—and just after Bobby's game had picked up, he received a devastating phone call: he had been traded for the San Francisco Giants' Bobby Bonds. Like most everyone else, I heard the startling news on television. I knew that ever since he was a boy he had dreamed of becoming a Yankee. Not only had he achieved his dream, but he had once been the star of the team. I was sure that Bobby must have been deeply hurt when he packed his bags, collected his rocking chair from the Yankee clubhouse, and headed for Arizona for the Giants' spring training camp in 1975.

That May '75 I had ten days off from the Bradenton Pirates. When I returned to New York from Florida I called Dick Howser and asked if I could practice with the Yankees. "Sure, Ray, come on over." While I was there one of the batboys became ill, so I volunteered to help out for a few days since I had experience.

A lot of magic was lost when Bobby left us. In the past when I would sit in the locker room, taking off my uniform after games, I'd watch the great baseball camaraderie. Now the place seemed empty without the antics around Bobby's rocker. I missed watching Bobby, Thurman, and Lou playing cards. Inevitably Lou would get that smirk on his face, and then throw his cards against the wall when he had a bad hand, while Bobby rocked on calmly. I also missed seeing Bobby's kids, Tori and Todd, around the clubhouse.

Now Bobby Bonds' son Barry, who was ten at the time, and Sandy Alomar's boys, eight-year-old Sandy Jr. and Robbie, who was six, were using the locker room as their playground. Bobby and Sandy had asked me to babysit for their boys a few times. Barry would, of course, grow up to be baseball's home run king, while Robbie would have a Hall of Fame career, becoming perhaps the greatest second baseman of all time. I could see, even at their young ages, a focus and intensity. That, combined with their superb hand-eye coordination whenever they battled it out at the Ping-Pong table, made me realize they might go on to greatness someday. As much as Robbie wanted to become a Yankee, his dream would never come true. His last act as a player would be to sign a baseball to Mr. Steinbrenner that read, *My only regret was not playing for you.*

Thurman managed to stay in touch with Bobby, often calling him, keeping up with his news. He reported back to us after he and Bobby had chatted. "He's not so crazy about Candlestick Park," Thurman told us. Later, when Bobby was traded from the Giants to the Chicago Cubs, Thurman would say, "Bobby's not real happy playing with the Cubs. You know, he left his heart in New York."

It was a sunny Friday at the end of June in 1979 when Bobby, wearing a blue shirt and looking tan and healthy, strode into the Yankee trainer's room, grinning from ear to ear. He had been traded back to the one team that he cherished. We needed a left-handed batter to play against some tough right-handed pitchers, and the Boss, never one to worry over a misguided decision, had called Bobby in Chicago. "What would you think of coming back?"

"I'd be back in a heartbeat," Bobby answered. The Boss welcomed Bobby by telling him, "You are always a Yankee now, no matter what."

Thurman gave Bobby a bear hug while glancing over at Bobby's locker, making sure his stuff was firmly in place, as if to confirm that he was there to stay.

"Welcome home, pal." Thurman didn't have to utter another word. His smile said it all. Since Billy Martin was now wearing Bobby's old number 1, Bobby fittingly wore the number 2.

"Hey, Ray." Bobby wrapped his arm around my shoulder. "We're going to win together now." Even though I knew Bobby wasn't going to be the big star that he once was—time was passing, and we now had Reggie as our right fielder—he and I picked up just where we left off in 1974. Within a few days after his arrival I found him sitting in that old familiar place, right there in his rocker, in front of his locker, expecting to be a winner. He was a Yankee and was ready to do anything he had to do to see our team win.

There's an old expression, "Once a Yankee, always a Yankee," and in Bobby's case nothing could have been truer. I pulled up a chair and sat next to him.

"You know, Bobby, I've been doing some commercials with Reggie. It's fun, and I've been thinking I'd like to try to be an actor," I said.

"Well, isn't that something? You know, I'd kinda like to be an on-air announcer one of these days myself," Bobby said. Without warning he grabbed a bat. It was almost as though a director was coaching the two of us as we used the bat as a microphone and pretended we were on air. I was the commentator with Bobby doing the play-by-play.

"Hey, ladies and gentlemen, this is Ray Negron, and I'm Bobby Murcer." Bobby became animated, even giddy. The two of us were lost in a fantasyland, having a great time. I felt as if Bobby had never left the Yankees.

A few days later Thurman, Bobby, and I were hanging out in the training room when Thurman turned to us. "Hey, where's Lou?"

Gene Monahan, our trainer, who had started his career as a batboy in 1962, was massaging our pitcher Catfish Hunter's shoulder while Catfish read the *Daily News*. "Lou's taken up dancing, if you can believe that," Cat muttered. Lou was always talking about either baseball, the stock market, or horse racing. But dance lessons? We looked at each other in disbelief and cracked up. A few minutes later Lou burst into the trainer's room, wearing that famous '70s uniform—bell-bottoms, boots, and a paisley shirt.

"I hear you're taking dance lessons." Thurman looked at Lou and laughed. I was sitting near a radio, and the song "Shadow Dancing," sung by Andy Gibb, came across the airwaves. Lou moved from side to side, and then started gyrating to the beat. He thrust out his hips, threw his hands high in the air, and thrust his head back and forth. The crazier his dance steps got, the higher I turned up the volume. Lou sang the last part of the refrain at the top of his lungs, "Baby you do it right," continuing to rock, shaking his ass. He pulled his comb out from his front pants pocket and ran it through his thick dark hair.

I turned the lights on and off and then grabbed a nearby lamp. I started slowly swinging it, creating a strobe effect. The light bouncing off the walls made Lou go even crazier. He ran over to the radio and turned it up to full volume, and as the music blasted, he shimmied his shoulders and raised his hands to the ceiling. A cheap white tile fell to the floor. Then Lou, dancing wildly, arms flailing, began punching out the ceiling tiles as he shook his head and hips and danced around the room. A thin white dust lightly covered us. I swung the lamp faster. Dizzy, we clapped our hands and continued egging Lou on. "Do it light . . ." We shouted the refrain, our hair now white with dust. Catfish, shirtless, sat there as if he didn't hear a thing, reading the paper, chewing tobacco and spitting into a cup, while Gene massaged his back and shoulders. Gene, however, was getting more agitated by the minute.

"Okay, out—all of you, get the hell outta here!" he yelled.

We paid no attention. We were shaking our bodies, singing as loud as we could.

"*Out! Now!*" The louder Gene yelled, the noisier and more boisterous we became. Finally Gene turned the radio off, grabbed us by the arms, and tossed us out of the room.

"What assholes," Catfish muttered as he sat on the trainer's table, staring at his newspaper.

I N THE MIDDLE of July 1979, when Thurman bought his fourth plane in eighteen months, a powerful twin-engine Cessna Citation 501 with his number N15NY emblazoned on the tail, he tried to get Lou and Bobby to fly with him. Even though Lou had flown with him before I overheard him tell Thurman, "That is one mighty jet, Thurman. I really don't know if I can get in that thing."

Over the next few weeks I heard Bobby voice similar concerns. "You don't have enough flying hours for me," I heard him say.

Thurman laughed. "I am so proud of this. Can't you see, guys? This plane is going to make it possible for me to see my family more."

At the end of July the Yankees were, as I described earlier, playing a three-game series in Chicago, and Thurman and Lou stayed at Bobby's house for three nights. One night after Bobby went to bed, Lou and Thurman stayed up half the night debating who was going to be the better pinch hitter. After the last day game in the series, on August 1, Bobby and Kay and their children drove Thurman to a small airport in Chicago. Thurman invited them to fly with him to Canton, but Bobby told Thurman he had to get back to New York for the game on August 3. Thurman wanted the Murcers to see his plane, and they all sat inside it for forty-five minutes listening to Neil Diamond tapes. Then Thurman asked Bobby to loan him some money for fuel, which Bobby did. The Murcers drove alongside the runway and watched as Thurman revved up the engines and took off by himself. Bobby described to me later how he and his wife had an uneasy feeling, sitting on the runway, watching Thurman's powerful jet disappear into the black of night.

THREE DAYS LATER, after the fatal crash, Bobby stood at the Canton Civic Center alongside Lou Piniella as they each delivered a heartfelt eulogy for their fallen comrade before their teammates and Thurman's friends and family. Bobby began quoting the educator and philosopher Angelo Patri, but his voice cracked and he had no choice but to sit down. Lou spoke of Thurman as a great competitor and how affectionate and friendly Thurman was. His voice choked, too, and he couldn't continue. He walked off the platform.

Later that same day, on our chartered plane that was headed from Canton to Newark, Billy approached Bobby. "Hey, don't even worry about playing tonight. You need to take the night off and get some rest."

"No," I heard Bobby say. "For some reason I'm not that tired, and I feel like I've just got to play tonight." Bobby said that Diane Munson really wanted the team to play. Bobby was playing for Thurman, and for Diane and their children. Personally, I wondered how he would find the strength to make it through the game.

When we landed at Newark Airport, half the team went home, and the rest of the players went to the ballpark. Guys were sprawled all over the clubhouse, sleeping on chairs and couches, anyplace they could find to stretch out their exhausted bodies. Nobody had gotten any rest the last four days, and Thurman's death was taking its toll on us all.

It had been a long and difficult day, and we still had nine innings of baseball to play. The game was going to be nationally televised on *Monday Night Baseball*. I wondered if Diane would watch from Ohio. Would she turn the game on, just out of habit?

I didn't feel like talking much the rest of the afternoon. Trying hard to act like it was just another day at the ballpark, I checked in with Mr. Sheehy. He had spent the night before at the clubhouse.

"Ray, I sent the uniforms out to Joe Fosina, you know, the guy at the dry cleaners in New Rochelle—he does special things with the uniforms sometimes," he said and held up a uniform. "We asked him to sew these armbands on."

Mr. Sheehy silently trod from locker to locker and hung a uniform in each with a black armband and the number 15 emblazoned on the left sleeve. He stopped at Thurman's locker, which now had a large bouquet of flowers in front of it. Everything was cleaned out, except for his catcher's equipment, which appeared there like a horse without a rider. Mr. Sheehy lightly touched Thurman's trademark orange chest protector, then looked around the clubhouse and hung his uniform, with the armband and the number 15 facing out to the center of the room. "I've never done anything like this before," I heard him mumble as I sat on a bench and cleaned the players' spikes.

Then I set up the equipment in the dugout. I tried not to disturb the guys; most of them seemed to be in a complete daze. As the hours wore on, I became increasingly tired. But I kept pushing myself, thinking if Thurman could perform his job while he was hurt, then surely I could do mine while I was tired. I made a couple of trips across the street to McDonald's and ordered for the team, because none of them felt like going out to eat. Out of habit I also ordered two cheesies. The old Puerto Rican guy with the pencil mustache who had been there for years to take my order—he always said, *"Rápido, rápido,* hurry up!"—glanced at me and sighed when I ordered the cheesies.

I was worried because the guys hadn't eaten much all day. It was a muggy night, and I hoped that no one would collapse out on the field from exhaustion. I kept watching Lou Piniella as I worked. Visibly upset, he was pacing around, as though he was wrestling with some important decision. Finally Billy Martin came in, and I watched as Lou went over to talk with him. "I can't play," I heard him say to Billy. "I'm just too emotional to go out on that field tonight."

I had never been in the clubhouse when it was so silent. Nobody was playing music; the guys weren't talking. Instead of telling jokes, everybody looked drained, kind of like they had just been beaten up. We all felt as though we were mourning a family member at a wake. Ron Guidry, our ace starting pitcher, sat in front of his locker and broke down in sobs.

A couple of hours before the game started, a brief thunderstorm cooled the air. From the minute Bobby ran onto that field, staring straight ahead, ignoring the roar of the crowd and the signs that read NY 15 IS IN OUR HEARTS 4-EVER and WE MUST GO ON, he was like a man with a mission. With the Baltimore Orioles leading 4–0 in the bottom of the seventh inning, Bobby calmly walked up to the plate. His first time at bat he had struck out, then in the third inning he flied out, and he lined out in the sixth. Things weren't looking good in the seventh. Bucky Dent was on third and Willie Randolph stood on second. Two outs. You couldn't hear yourself think as the fans yelled, *"Charge! C'mon, Bobby!"* Starter Dennis Martinez pitched high and wide. Ball one. Dennis's second pitch floated over home plate, a strike. Bobby was looking for a pitch in the middle of the plate, a pitch that he could blast out of the park. And on the third pitch he got it. Bobby belted a three-run homer, a terrific line drive into the right field stands, just as he used to do into the old days. As he entered the dugout and the players lined up to shake his hand, Bobby said, "Well, that sure was a Reggie Jackson shot."

The old Bobby Murcer was suddenly back. Bobby and Lou hugged in the dugout, and it seemed like Thurman was right there in the middle of their tight embrace. The team was happy, but nobody was happier than Lou. It was as if Lou Piniella knew this was going to be Bobby Murcer's night to shine, and he was going to sit back and watch the fireworks.

We were still one run down in the bottom of the ninth. The Orioles led 4–3. Dent once again walked, this time off reliever Tippy Martinez. Randolph tried to bunt Dent to second, but Martinez fielded the ball and threw it into right field, setting up the same runners, Dent and Randolph, on second and third as in the bottom of the seventh. Bobby kept looking over his shoulder to see if Billy was going to take him out for a pinch hitter. Normally Billy would have pinch-hit for lefty Bobby against a tough lefty like Tippy, but he decided to let him hit that night. Maybe Billy knew that Bobby was on overdrive or maybe not. Billy just clapped his hands and yelled, "Come on, Bobby, you're a good hitter! I know you can do the job! Bring 'em in!" Every eye in Yankee Stadium was on Bobby, and he knew it. He coolly walked up to the plate. He fouled off the first two pitches. Tippy was being careful, knowing Bobby's strength for blasting to that short porch in right field, only 296 feet down the line at Yankee Stadium, as opposed to 330 feet at Shea. We were down to our final strike, but Bobby remained composed. At that moment, everyone on the team seemed closer than I had ever seen them in all my years with the Yankees. The dugout was silent and the team's energy was directed at Bobby, standing rapt at home plate. You could almost hear the swish of his bat as he swung at a knee-high slider and punched a line drive down the left field line. Two runs crossed the plate on his game-winning single. We won the game 5–4. Bobby had vindicated Billy's decision to keep him in.

I sat in the dugout and started crying. At first I thought that my tears were for Thurman, but then I realized they were tears of joy. With Thurman's passing I was convinced that none of us would ever be happy again. At that moment, I knew that we would not only survive, but we could again become what we had always been. The crowd went wild and cheered for Bobby to take a bow. He didn't want to, but after a few pushes from his teammates, he responded by running up to the top step and slightly tipping his cap to the crowd as they roared.

Mr. Steinbrenner was waiting to congratulate everybody, right down to the batboys. It was almost like we had won the World Series, but in a way we had won a whole lot more.

Bobby RETIRED FROM the Yankees in 1983 and went on to a varied and unusual career that included recording two country songs, "Bad Whiskey" and "Skoal Dippin' Man." He appeared on several TV game shows and even as a guest DJ with Billy Martin on MTV. He was in two motion pictures as himself and in 1988 entered the New York City Marathon and finished it. After a family member died of cancer, he realized that his habit of dipping tobacco during his playing days was dangerous. He became an anti-tobacco activist and worked hard for the passage of Oklahoma Senate Bill 619 that helped to ban tobacco sales to minors.

Yet it was his career in the Yankees broadcasting booth that brought Bobby the most fame. Bobby was a natural. In addition to his friendly, folksy drawl and sense of humor, he had an amazing knowledge of baseball that he passed on to the fans. He worked with Phil Rizzuto, Frank Messer, and others calling Yankee games. I always loved Old-Timers' Day when he went out on the field wearing a microphone and chose one of the current players to be his hitting coach. A-Rod did it. So did Jason Giambi. Even Hideki Matsui did, with his translator. It was a great idea, and he always got lots of laughs out of it. He won three Emmy Awards for live sports coverage—awards that he treasured.

During the 2006 season, we all noticed that Bobby wasn't himself. He suffered from a lot of headaches and seemed to be dragging. His broad smile and sense of humor never disappeared, but it was obvious that something was wrong. When the season was over, he went home to Oklahoma and eventually saw his doctor. On Christmas Eve, he was diagnosed with a brain tumor. Four days later he underwent surgery in Houston. On January 10, 2007, the family released a statement. Bobby's tumor was malignant.

Todd called me after the surgery. "I don't want you to hear rumors from the press. The prognosis isn't good, Ray. But Dad's attitude is excellent, and you know he is a fighter." Todd and I agreed that if anyone could get through this, Bobby Murcer could.

On the twenty-third of January, Bobby appeared on Michael Kay's radio show taking questions from the fans. He concluded by saying, "I want to thank you very much for giving me the forum to do this because even though this looks bad, I'm doing great. I really am. God has given me peace, and the overwhelming love has helped me deal with this diagnosis. I can feel the fans. I can feel their thoughts and their prayers, and I wanted to tell them how much I love them."

He made a promise to the Yankees and their fans: he would be there on Opening Day, in his usual place in the broadcast booth. Opening Day was just a little over two months away, but those of us who knew him believed him. After all, Bobby was a man of his word.

Naturally it was a chilly day on April 2 in New York when the Yankees opened in 2007. When the game started without Bobby in the booth, all of us felt sad and scared. Was his condition more serious than he let on? That would be just like Bobby—keeping the bad news from his friends. But then a bald man bundled up in an overcoat and bright blue scarf flashed on the stadium's viewing screen. It took the crowd and the team a few seconds to register who it was. The crowd broke into a standing ovation. Bobby had kept his promise. The players ran up the steps of the dugout to peer into the booth. Jorge Posada was waving at him and giggling like a little kid. Bobby brought Yankee Stadium to a complete stop. I had never seen so much love in that place for anyone.

Bobby returned in May to broadcast on a limited schedule. It was difficult for all of us to see him undergoing experimental treatments in the face of the odds that were clearly stacked against him. At the same time, he was writing his autobiography—a frank and honest look at his career and at his fight against cancer.

Bobby and I had been talking for a few years about my aspirations.

He asked me about the children's books I was writing. We discussed taking them to higher levels—to directing and producing movies about my stories, my ultimate dream. I told him how I wanted to use my talents to raise money for kids. He asked me about the schools, camps, and hospitals that I visited. Using the Yankees and Yankee Stadium as a backdrop for my stories, and eventually movies, I could not only give hope to inner-city kids, I could raise the money to give them a leg up in life. Maybe not all of them could have the break I had gotten, but that didn't mean that I couldn't help them make their own breaks . . . and I told Bobby that.

When my first children's book, *The Boy of Steel*, was published, Bobby was its biggest supporter. He showed it on the air and was excited when it became a best seller. When he discovered that I planned on an animated feature based on my books, he immediately announced that he was going to be the narrator. In fact, I received a call from him once when he was in the hospital. We talked for a while, and he ended the call by saying, "Don't give away my job, Ray. I am going to be around to narrate that movie." I didn't want anyone else to do it. Bobby or nobody.

When I mentioned Bobby to Joey Gian, my actor/songwriter friend, he said he had just the right song to send Bobby to keep his spirits up. During the latter part of the first week of July in 2008, I received a phone call from Bobby, but his call went straight to my voice mail. I had been unaware that he called.

On July 12, Todd called me to tell me that his father had died. I could tell that he knew how heartbroken I was. I had lost one of my heroes, but Todd had lost a father. He knew that I would have done anything for Bobby.

Later that day, I retrieved Bobby's old message from my phone.

His voice sounded just like the color commentator that everyone listened to on air.

"How ya feelin' today, Ray? Well, I'm sorry I missed you. Glad you and Todd are talking regularly. I know you'll always be friends. Please thank Joey Gian for sending me his song, 'I Believe.' The words are so appropriate for what I'm going through. Please understand, Ray, that I do believe that everything is going to be all right."

Bobby sang a couple of bars from that song. Then he hung up. His voice on my answering machine became etched in my memory.

By then, the plans were under way for the animated feature film *Henry & Me*. I knew that if Bobby couldn't narrate the movie, there wouldn't be a narrator. At that time, my third children's book, *One Last Time: Good-bye to Yankee Stadium*, was in production. In the story, all the Yankees who have passed on come back to play one last game in the old stadium before it is torn down. I wanted to halt production and do a rewrite with Bobby in it. I had still been writing it the previous August when Phil Rizzuto died, and I wrote him into the story before it was sent to the illustrator. This time it was too late. The book had already been sent out for printing. I made my mind up then that I would find some other way to honor Bobby Murcer.

A memorial service for Bobby was held on August 6 in Edmund, Oklahoma. It was fittingly the anniversary of Thurman Munson's funeral—hard to believe, the twenty-ninth—and the night that Bobby had won the game afterward, which became known as "The Bobby Murcer Show." It was also the twenty-fifth anniversary of Bobby Murcer Day. Bobby's widow asked four people to write a quote for the program that was handed out. I was honored to be one of them. I thought about it long and hard before I came up with "I always wanted to be Bobby Murcer."

I still needed to do something else for Bobby, though. It had to be something that involved the people of the Bronx. Bobby was their guy. Back in the early '70s when the Yankees were losing, they still had a hero in Bobby Murcer. A couple of years earlier, I had asked a famous graffiti artist, Cope2, to paint a wall on the side of the building where the kids in the neighborhood played stickball. He did a rendering of the way I saw Yankee Heaven. Babe Ruth, Lou Gehrig, Mickey Mantle, and Thurman Munson are among those depicted on the wall. Above them all is a picture of the Boss.

I had arranged a ceremony to unveil the latest addition to the painting—the image of Bobby, who represented the bridge between the old Yankees and the new Yankees. He was the only player to have played with both Mickey Mantle and Don Mattingly. And he belonged on that wall. Kay, Todd, and Tori attended, along with important Yankees like Joe Girardi, who came to the ceremony dressed in his pinstripes, Willie Randolph, and Derek Jeter and most of the Steinbrenner family. It was meant to be a ceremony for the people of the Bronx, and they came out in huge numbers to say good-bye, including Lucky Rivera and three hundred of his construction workers from Positive Workforce. They loved Bobby because they thought he was blue-collar, like they were.

Bobby may not be in Monument Park, but he is in my own Monument Park, where he can watch over young kids playing stickball every day.

In the locker room before the ceremony, I went over to talk to Derek Jeter. I told him that as captain of the team, it would be nice if he presented the family with a gift. Derek agreed and asked me what he should give.

I thought a minute, then suggested that since Bobby wore number 2 and Derek wore number 2, it would be appropriate to give them a jersey. Derek immediately reached into his locker and brought out his "gamer"—his game-worn jersey. He asked me what I should write on it. Celine Dion's song "Because You Loved Me" had been on my mind all morning.

I looked at Derek and said, "Because we loved him."

Catfish Hunter: Thank You for Being a Friend

While Lou was known as the Iron Horse for his longevity,
Catfish was a shooting star—only with us for what seemed
like a brief moment.

CATFISH HUNTER WOULD have made a great poker player. Whether the opposing batter struck out or hit a home run, his expression didn't change; he'd get right back on the mound and throw the next pitch. One of the quietest players I had ever known in my years with the Yankees, he would simply smile and nod back when I saw him around the stadium and said hello. I was never sure that he knew my name, but I didn't care. I was just happy to be around such a great pitcher.

When he first arrived in 1975, Catfish was the Yankees' great hope. He was also the highest-paid pitcher in baseball, after signing a record $3.75 million five-year contract on December 31, 1974. That New Year's Eve I wasn't focusing on the countdown as I watched Dick Clark in Times Square on television—I was thinking how exciting it was that I'd just seen the press conference with Catfish. His longish hair, tucked behind his ears, his mustache, and his southern drawl made him look and sound cool. There was no doubt, the Yankees were getting the best pitcher in baseball.

That '75 season Catfish lived up to everyone's high expectations. That year I was playing with the Bradenton Pirates, but back in the Bronx Catfish had started thirty-nine games and finished thirty of them, with a record of 23–14 and an ERA of 2.58 in 328 innings. When I returned to the Yankees later that fall, I, like everyone else, was in awe of every aspect of Cat's game. He had a precision that was unmatched by other pitchers and had been consistently performing for years. Eight years earlier, he had pitched a perfect game with the Oakland A's (only the seventh perfect game in baseball history) and helped them win their third straight World Series in 1974.

Right away I noticed that Catfish had a little limp. I mentioned this to Mr. Sheehy. "He had a horde of scouts after him during his senior year in high school. Imagine what that was like for a shy, low-key kid from a small town in the South." Mr. Sheehy handed me some uniforms to hang in the players' lockers. "Practically every scout thought he was one of the best high school pitchers in the country. You know, those guys arrived down there in his town of Hertford, North Carolina, in droves. I don't think there could have been more than three thousand people living in that little town. Catfish was on top of the world, but in the middle of all of this attention he was in a serious hunting accident and lost one of his toes. He also had shotgun pellets lodged in his foot that the doctors couldn't remove."

"Oh, so that's why he limps," I said as I followed Mr. Sheehy around the clubhouse.

"When the scouts found out about that accident, most of them backed away from Catfish right then and there. They thought he'd never amount to a thing with that kind of injury," Mr. Sheehy said. "But Charlie Finley, you know, he's the owner of the A's, well, he always went outside the pack, and he signed him to a contract."

Charlie Finley had been on the cover of *Time* magazine a few weeks earlier, around the middle of August. I read that Finley gave Catfish his name—that everyone in Cat's town called him Jimmy, but the A's owner wanted him to have a flashy name. I told Mr. Sheehy what I'd read.

"That's right, Ray. He's the one who introduced colored uniforms and white spikes. He's also the guy who wanted to change the color of the baseball to orange. In fact, he paid his players a three-hundred-dollar bonus if they grew a mustache. Well, anyway, he was quite a character. Boy, did Catfish at nineteen years old perform for the A's. Except for Cat's facial hair, he would have been a perfect Yankee in the '20s and '30s. He was such a simple country boy—he loved nothing more than hunting and fishing—and the Yankees were full of guys like him back then," Mr. Sheehy said.

Since Cat's first season with the Yankees was so successful, all eyes were on him. As it turned out, his numbers dropped some. While he still managed to toss twenty-one complete games and once again be named to the All-Star team, his record was only 17–15. And though he helped the Yankees reach the World Series that year, our first time in twelve seasons, Catfish grew even quieter in the clubhouse.

On a cloudy February afternoon in 1977, we were coming home to Fort Lauderdale from a trip to St. Petersburg, where we had played the Mets during spring training. This was the hardest time of year for me because only three guys were working the clubhouse with forty players to take care of. We had to wake up at 5:00 A.M., get all the equipment together, and after a long ride to the game unpack the bus and set up. Then, as soon as it was all over, we would pack up the bus and head home, knowing that when we returned to our stadium we had to wash the uniforms, clean countless pairs of spikes, and pack the bus yet again for the next day's game. The players and the crew generally sat in the same place during each long bus trip. Some guys slept, others talked to friends and joked, some listened to music and read.

That day I was sweaty and exhausted. Instead of sitting in my usual spot, I dragged myself to the back of the bus and stretched out on a long bench seat, instantly falling into a deep sleep. Suddenly I heard Catfish shouting, "Stop the bus! Stop the fucking bus!" The bus driver swerved over to the side of the road and the bus screeched to a halt. Books, shoes, newspapers, bags, and magazines cascaded onto the floor from the racks above the seats.

"Turn this bus around." Catfish sounded frantic. "We've forgotten somebody! Damn, we've forgotten somebody. Where's Negron? Where's Ray Negron?" Cat yelled.

Was I dreaming? Did I hear my name?

I shot up from my horizontal position and stumbled down the aisle.

"I'm, I'm here, Cat." I rubbed my eyes and tucked my shirt in. "I was sleeping in the back," I said sheepishly.

Catfish sighed deeply and relaxed his shoulders.

Paul Blair, an outfielder who had joined the team from the Baltimore Orioles that year, broke out laughing. "You stopped the goddamned bus for that kid? What the hell is going on around here?"

Mickey Rivers, our cool center fielder, joined in the laughter and yelled out, "Yeah, why'd we stop this damn bus? Shoulda kept on going."

I smiled and slid into the spot in the middle of the bus where I usually sat. Across the aisle Mickey and Lou Piniella were telling jokes. I heard the Stylistics' hit, "Stone in Love with You" blasting from a nearby boom box.

The bus driver pulled back out on the busy highway. I leaned my head on the window, quietly staring out to the long expanse of flat road, listening to the Stylistics' lyrics about being a movie star, an overnight success. I didn't even know that Catfish knew my name. I swallowed and felt a lump in my throat as I watched the cars speed down the highway. Had Catfish Hunter really stopped the bus just for me? Had the

World Championship Yankees pulled off the highway for Ray Negron? I looked up and Catfish was standing above me, looking down at me.

"Thanks, Catfish," I said. I could see by his smile that he understood how grateful I was. But I could also tell that this great pitcher knew exactly what it was like to be a confused twenty-one-year-old kid. I was going through so much—trying to get a grip on the fact that I might never become a major league player, struggling to figure out who I was. For the next couple of hours I thought about both Catfish's kindness and how the entire team was now looking at me differently from before. By the time we got off the bus, I was filled with a new confidence.

After that incident, I began to seek Catfish out in the hotel after games. A couple of times we talked about the Boss and how he compared to Charlie Finley. "Well, I'll be goddamned. I went right from Barnum to Bailey," he laughed.

His roommate on the road—in the days when players still had roommates—was a sloppily dressed, gruff, crude equipment guy who despite his demeanor took good care of the players. One evening in March while we were staying in the Bay Harbor Inn in Tampa, I knocked on Cat's door to see if he wanted to go out to eat. I heard laughing and screaming coming from the room. When Cat opened the door, I could see that the equipment man was wearing Cat's uniform and pretending to be Cat, tobacco in his mouth, no shoes and socks. I smiled, thinking how Cat could have his choice of roommates, yet he seemed to be enjoying this guy.

In July of 1977, Catfish really got lit up in Boston. Every fastball that came to the plate left the bat faster. He pitched six innings and was tagged for six earned runs. I drove back to New York that night with Thurman, who was known for never taking his work home with him. "Poor Catfish. I'm worried about him, Ray. He just isn't on his game. Dom Scala told me that when he was warming up Cat in the bullpen, there was nothing there. I didn't realize what he meant until I caught him in the game."

That summer I stood at the door of the trainer's room and watched as Gene Monahan did manipulations on Cat's arm and shoulder. It hurt to watch Gene rotate and pull at his arm, but while Catfish grimaced, he never uttered a sound. By the end of the season he had dropped to a 9–9 record.

In late February 1978 I was just arriving at spring training. Mr. Steinbrenner had called me the day before, just like he did in other years, and said, "Ray, George Steinbrenner. Get down here by 2:00 P.M. tomorrow." Click. The players were assigned roommates, but obviously on such short notice I didn't have one.

"Shit! What are you doing here? George doesn't tell me anything." Bill Kane, our traveling secretary, stood in the Fort Lauderdale clubhouse and threw his hands up in the air. "I don't know where I'm going to put you. What the fuck? I don't have any more rooms. Where am I going to put you?"

"Why don't you put him in with our sex symbol here?" Billy Martin said with a laugh as he walked by.

"I don't have a problem with that." Bucky Dent stood by his locker, getting dressed. Billy and Bill looked at each other. "He can room with me." Bucky, our handsome, dark-haired star shortstop, smiled. From the moment he arrived on the team, he was an instant fan favorite to the teenyboppers.

I thought back to Catfish's kindness. Bucky, too, had hailed from the South, Georgia and Florida.

That night I moved in with Bucky. He, along with the other players, received a weekly meal stipend. Mine was only about a quarter of theirs, and I sometimes made peanut butter and jelly sandwiches in the clubhouse to make the money last all week. Bucky kept his cash in a brown Cartier attaché case underneath his bed.

"Here, need some of this?" he'd ask, counting out his money for the evening. I was touched by his offer, yet I never once accepted.

A few days later, on March 2, the trainers told the players that Catfish had been diagnosed with diabetes. Some players watched Cat uncap the plastic cylinders that he carried with him that season. They talked about how he'd slip off to the trainer's room and inject himself with insulin before games, never complaining, going right out on the field and giving it everything he had. Bucky saw how bothered I was over Cat's medical situation.

"Don't worry, Ray, if anyone can handle this, Catfish can," he said a few times.

Sure enough, Cat tried to continue on like nothing was different. "I'll just take my shot. I'll be able to pitch. No big deal," he would say to his teammates from time to time. But he was often dragging, exhausted after the games. His pitching was requiring more and more energy and effort. Sometimes I'd see him leaning on his locker and think of Gary Cooper playing Lou Gehrig in *Pride of the Yankees*, sitting by his locker, trying to hide his illness.

By the age of thirty-three, Catfish Hunter's body was failing him. He didn't want to embarrass himself or the Yankees. By the middle of the 1979 season he just couldn't pitch. At an age where most baseball players are hitting their stride, Catfish Hunter announced his retirement. "I'm going home to North Carolina." Catfish easily could have negotiated another two- or three-year contract, but his pride wouldn't allow him to do that. I knew he did most of the work on his

110-acre farm himself in the winter. I wondered if he would be able to keep the work up. Would he still be able to hunt and fish, just as he always did?

On his last day at Yankee Stadium, the last weekend of the regular season, I found him sitting at the picnic bench in the locker room, signing baseballs. I didn't have a ball for him to sign, but I saw a pile of photos on the table that the team had printed up for him to autograph for his teammates. I grabbed one and went over. "Hi, Cat, would you sign one for me?"

He looked up and smiled, so warmly I couldn't help but think he was remembering back to over a year ago when he stopped the bus for me. Now that seemed like a very long time ago.

He took the picture, wrote on the front of it, and handed it to me. "Thank you, Catfish," I said and walked away. I sat on a bench and read what he wrote. *To Ray. Don't take no shit from anyone in the game. Best wishes, Catfish Hunter.*

I saw Cat from time to time after that. The next year he came back to New York for Old-Timers' Day and as always was a big hit with the fans and the rookie players. Every year he showed up at spring training to work as a pitching coach. Nobody worked harder with rookie pitchers than he did. In the spring of 1982, he was the first guy I saw when I arrived at camp. We sat and talked a while, and then Mr. Steinbrenner walked into the locker room.

"Boss, you gotta give Ray here a raise," Catfish said.

Mr. Steinbrenner smiled and sighed. "I guess your agent Mr. Hunter is speaking for you now," he said.

A week later that increase showed up in my paycheck. It was a nice one.

. . .

I<small>T WAS ANNOUNCED</small> in 1998 that Catfish had been diagnosed with ALS—also known as Lou Gehrig's disease. When I heard the news I thought back to the day Catfish inscribed his picture for me, and for an instant I could picture Lou Gehrig standing over Catfish's shoulder, offering prophetic words to his fellow Yankee. Catfish spent the last year of his life speaking out for ALS awareness. The perfect spokesman for the task, he helped raise millions of dollars for ALS research. While Lou was known as the Iron Horse for his longevity, Catfish was a shooting star—only with us for what seemed like a brief moment. Now his moments were about to become even shorter.

In 1999, at the age of fifty-three, he fell down the stairs at his home and suffered a head injury. Released from the hospital on a Saturday, Catfish Hunter was dead by the following Thursday. He didn't live long enough to see the Yankees, after a drought of nearly two decades, win their third World Series in four years. I thought back to the sign on Cat's locker that read WINNING ISN'T EVERYTHING, BUT WANTING TO IS.

A decade before, Cat had been elected to the Hall of Fame. Rather than choosing between the Yankees and the Oakland A's, he went in with a logo-less cap. But for all of Cat's great successes on and off the field, I will cherish that day during spring training when he stopped the bus for me. Even now, when I visit children in hospitals and schools, I seek out the quiet kid hiding in his own bus and try to bring him or her into the middle of what we are doing. Every time I see a child's face light up, I think of Catfish. I hear his voice, yelling to the driver. I know Catfish would have been right there beside me, helping the children who need it most, in his own quiet way.

7

Alex Rodriguez: The Man in the Mirror

Any fatigue that Alex experienced that day quickly disappeared as he stood on the stage and gave an impassioned speech about the importance of reading.

Tony Melendez was "the man" in his Bronx neighborhood. A dark, athletically built twenty-four-year-old salsa dancer and the third baseman for an amateur AA baseball team, Tony ran a small souvenir shop across the street from Yankee Stadium in 1989. It was a favorite drop-in spot for his friends, who not only coveted a spot on Tony's team but also wanted to learn his dazzling dance moves and go disco hopping with him.

Almost thirteen hundred miles away in Miami, handsome Alex Rodriguez, ten years younger than Tony, was becoming "the man" in his high school, excelling in both baseball and in the classroom. Alex's extraordinary hard work and talents were beginning to catch the community's attention. "Who's that kid?" people often asked.

No one would have guessed—least of all Alex and Tony—that their lives would become profoundly intertwined almost twenty years later.

When I first met Tony in the fall of 2006, he was sitting outside the stadium with a few young kids dressed in baseball uniforms. They were waiting patiently for their favorite players, catcher Jorge Posada, second baseman Robinson Cano, and third baseman Alex Rodriguez, to walk by, hoping for a chance to meet their heroes and get their baseballs autographed.

At that time, the guys on the team walked from their parking lot to a small street, Ruppert Place, and then across to a private stadium entrance by the press box. I watched Tony and was impressed with the sincere way he spoke to the kids and players. After seeing him several times, I started up a conversation with him. He told me he owned a small store nearby and eventually invited me over to see the place. When I came by one night, we sat together and watched a Yankees game on his small television. I listened as Tony told me about an event that had changed his life.

It was late afternoon on September 1, 1989. Tony parked his red Chevy Camaro on Fifth Avenue and 103rd Street and headed for the baseball field deep in the northern section of Central Park. The sky was clear and there was a little breeze. Tony loved playing baseball during the last fleeting days of summer. His teammates, some of them ex-professionals, were in good spirits, especially considering they were only one game away from winning an all-expense-paid trip to the league championship in Tony's birthplace, Santo Domingo.

That night, Tony whacked a triple in the bottom of the ninth, bringing in the run that clinched the game 4–3. Surrounded by his cheering teammates and his longtime girlfriend, Ada, Tony thought, "Just one more game."

"You made it happen for us, Tony!" his teammates shouted. Tony was on such a high that evening that for a brief moment he entertained the notion that maybe someday he might play for the majors. After all, occasionally a scout came to watch his team play.

As Ada and Tony strolled hand in hand across the park to Tony's car, he could still hear his teammates calling his name. He drove back to his apartment in the Bronx, where they changed into their dancing clothes. Tony wore his best slacks and a fitted shirt; Ada wore a low-cut orange dress and high heels.

"Hey, Tony, what's up, bro? You hear the Yankees won tonight?" a man in his twenties shouted out to Tony as he and Ada headed toward Tony's car.

"Yeah, just heard on the radio that Velarde and Hall homered."

"Hey, and your man Mattingly didn't do too bad either tonight." Tony, a good hitter with a great glove, was often compared to New York Yankee first baseman Don Mattingly by his friends.

"So, how'd your team do?" the man asked.

"They won!" Ada shouted as she climbed into the car beside Tony.

He drove to Fuego Fuego, a popular Latin Club at 158th and Broadway, where the DJ was spinning songs by Gloria Estefan. When the hit "Don't Let Me Be Misunderstood," by Santa Esmeralda, blasted through the club, Tony grabbed Ada's hand and led her out onto the crowded dance floor.

Tony wanted to stay out all night. "Let's beat the fuckin' tired," he said to Ada a few hours later.

"*Cómo no*," Ada agreed, laughing, as they drove to the next club, Studio 84, just a few blocks south on 145th Street, where some of Tony's teammates were also out late, "breaking the night."

"Tony, you're the man." "One more chance, one more dance." "You hit like you dance." "You're the king." Tony quietly laughed as the guys called out to him while he danced with Ada to the beat of a Latin band. It seemed like every girl on the dance floor was watching Tony swivel his hips just like John Travolta in *Saturday Night Fever*.

When Ada looked at her watch, she was surprised that it was 6:30 A.M. "Come on, Tony, you've got your big game in a few hours, and I've got to be at work by eight." They left the club and headed home. Tony dropped Ada off at her apartment so she could get ready for her waitressing job. Then he parked his car near his apartment and headed for his favorite neighborhood diner.

"Hey, Tony, you and the Yankees did all right last night." The old waiter handed Tony a menu. "What'll you have?" Tony sat at the counter and ordered ham and eggs.

"Get some rest before your game, Tony. I'll try to stop over at Crotona Park and watch after I get off work," the cashier said as Tony paid his tab.

The early morning was cool and gray. Even though Tony was weary, he was still feeling the good vibes from a few hours before. He strolled down River Avenue and headed home. Two young guys, one wearing a black hooded sweatshirt, the other smaller and slimmer, passed him on the sidewalk.

"Hey, Tony," the bigger one called. Tony smiled.

"Wha's up?" The younger guy sidled up to Tony. His speech was slurred. The two stood on either side of Tony.

"You ain't answerin'," the guy wearing the sweatshirt said.

"Huh?" Tony took a step back.

"Need your cash, motherfucka," the other guy mumbled. He grabbed Tony by the arm. "Take me to your car." When they got to Tony's red Camaro, he put his key in the car door lock, and the smaller guy shoved Tony into the driver's seat.

"Hey, why you guys hurtin' me? I always take care of you—"

"Shut the fuck up." They climbed in the backseat and ordered Tony to drive south to the 138th Street Bridge.

"Make a left." The smaller guy, who was sitting directly behind Tony, stuck a gun in Tony's neck. Tony flinched. "Don't move or I'll blow your head off!" the guy screamed.

They forced Tony to stop at a deserted wasteland filled with old tires and garbage right underneath the bridge.

"Get out," the guy in the sweatshirt yelled.

He pulled a pair of handcuffs from his back pocket and snapped them tightly around Tony's wrists. He snatched the gold chain from Tony's neck and demanded that Tony hand him his watch and wallet.

"Why you doin' this?" Tony was shaking.

"Just get the fuck outta here. I'm not gonna shoot you. *Run!*"

Tony took off. *Pop.* Tony felt burning in his left leg. *Pop.* Another shot. Pop. Tony hobbled toward the river. *Pop. Pop.* He felt the warmth of the bullets hit his arms, his back, and his legs. He tried to sprint, but he could barely move. *Pop, pop.* He felt a razor-sharp pain in his legs.

Tony collapsed headfirst into the frigid Harlem River while cars in the distance whizzed by. His legs were frozen. His hands were cuffed. He looked up to see silhouettes standing in the windows of a building near the water.

"Don't get out!" they screamed. "Stay there!"

Tony heard them yell, but he wasn't sure what they were saying.

Somehow he crawled out of the filthy water. He had to get to the highway and flag a car down. But he could barely move. Heavy wet clothes clung to him. His bloody legs and arms throbbed. He froze. The smaller of the two guys who'd made him drive to this godforsaken spot was hiding behind a tree. Tony didn't know which way to turn. He tried to run.

Pop! Darkness. *Pop!* Silence.

Two weeks later Tony finally stirred. Hooked up to tubes, he opened his left eye, then his right. He wiggled his fingers and examined his wrists, trying to recall what had happened that made his wrists red and swollen.

"Please try to raise your arms, Mr. Melendez," a nurse said

He pulled his left arm from under the blanket, then his right. His arms were bandaged, yet he could lift them. However, when the nurse asked him to wiggle his toes, he couldn't. Nor could he move his legs. He glanced around at his bare room in a northern Manhattan hospital, trying to recall why he was there. Then he remembered the *click*. He visualized the distorted angry face of the man who grabbed him and fastened the handcuffs around his trembling wrists. Tony had feared for his life . . . but what had happened after that? He drifted back off to sleep.

For six months Tony recuperated in the hospital. Slowly he began to remember the horrors of that September morning, when his life had so much potential.

Tony asked the doctors if he'd ever walk again, but the answer was always the same.

"You're just out of your coma, Mr. Melendez. We just can't say for sure whether you'll be able to walk."

While Tony was recovering, trying his hardest to get his once gifted legs to budge, he met a nurse's aide. "I live in your neighborhood, Mr. Melendez, and I know some at-risk kids who live near the stadium. They need to be part of a team, so they can stay out of trouble. Maybe you'd be interested in coaching?"

At that point the only thing that Tony wanted was to be back in the park playing third base for his AA team, then dancing to his favorite songs in discos with Ada. It wasn't until a few days before he was released from the hospital that he began to fully grasp that he might never walk again. His legs were broken, frozen. They just wouldn't work. He couldn't go anywhere without sitting in a wheelchair. He had to be lifted on and off the toilet.

On the day he was to be released, the nurse's aide came into his room to say good-bye. "You know, maybe I should meet those kids," Tony said.

He knew he needed to find an anchor. His old life as he knew it was over.

A year and a half after the shooting, in the spring of 1991, Tony, back at work in his store, spread the word throughout his neighborhood. "I want to organize a dozen kids to play on a baseball team," he told his friends. A few days later, on the first Saturday in June, thirty kids who had never played organized baseball showed up at Franz Sigel Park, a tape-measure home run away from Tony's store and the stadium. Because Tony didn't have any staff to work with so many players, he had no choice but to turn half of those who showed up away.

Surprised at first to find their new coach sitting in a wheelchair, the kids who were on the team quickly forgot about Tony's disability. In fact, Tony almost immediately became their father figure. "Do your homework before you get to practice," he would tell them. "Make sure you help your mother with chores before our Saturday game." Because Tony's initial team had so much success, he was able to rally many of his friends to coach. With the help of local merchants, he put twenty-one teams together the following year, comprised mostly of Hispanic kids ages five to nineteen.

While Tony was creating a new life for himself and the league, young Alex Rodriguez was having a remarkable junior year as the star shortstop at Miami's Westminster Christian High School. Top scouts for Major League Baseball teams began arriving at Alex's practices and games, witnessing his record number of steals and his .419 batting average. They were watching when Alex went on to help his high school win the national championship.

The following year, while Alex was a senior, he was first-team prep All-American, hitting .505 with nine home runs. Selected as the USA Baseball Junior Player of the Year and as Gatorade's national baseball student-athlete of the year, he was the first high school player to ever try out for Team USA.

Alex was regarded as the number-one baseball prospect in the country. It was no surprise that he would be drafted in the first round as the top pick for the Seattle Mariners. Only the third eighteen-year-old major league shortstop since 1900, Alex's star rose rapidly. Seven years later he became a free agent and signed with the Texas Rangers. During his first season in Texas he belted in fifty-two homers, a record for shortstops. In 2003 he won MVP. As a shortstop for the Rangers and as the Yankees third baseman when he first arrived in the Bronx in 2004, Alex had the highest salary in baseball, at $25 million a year.

"I'm pretty excited about this," the Boss told the press in mid-February 2004 when Alex was traded to the Yankees, for second baseman Alfonso Soriano along with minor leaguer Joaquin Arias. "This is a big, big one, just like when we signed Reggie."

Like Reggie, Alex assumed that the fans would idolize him when he arrived in New York. But Alex, too, discovered that he had to earn the respect of New Yorkers. Scrutinizing Alex's record-breaking salary, the New York fans didn't care what he had accomplished as a Mariner or a Ranger. They focused on one thing: what was A-Rod going to do for the New York Yankees?

During his first year Alex was anything but idolized. Instead many fans and some of the press quickly trashed him. Commentators repeatedly questioned why he couldn't hit in the clutch, criticizing his huge salary.

I had been following the Yankees in the news and watching the games on television from Arlington, where I had been working with the Texas Rangers' management helping sports psychologist Don Kalkstein. He was working with Latin and minority players who were struggling with performance issues as well as a few addiction issues.

During the late 1990s I had also worked for the Cleveland Indians. Tom Giordano, assistant to general manager John Hart, had asked me to join the organization and work with famed sports psychologist Charlie Maher. "If we sign Dwight Gooden, then we're going to need Ray Negron," Tom told John.

When John left Cleveland in 2001 to go to the Texas Rangers, he asked me to go with him. He knew that Alex, who had joined the struggling team the year before—at the time they were last in their division—was an advocate of sports psychology. I've always believed that part of Alex's greatness has to do with the fact that he embraces the mental aspect of baseball.

Alex and I knew each other casually when he played for Seattle. During our time together with the Rangers, he and I had been friendly, stopping to chat with each other in the clubhouse. I was now curious how Alex was coping with the negativity of the New York fans and press.

It was painful watching Game 6 of the 2004 ALCS. At Yankee Stadium, in the eighth inning, Alex, in a reversed ruling, was called out for interference for swatting at Boston pitcher Bronson Arroyo's glove and knocking the ball loose. As a result Derek Jeter, who had scored, was ordered back to first base. The Yankees then had two outs instead of one, which killed any possible rally. Terry Francona, the

Boston manager, yanked his players to protect them from the balls and bottles that furious Yankee fans hurled onto the field. Dozens of New York City police offers took to the chaotic grounds in riot gear. The game resumed, and we lost 4–2 that night.

I read in the newspapers the next day that the 2004 Yankees were notable as the only team in Major League Baseball history to lose a seven-game playoff series after taking a three-games-to-none lead. "It is considered one of the worst collapses in baseball history," wrote one reporter.

The Red Sox eventually went on to the World Series, defeating the St. Louis Cardinals. However, the newspapers couldn't get enough of what happened in Boston during the playoffs, thrusting Alex into the spotlight.

At the beginning of the 2005 season, when I came back to the Yankees after an eight-year hiatus, Alex had pulled an eight-year old child to safety, out of the path of a truck, while he was in Boston. Papers carried the story, but it almost immediately got lost amidst the negative reporting. Reporters had no qualms about following Alex's personal life, though, publishing photos of him with various women, indicating that his marriage was crumbling. I wished someone would write a story about how extra hard Alex worked in practices, how he arrived early and stayed late at the stadium. But the media machine in New York was much rougher on Alex than the almost nonexistent press in Texas had been. Reggie could have told him that.

While the 2006 season started out on a good note—Alex was the American League Player of the Month for May, when he batted .330 with eight homers and twenty-eight RBIs—by June he had lost his groove and couldn't hit a ball out of the park even in batting practice. During that time, Reggie Jackson took him to dinner. "Act yourself,

Alex. You've got the talent," he advised. The fans were regularly booing Alex, especially when he failed to make a hit. Finally, in late July,
former mayor Rudy Giuliani, while being interviewed on a sports radio
show, asked the fans to show some respect. "Stop booing A-Rod," he
said on the air.

Some of the sports headlines that summer read E-ROD when he
made a crucial error or K-ROD when he struck out in the clutch. The
constant jabs from the media combined with snipes from fans and
players on other teams were clearly wearing Alex down. His hitting
improved in late August, but by mid-September, with three seasons
under his belt and no hint of the team heading to the World Series,
Alex seemed resigned when he told Bob Costas on a nationally syndi-
cated radio show, "I think the demand that is put on a player like me
is so much more than the generic everyday guy."

Alex had increasingly struggled in postseason play, to the point
where he batted eighth in the Yankees' final game in October, when
they were eliminated in the first round by Detroit.

Knowing how much Alex looked up to the Boss, I decided to take
him up to Mr. Steinbrenner's office during spring training in Tampa
in 2007.

"Look, Alex, I went through this type of thing with Reggie years
ago." The Boss's tone was comforting. I glanced at his jowls and his
receding hairline and thought how age had mellowed him. "Reggie
delivered for me. You will, too. I expect you to be the big guy with the
bat. You're a good kid. I want you to continue that way."

Alex looked at the Boss as if he were a god.

"Thanks for bringing me up here, Ray," he said as we left the office.

I knew that Mr. Steinbrenner was counting on me to help distract

Alex from the unrelenting pressure. I had been in this position almost thirty years earlier when he asked me to help Reggie out.

ONE JUNE AFTERNOON at the beginning of the 2007 season, Alex noticed a middle-aged man sitting outside the stadium in a wheelchair, surrounded by kids wearing baseball uniforms.

"Ray, who's that guy?" Alex asked me before a game.

I told Alex Tony's story. "See what he needs, Ray, I want to help his league out," Alex said, then went and got his checkbook, sat down on a bench in the clubhouse, and wrote a check to the United Youth Baseball League. "If I give you this check, will you deliver it to Tony?"

"Maybe it's best if you hand it to him, Alex," I said. "Let's go over there right now."

"Seriously?" Alex asked.

"Yeah," I said. "Let's get over there before the ink dries up on this paper."

Tony could not have been more startled when I walked into his store with Alex.

"Let's go over to the park so Alex can see the kids practice," I said to Tony. When the three of us arrived at the park, the kids looked at Alex, then at each other. Alex talked to some of them while they were waiting to go out on the field. "You like playing ball? Doing okay in school?" he asked them.

Alex watched them interact with Tony.

"Hey, Tony, when am I gonna pitch?"

"Gotta show your stuff first."

"Tony, I can't come up with no more money for my uniform."

"Don't worry, play ball. I'll take care of it," Tony said.

"I just want the kids around here to get the same great start in baseball that I was able to get when I was a kid," Alex said as he handed Tony the check when we got back to his store. Tony was so touched that he was speechless.

"You know, Alex, I'd had a little connection with the Yankees back in 1996," Tony finally said. "I'd been running the program a few years, and Joe Girardi, the catcher, you know, he caught Dwight Gooden's no-hitter that year, well, anyways, he showed up one day to see what I was doing with the kids. Joe and I were just starting out. He and I talked a lot that day. When Joe was first traded from the Rockies to the Yankees, he replaced Mike Stanley as catcher. Do you know the fans actually booed Joe early on because they liked Stanley so much?" Tony said.

Alex sat with Tony and listened.

"When Joe hit a triple in Game 6 of the '96 World Series, they started to love him. Anyway, that day, Joe went back to his car and wrote out a check to my team and handed it to me, just like you did today. This means so much to our team. Thank you, Alex. We couldn't play without this."

"Just take care of the kids, okay?" Alex said, and we headed back to the stadium. Alex was in a great mood. We passed the wall adjacent to the local bowling alley, the one right next to Tony's store where the Yankee greats mural was, with the portraits of Bobby Murcer and the Boss I had recently commissioned

"That's Yankee Heaven," I said to Alex. "You'll be up on that wall one day."

"I hope it's not anytime soon," he said laughing.

That night after the game, I told Joe Girardi about meeting Tony.

"Yes, Ray, I really wanted to help that guy out. I liked what he was doing. I wish I could have given him more. Tony would never tell anyone how much I gave him. All he would say is that he was so happy that someone gave a damn," Joe said. "You know, he used to be a pretty decent ballplayer before he was shot. How could I not help him? I think Tony was one of the people I met along the way who gave me an incentive to be a better player."

That same summer, Alex started paying Tony's team regular visits, giving the kids a free clinic, talking to them about the importance of reading. One afternoon in late July, Alex brought his three-year-old daughter, dressed in patent leather shoes and a frilly pink dress, out to the field. Soon it seemed all the kids in the neighborhood knew Alex.

Later that fall, even after he won his third MVP, Alex's second with the Yankees, the New York fans still hadn't completely accepted our third baseman. Instead, the *New York Post* dubbed him "Stray-Rod" as they continued to dissect his personal life. To make matters worse, Alex's agent, Scott Boras, chose to announce Alex's free agency, through an opt-out clause in his contract, during the 2007 World Series, taking the spotlight away from the Red Sox and their Series win. Alex, who loved being a Yankee, renegotiated his own new contract with the team.

The year 2008 should have been a good one for Alex. He had passed the five-hundred-home-run mark—the youngest player ever to do so. He had negotiated a new multiyear deal. The Yankees had a promising new manager, Joe Girardi, and right across the street, a brand-new stadium would be ready for the 2009 season. The newspapers continued to crucify Alex, writing that he couldn't hit in the clutch, that he was cursed, image-conscious, not tough enough, and that he put too much pressure on himself to justify his huge salary.

The 2009 season started off with another big problem. Rumors of previous steroid use surfaced. Alex called a press conference in the backfield of Steinbrenner Field in Tampa, during spring training, on February 17, 2009. Underneath a tent behind the third base stands, sitting at a dais, looking vulnerable, Alex admitted that he had used steroids from 2001 to 2003 while he played for the Rangers. In front of a large media contingent and surrounded by all twenty-four of his teammates as well as his coaches and manager, Alex got through one of the hardest moments of his career.

I thought maybe the media circus would calm down after that, but Alex was cast even further into the public eye. During the next month he would be on the back page of the *Daily News* almost twenty times. A reporter asked Alex at the February press conference, "How do you address parents in terms of talking to their kids about what you did?"

"The first thing I say is I'm sorry," Alex said. "But this may have happened for a much bigger reason than baseball. I'd like to help spread a message to kids, not to use steroids."

E VER SINCE EARLY 2000, the Boss had urged me to return to the Yankees as a community adviser for the team. While I had enjoyed my time helping the Rangers and Indians, I couldn't wait to build a program where I, together with the players, could give back to the Bronx community that had given me so much. When the Boss had asked me to come back again in early 2005, I was ready to get to work.

"No one in this organization has had the background that you've had, Ray. You'll be an important connection to the community. You know the streets," the Boss had said at the time.

In the four years since then, I had been trying to create a bridge between the team and the neighborhood people. I knew that Alex needed to get out there, just as much as the kids needed Alex's support. But after his steroid-use admission, many close to him advised him to keep out of the public eye. "People need to get over this before you can move on," someone told him shortly after the press conference.

"I can quietly continue to help others in the community," he answered. "No one needs to know what I'm doing."

He refused to stay away from the neighborhood kids, the ones who played on the United Youth Baseball League—Tony's kids, the ones he needed to be around so that he could make sure they learned from his mistakes. Alex needed to rediscover that young player in Seattle who had taken baseball by storm.

Over the last couple of years he had developed a solid bond with the kids in the Bronx neighborhood, but he wasn't prepared for the reception he received when we arrived back in New York after spring training on a Saturday morning in early April 2009. There were almost four hundred kids from the United Youth Sports Organization, ranging in age from six to sixteen, along with Tony, all gathered in Franz Sigel Park, chanting, "Go Alex, go!" Some of the kids carried signs that read, WE BELIEVE IN YOU, ALEX! WE LOVE YOU, ALEX! When Alex stepped out of his black SUV, the kids rushed up to him, surrounding him and walking across the field by his side. Not one asked Alex for his autograph. I watched the scene and felt like I was watching Moses parting the Red Sea in some '60s movie. If he ever doubted his decision to keep supporting them publicly, that day took away any doubts.

During that same spring training, Alex had been talking to Richard Gere, who became a friend of mine when he starred in the film *The Cotton Club*. I had a small part as a waiter in that movie. Meeting

Richard and working with the legendary director Francis Ford Coppola were highlights in my life. For those two months in 1983 when I was on the set, Coppola, like the Boss, made me feel like my part was bigger than it actually was. In fact, as Richard jokes with me today, "If you watch that film and wink, you'll miss Ray altogether."

Alex and Richard came up with the idea of setting up a Little League All-Star Game when we returned to New York for the regular season. The teams would be Manhattan against the Bronx, with Richard managing the Dominican Federation Team from Manhattan, while Alex would coach the kids he had been supporting, the United Youth Baseball League in the Bronx. They would play at Franz Sigel on Saturday, June 6, after the Yankees' afternoon home game against the Tampa Bay Rays.

The Yankees lost to the Rays 9–7 that afternoon, in a game that lasted three hours and forty-five minutes. Alex had played well, hitting a homer in the second inning. It had been raining lightly all day on and off. A sea of wet faces, ages twelve to fourteen, along with Tony, who sat with the parents, were waiting patiently for Alex to come to the field so they could play ball. Richard, wearing jeans, a red T-shirt, and a red cap with the number 7 on it, was already warming up his team, but there was no sign of Alex.

I ran back to the stadium and saw that Alex was surrounded by a swarm of reporters. When I returned to the field, I was trying to figure out how I was going to tell everyone he might not be coming. Even though I stood ready to manage the team in Alex's place, I knew the kids would be greatly disappointed.

Just as I was about to approach the crowd, Alex, dressed in jeans, a pink shirt, and a gray V-neck sweater, strode onto the field, quickly taking his place as third base coach, as the kids cheered. During the three-inning game, a young player drilled a line drive toward the coach's box, practically grazing Alex's head. He laughed and edged closer to the dugout, which made everyone else laugh, too.

At one point, Alex went out to the mound to change his pitcher after a rocky inning. Facing the dread that every Little League coach faces—*how is this young player going to take being pulled out of the game?*—Alex held his hand out for the ball and waited a second. Instead of handing Alex the ball, the boy reached out and wrapped his arms around Alex's waist, hugging him for a long time. Alex grinned.

I looked around and saw the smiles on the faces of the parents who were standing behind a chain-link fence on the sidelines. Alex interrupted the game to go over and greet the moms and dads, many of whom had stretched their fingers through the chain links just so they could touch him. Then they turned to Tony and thanked him for getting Alex involved.

Alex's team won 3–0. It was getting dark that afternoon as Richard and Alex handed out medals to all of the players. As Alex placed a medal over each player's neck, he made a point of talking to the kids. "Good hustle on that throw," he'd say, or "Way to cover that base." A few weeks later, Alex visited Tony at his store and brought another check to the United Youth Baseball League.

ALEX HELPED TO LEAD the Yankees to another postseason. The day after we won the Eastern Division title in 2009, he and I were joking in the locker room together. I started to leave, but Alex stopped me. He was carrying a pair of fungo bats and an armful of tennis balls.

"Hey, Ray, you ever play stickball?"

"I used to be the king of stickball," I replied.

"Okay, let's see what you got. Let's go by Tony's store and play by the strike box by that mural, you know, your Yankee Heaven wall," Alex said.

Still a kid at heart, I smiled. Alex rounded up a couple of his teammates in the locker room, utility player Jerry Hairston Jr. and Sergio Mitre, a relief pitcher. I figured it would be just a matter of time before we found some guys to play against.

Alex stood against the wall as I pitched the tennis balls to him. I could tell he wanted to hit an A-bomb up to the top of the El, where the 4 trains thundered by.

A couple of kids walked by as I threw a fastball. "Wow, is that, is that really . . ."

"Nah." A small boy wearing a Yankees cap kept walking.

"Yeah, yeah, that's him!" A teenager grabbed the small boy and stopped him, instantly recognizing the guy at bat. During the next ten minutes, kids shouted up and down the block, "A-Rod's here!" The word went through the neighborhood like wildfire. "Alex Rodriguez is playing stickball."

Tony came out to see what all of the commotion was about.

"C'mon, Tony, we need an umpire. Get over here and call balls and strikes. You know we don't want any cheating," Alex called to him.

"Okay, Alex!" Tony squared himself right behind Alex.

The lot was quickly packed with kids and adults. Alex organized the kids into teams. "Okay, I want kids only," he said. "Adults, you'll have to stand outside the play area." Tony shouted *stee-rike* in his best umpire voice while Sergio and Jerry belted homer after homer.

A chubby twelve-year-old, a ringer for Spanky from the Little Rascals, dressed in a backwards Yankee cap and baggy dungaree shorts, stood on the pitcher's mound facing Alex. I wanted to hear the crowd go wild as Alex let one loose. The boy hauled off and threw the tennis ball with everything he had—a funny curveball, almost like a slider. Alex swung for the fence across the street and missed.

I looked at the boy's gleeful expression and thought that he was probably always the last kid to be picked for a team. I glanced at the mural, and for a minute I thought I saw Mickey Mantle's expression change into that famous grin of his as watched over the scene in the lot. It was a *Field of Dreams* afternoon right in the backyard of Yankee Stadium.

"Hey, Alex, how come they don't write about these kinds of things in the papers?" some guy called out as the game ended.

After playing, Alex took the kids to Billy's, a restaurant near the stadium, and bought hamburgers, hot dogs, and sodas for as many of them as the place could hold. I smiled at Alex and said, "Just like Willie Mays." When Willie, as the center fielder for the New York Giants in the 1950s, had a day game, he would run outside of his home on Sugar Hill at 115th Street in Harlem and play with the neighborhood kids for fifteen minutes, but not before slipping a five-dollar bill into his back pocket. When they were finished playing, he would reach into his pocket and buy ice cream for all.

The 2009 season was A-Rod's twelfth straight with thirty home runs and a hundred RBIs. More importantly, the Yankees ultimately delivered the twenty-seventh championship to the New York fans, Alex's first World Series ever.

The team partied into the wee hours of the morning after the Yankees won the American League title, defeating the Los Angeles Angels 5–2 in Game 6. Yet Alex still managed to pull himself together the next day and show up at a struggling Bronx parochial school. As Alex sat in a stairwell, waiting to walk down the center aisle of the school's auditorium, a reporter approached him.

"Are you tired?" the reporter asked Alex.

"Yeah," Alex said. "It's been a long season."

"Well, why aren't you resting up?" the reporter asked. "After all, this isn't that important."

Alex's face hardened. "If you aren't going to ask me about these kids, then don't ask me any more questions."

Alex stood up, brushed past the reporter, and walked down the aisle to Michael Jackson singing "Man in the Mirror," a song about changing the world for the better, beginning with yourself. He traded high fives with the ecstatic kids on the aisles. Any fatigue that Alex experienced that day quickly disappeared as he stood on the stage and gave an impassioned speech about the importance of reading. I looked around at the young students' rapt faces.

Alex finished speaking and stood on the stage for a minute while the audience cheered wildly. His relaxed demeanor, his wide grin, and the slight nod of his head told me that he finally understood the magnitude and importance of what he represented to these kids, and to kids everywhere, as a member of the fabled New York Yankees.

8

Another Bronx Tale: No Favors Between Friends

I was breaking every rule there was, but I kept telling myself
that this was what the Boss would want me to do, and that
thought pushed me forward.

CHAZZ PALMINTERI, an actor and author, was born and raised in the long shadow of Yankee Stadium in the 1950s and '60s. In 1989 he wrote and performed in a semiautobiographical one-man show, *A Bronx Tale,* based on his rough childhood in the Bronx. After Robert De Niro saw the off-Broadway production, he ended up directing and costarring with Palminteri in the 1993 film version, which became a big box office hit. I knew that Chazz often came to Yankee games, and I wanted to meet him. Imagine how excited I was when I found myself in the owner's suite at Yankee Stadium one afternoon with Chazz Palminteri standing right in front of me. I had watched *A Bronx Tale* literally dozens of times, and I idolized the guy.

As we sat at the ball game together, Chazz and I discussed our mutual tough childhoods, our devotion to the New York Yankees, and our love of films. When the game ended we exchanged phone numbers.

About a year later, when I was in the process of putting together my animated film, *Henry & Me,* I needed someone to be the voice of Babe Ruth. I thought of Chazz, and when I asked him, he jumped at the opportunity.

Chazz called a few weeks later. His strong, powerful voice was subdued. "Ray, listen, buddy, I need a favor."

"There are no favors between friends," I said. "If you need me to do something, I'll do it."

"I have a very dear pal who has a young son named Michael. Big

Yankee fan. Michael is suffering from cancer, Ray. We've just learned that the boy only has only a month to live," Chazz said. "Michael especially likes Derek Jeter."

Chazz started to cry. I didn't say a word. As I listened, I thought back to Sonny, the local Mafia boss Chazz plays in *A Bronx Tale*. I remembered what he told Calogero, played by Francis Capra, the young boy he befriends. "Mickey Mantle makes a hundred thousand dollars a year. How much does your father make? If your dad needs money, go ask Mickey Mantle. See what happens. Mickey Mantle don't care about you. Why care about him? Nobody cares."

In the many years I had spent working for the New York Yankees, I had worked hard to prove that statement wrong, trying to show that baseball players do have hearts and that they care about their fans, especially kids. I always like to think that Mickey Mantle would have proved that gangster wrong.

"Chazz, I'm going to find a way to get Michael to meet Derek Jeter, no matter what it takes. I'm here for that young boy," I said.

After I hung up the phone, I knew I had to do something. The Boss never thought too long about how he would handle a situation with a sick child. He would offer help wherever he could, trying to make the situation better right away. Countless times I had seen his instant kindness and instinctive generosity, and I learned not to hesitate in dire situations.

The next day, I went into the stadium and set up a meeting. I called the boy's mother and gave her the details. I could hear in her voice how grateful she was that somebody she didn't even know was going to go out of his way to make sure her son met Derek Jeter.

I told her to bring Michael to Yankee Stadium on the following Sunday at eleven o'clock because I knew Derek would be on the field taking batting practice. My plan was to take Michael and his mother right up to the batting cage and introduce them to the boy's hero.

As I waited outside the stadium, I began to get nervous. Eleven came and went, and there was no sign of Michael and his mother. I was worried that something had happened to the boy, and I found myself wishing that Chazz had told me about him sooner. But at eleven thirty, Michael and his mother arrived, out of breath. They had been stuck in stadium traffic. I quickly put the credentials around their necks and hurried them into the stadium and onto the field. I knew Derek took batting practice in the next-to-last group and that he usually left the field afterward, rarely hanging around to watch the others.

But this time Derek was gone. He had finished his batting practice and quickly left for the locker room. I had to improvise. The last group was still batting, so I took Michael and his mom around and introduced them to Alex Rodriguez, Mark Teixeira, Melky Cabrera, and the other players who were still out on the field. Michael smiled a lot as he shook hands and got autographs. I kept looking at Michael, asking him if he was having fun.

"Yes," he said, nodding.

"Are you happy with everything here?" I asked him.

"Mmm-hmm," he said. But as I peered into his dark eyes, I could tell that there was something missing: Derek Jeter. While it was great to talk and joke with the other players, Michael had come to Yankee Stadium with his mind set on meeting Derek. I had to make that happen.

There is a rule in baseball that no visitors are allowed in the locker room before the games. The locker room is the players' safe haven where they prepare for the game away from prying eyes. It is almost a sacred place that they share. That is why they refer to it as the club-house. Nobody is allowed behind those closed doors except for players and coaches.

I grabbed Michael's hand, turned to his mother, and said, "Please wait here. We'll be back." Michael and I walked down the dugout stairs and into the hallway. If anyone asked, I said to myself, we were going to use the bathroom. I took Michael through the video room and into the tunnel that led to the back door of the locker room by the manager's office. As I breezed past a guard, I whispered, "You didn't see me."

I was breaking every rule there was, but I kept telling myself that this was what the Boss would want me to do, and that thought pushed me forward. My biggest worry was that some of the toughest security guards in the stadium were assigned to the locker room. Their job was to protect the team at all costs, and I respected that. They followed the rules to the letter. No exceptions. I was worried sick that they would turn this kid away and break his heart.

The next thing I knew, Michael and I were inside the locker room. Somehow, the guards weren't anywhere around. The room was completely empty except for Derek, sitting in front of his locker. I could almost feel Michael's heart beating. We walked over to Derek, whose back was turned to us.

"Someone would like to meet you," I quietly said.

Startled, Derek turned around to see Michael standing in front of him.

I could tell from the look on Derek's face that he realized right away that Michael was a sick little boy. Michael's skin was pale, he had dark circles under his eyes, and he was painfully thin. Like so many families, Derek's family, too, had been touched by cancer.

Derek extended his hand, and Michael shook it, his body trembling.

"Let's take a walk to the back there," Derek said. He and Michael went over to a corner and huddled for a few minutes. I didn't hear what they said because I stayed in front of Derek's locker. I wanted them to have a private moment together. "I'll be rooting for you," I finally heard Derek say as they walked toward me.

"I'll be rooting for you, too," Michael said.

I was elated that Michael was able to have this special time with Derek. Then I asked Derek if he would pose for a picture, and he put his arm around the little boy. My hands were shaking, too.

The first picture came out a little blurry. I wanted to take another one, but Michael said no. He insisted that he wanted the first picture. It was as though that first moment was special. Taking another picture just wouldn't be the same.

Michael and I left the clubhouse, and I took him back on the field to his mother. She looked at her son and then at me. I guessed she knew right away where we had been. I glanced at the little boy and then around at the big new stadium.

At that time, it seemed like everyone in New York was already caught up in Derek's race to pass Lou Gehrig as the all-time Yankee hit leader. When it would finally happen, Michael probably wouldn't be around to see the big day. I knew that he wasn't going to be with us in a few weeks. I wiped away my tears and then put sunglasses on to hide my eyes. Someone tapped me on the back.

It was one of the locker room guards. I stepped away, out of the boy's earshot. "Hey, did you take that kid into the clubhouse?" the guard asked me. I wasn't afraid of the security guard. He wasn't going to give me the chance to tell him how sick the boy was, or that Chazz

Palminteri asked me to introduce him to Derek, or that meeting Derek was the boy's dream.

I took a deep breath and thought of what the Boss would say.

"Yes, I took the boy into the locker room," I said. "In fact, I would do it again for any kid who could be helped by spending one minute with their hero." The guard muttered something and walked away. I shrugged, guessing that I was going to be reported.

Sonny Hight, the stadium manager, came out to talk to me. He asked me what had happened. I told him and repeated what I told the guard. "Yes," I said, "I would do it again if the situation arose." Sonny looked at Michael and his mother and nodded. He said he would handle the matter with the guard.

Michael's mother hurried over. "Are you in trouble?" she asked.

"Just regular stadium business. There's no problem," I said. I took Michael and his mother upstairs to watch the game from one of the suites, where Michael could be cool and out of the sun. Then I arranged for them to have food and drinks.

As the 2009 season went on, every time Derek got another hit and inched closer to breaking Gehrig's record, I thought about Michael. On the night that Derek broke the record, hitting a single off of Baltimore Orioles pitcher Chris Tillman, fans yelled, "Derek Jeter, Derek Jeter," while thousands of cameras flashed. Derek's teammates surrounded him at first base.

He humbly waved to the crowd. I watched as he looked up to the box where his mother was sitting. The two smiled at each other as he waved and held out his arm for an extra few seconds.

I wondered how Michael's mother was doing.

A few days later, I received a text message from her. She told me that Michael had become so involved in Derek's pursuit of Lou Gehrig's record that he had rallied. He had followed the games every day and kept track of how many hits Derek needed. Michael hung on until he knew that Derek had become the Yankee all-time hit leader.

She went on to tell me that her son had finally left our world on the night of September 13, 2009—two days after Derek Jeter broke the record with 2,722 career hits. Michael had followed Derek until the very end. He and his mother had watched all the games together. She was extremely grateful for the extra months she had with her son. I reflected back to the little gesture between Derek and his mother that winning night. Now I thought about another mother and son sharing that same moment as they watched the hit together on television.

When I composed myself, I went to find Derek. I told him about Michael and showed him the text message. He read it quietly. He handed me back my BlackBerry. His customary cool, detached expression turned dark.

"Send Michael's mother my love." Derek wiped his eyes with the back of his hand.

That was all he could say, but that was enough.

Now when I think back to *A Bronx Tale,* I think about that young boy, Calogero, saying that he read in the paper that Mickey Mantle cried in the locker room after they lost the 1960 World Series. It was a different locker room then and a long time ago; however, I knew that if Mickey did cry it was because he let his fans down. I hope that Derek Jeter felt a tremendous sense of pride that day. Surely he hadn't let his fans down. After all, he had broken Lou Gehrig's record and, perhaps most importantly, he had made a difference in one little boy's life. The gangster in *A Bronx Tale* had been wrong. In my Bronx tale somebody *did* care.

9

Brett Gardner and the Girl with the Yellow Bracelet

"Hey, when you put on that uniform you become Superman in the eyes of these kids," I told Brett.

I T WAS EARLY May of 2009, the same year Jeter broke Gehrig's record. I received a call from Project Sunshine, a New York–based nonprofit, requesting that I bring a Yankee to read baseball-themed books to children in a Manhattan hospital. I looked around the club-house. Brett Gardner, who had recently come to New York as a rookie, was sitting on a bench near his locker, changing out of his uniform. In the beginning of the season Brett was named the starting center fielder, beating out Melky Cabrera. Even though Brett had had a great spring training—he had been quick, excelling as a fielder—his hitting now just wasn't taking off. Suddenly Melky had his old job back. I thought Brett needed to think about something other than baseball. A visit to pediatric patients would do him just as much good as it would for the children he would see. I went to Brian Cashman, our general manager, for permission and support. As always, he said, "Whatever we can do for these kids, do it."

When Brett arrived in New York, he saw how many of the Yankees were helping children in need. Mariano Rivera, our star closer, continually befriended children, and had a special bond with Jack Szigety, a young cancer patient. Mariano invited Jack to work out with the entire team during calisthenics several times. When things looked bad for Jack, some of the players watched Mariano sit in front of his locker and pray for the boy. In 2006, when Jack became very ill after a stem cell replacement, he received a call from Mariano.

"Jack, buddy, how are you doing?" Mariano's phone call gave Jack a much-needed boost during the lowest moment in Jack's life.

On Friday, May 4th, 2012, the day after Mariano tore his ACL in Kansas City, the very first call that Clara, Mariano's wife, received was from Jack. The boy, now a freshman at Notre Dame, found himself consoling Clara: "Mariano has always been there for me, and I want Mariano to know that I will be there spiritually for him forever."

Brett also knew of Robinson Cano's commitment to Hackensack University Medical Center in New Jersey, where young Jack had been a patient. He heard of how often Robinson cheered pediatric patients, eventually having a children's physical therapy room named after him. Brett often stopped and noticed when Joe Scafidi, the Boss's office attendant, called me with an urgent request to bring a Yankee to visit a critically ill child. One of our catchers, Francisco Cervelli, was an especially dedicated player, and Brett asked about Francisco's frequent hospital visits.

Yet when I approached Brett, he said he wasn't sure he was worthy of going into the hospital. "How can I help when the kids really want the big stars?" he asked.

"Hey, when you put on that uniform you become Superman in the eyes of these kids," I told Brett. He looked skeptical but agreed to help out.

On Friday, May 15, a seasonably warm day, he arrived at the hospital, just minutes from the stadium, accompanied by Lenny Caro, the president of the Bronx Chamber of Commerce. Brett had returned home at 4:00 A.M. from a night game in Toronto. He hadn't shaved and had dark circles under his eyes. Despite his fatigue, I could tell that he was excited, and a little nervous, about his hospital visit. Linda Ruth Tosetti, Babe Ruth's granddaughter, was there, joining Brett. In a large event space, the two read baseball-themed books to a group of children, many of whom were waiting for organ donations. Brett was focused on the young patients. I watched how attentive he was with each child, quietly sitting with them, asking the children about themselves, deflecting the attention away from himself. Then he and Linda visited with patients at their bedsides. Brett looked out one patient's window.

"Wow." He turned to the child. "There's Yankee Stadium there in the distance. Can you see it?"

"Yes, most of the beds in this wing have views to the stadium," a nurse said. "In fact, did you know that this hospital sits on the site that previously housed the baseball field where the New York Yankees played?"

"No, I didn't, did you?" Brett turned to the young patient and then to Linda.

The little boy shook his head; so did Linda. The nurse looked at both of them. "What was the name of the Yankees back then?"

Brett and the boy looked at each other and smiled.

"The New York Highlanders, that was their name. They first played right on the ground below us in 1903," Linda said.

Brett and Linda visited a few more patients. As they were leaving the hospital, they came upon Alyssa, a small blue-eyed girl in her late teens, who was sitting in a wheelchair in the big conference room. She handed Brett a Project Sunshine bracelet, a yellow band with a gold disc that read SHINE on one side and had the Project Sunshine logo on the other. "If I give you this bracelet, I think you'll hit a home run."

I took a deep breath and looked down at the floor. I thought that Brett probably wasn't in the starting lineup that night. I was also quite aware that since the Yankees had arrived at the new stadium, Brett had only hit one home run in his 202 major league at-bats. The odds of him hitting a homer that night were slim, to say the least. I hated the thought that this little girl was likely to be disappointed. But Brett handled it beautifully, like a seasoned pro, even though it was his first time visiting hospitalized children.

"Keep an eye on me, okay?" The lower half of the young girl's face, bloated from steroids, was covered with a sterile mask, but I could tell by her sparkling eyes that she was smiling. "Keep fighting." He hugged her and left, still holding the yellow bracelet.

On the ride back to the stadium I could see that Brett was deeply moved by meeting all of the pediatric patients, especially Alyssa.

That night, Brett sat on the bench watching as we trailed Minnesota. It didn't look like he was going to get into the game. However, in the third inning Johnny Damon, our left fielder, was ejected for arguing balls and strikes with the home plate umpire. Joe Girardi called on Brett to take over in left field.

When Brett got up to bat in the seventh inning, the Minnesota Twins were beating the Yankees 4–1. I remembered Alyssa's prediction and wondered for a brief minute if Brett might have a home run in him. The first two pitches were strikes. I laughed at myself for my silly notion. Then I was startled by the crack of his bat. The fans suddenly roared. Brett had looped a lazy fly ball to left field, which curved toward the seats. I doubted it would stay fair. The Twins' left fielder, Denard Span, took off running after it. I figured, *That's it, Brett is out.*

Then an image of Bobby Murcer came to mind. I closed my eyes and saw the ghost of Bobby up at bat, giving the game everything he had, right after Thurman Munson died. I opened my eyes and watched the left fielder reach out his glove and then miss the ball by inches. It skidded past him and headed for the corner, rattling around instead of bouncing back. As the Twins' left fielder went to chase it down, Brett had taken off, putting on every ounce of speed he had.

I watched and thought, *This is a double, maybe a triple at best.* When Brett got to third base, the coach waved him home. Brett, often referred to as "the fastest man in pinstripes," gave it one final push and slid across the plate, headfirst, as the crowd went wild. There wasn't even a play at the plate. Brett had just hit an inside-the-park home run while the Yankee bench and the fans clapped, whistled, and yelled out his name.

So exactly how big a deal is it to hit an inside-the-parker? Well, statistics show that of the 154,483 homers hit between 1951 and 2000, only 975, or 1 out of 158, were inside-the-park home runs. That number is decreasing due to more power hitting and smaller ballparks. The last time the Yankees had one was in 1999—ten years earlier—when Ricky Ledee hit one in the old stadium. Brett's was the first inside-the-park home run in the new stadium.

The Yankees went on to win the game 5–4, and Brett went 3-for-3, including smacking a triple in the last inning, scoring the winning run on Melky Cabrera's walk-off single. When the reporters interviewed Brett after the game, the yellow bracelet was hanging on a hook in his locker. Brett credited the young hospitalized girl and the bracelet for his success on the field that night.

As newspaper writers hovered around Brett, I saw Hideki Matsui standing in front of his locker. I thought back to the time five years earlier when he visited Sunny Kawamura, a boy who was at Hackensack University Medical Center. Through David Jurist, copresident of Tomorrows Children's Fund, Hideki had heard that Sunny was fighting for his life. But he wasn't prepared for how deeply emotional he would be upon greeting the boy, whose body was limp and swollen. Instead of staying at the hospital the planned twenty minutes, Hideki visited with him and his family for over two hours. That night he miraculously hit two homers and drove in six runs against the Blue Jays at Yankee Stadium. Sunny wasn't as lucky as Alyssa, though. He died two months after Hideki's visit. I watched Brett cheerfully speak to reporters and remembered how devastated Hideki had been over the boy's untimely death. Yet I knew that Hideki understood the power of his visit and what those two home runs meant to Sunny.

"I wonder if Alyssa was able to see the home run, or do you think it was past her bedtime?" Brett asked me. "If she didn't see it, I hope she'll be able to see the replay tomorrow."

The following morning I received a call from someone who had been at the hospital event the day before. He told me that Alyssa had been waiting for about three months for a new heart, and while Brett had been winning the game for the Yankees, a donor had been found. Alyssa was being prepared for surgery and received the gift of a new heart the next day. When she woke up in the recovery room, the replay of the game the night before was playing. "He did it for me," she said with a smile.

The surgery was successful. To celebrate her one-year anniversary with a new heart, Brett and Alyssa had a quiet meeting on the Yankee field in May 2010.

"You will always be my hero," she told Brett.

The bracelet goes wherever Brett goes these days. Even though he can't wear it because it interferes with his fielding, it hangs in his locker in every stadium he plays in. These days Alyssa watches the Yankees games from home, instead of looking at the stadium lights from a hospital bed. Every major New York newspaper and television station, as well as the *CBS Evening News,* covered the story of the unlikely pair—whom they soon dubbed "a couple of good luck charms."

10

Last at Bat

"If there are spirits here in this stadium, then they'll find a
way to get across the street, Ray. But you've got to understand,
with time comes change," the Boss would say.

MR. STEINBRENNER ASKED if I would sit with Eleanor Gehrig, Lou Gehrig's sixty-nine-year-old widow, in August of 1973. She was being interviewed by a reporter at the stadium while she watched a game. That summer I had already escorted a few VIPs to their seats as guests of Mr. Steinbrenner's. I would see to it that they were comfortable and had their drinks, seat cushions, and new yearbooks.

"Tend to Mrs. Gehrig's every need," Mr. Steinbrenner said.

Mrs. Gehrig, refined and well spoken, was easy to talk to.

"One of the big reasons that I love the Yankees," I sputtered, "is because of Lou."

"How did you first learn of my husband?" she asked.

I told her how I had watched the movie *The Pride of the Yankees* and was fascinated with the left-handed slugger from that moment on. "That's when I knew that I wanted to be a Yankee. How true is the film, Mrs. Gehrig?"

"It's quite accurate," she said. "But I wished that more of the, you know, mystique of Yankee Stadium had been shown. For instance, they didn't show the room."

"The room?" I asked.

"Yes, deep inside this stadium there's a small space, almost a cubbyhole. It was mainly used for storage. But it's the place where Lou would escape to when his ALS began to take over. There was an old stadium chair in there. He'd sit on it, just meditate and cry sometimes," Mrs. Gehrig remarked. "I'd park my car outside the ramp that led to the room. After he came out, he'd go straight to the car. The fans and the media couldn't get to him when he was alone in that room."

The next day I raced down a narrow blue concrete hallway, flying by the umpires' room, the weight room, and then the carpenter's shop. I remembered that Mrs. Gehrig had said to turn right. I made a right and then, as she instructed, a left. I passed a storage room, jammed with assorted junk. There, behind a rolling metal gate, was a small space packed with wooden chairs, copper piping, and industrial drums filled with cleaning liquid. I shuddered as I sat down, in what I thought was the very same wooden chair from 1939, next to a pillar, where the Iron Horse had once said his prayers, where he communed with a higher being. I closed my eyes and pictured Lou during that last season, his large body worn and tired. I thought about his incredible streak of 2,130 consecutive games, and how it all came to a crashing end on May 2, 1939, when at the age of thirty-five Lou took himself out the lineup. I opened my eyes and felt that the Iron Horse was standing right next to me.

For the next few years, I went by myself to the room whenever I was feeling blue. I also went there when I was happy and excited. I found myself in Room 107 whenever I needed to be quiet. When I wanted to converse with the spirits of some of the Yankee greats, I'd head for the small storage room. It always provided comfort and magic for me.

After Thurman became our captain in 1976, I let him in on my secret, taking him to Lou's private room. Thurman, in his late twenties then, wasn't particularly spiritual, but I thought he might have connected with the former Yankee captain that day, as he sat in Lou's chair and glanced around the room. Over the years, I would take many more players as well as reporters there. I would go on to write several children's books in that small space. In 2005, I would ask my friend James Fiorentino, an artist, to paint a mural on the pillar there—the three legendary Yankee captains. He depicted Gehrig in tears in the chair, Munson in his catching gear, and Jeter taking a swing.

Yet even though Derek's portrait was there, I couldn't get him to visit that room. I tried, but Derek always had an excuse. "I've got to meet someone. Maybe another time, Ray." I stopped asking him after a while. I didn't want to be a nuisance. Derek was the captain and I had to be careful not to overstep my boundaries.

But in 2008, I began to fully comprehend that the Old Lady—my name for the stadium, because I always felt I was running home to Mama—was not going to stand forever. After all, she hadn't had a face-lift since 1973 and she was showing her age at eighty-five. All season I found myself in mourning over the fact that I was losing her.

"I'm really messed up about losing this stadium," I had told Mr. Steinbrenner many times. "I feel bad about leaving the spirits behind."

The Boss would look at me like I was crazy. Yet he knew everything that ever went on in that stadium, from the time he first purchased the team. He knew of the many nights the other batboys and I had run the bases and had pursued our own fantasy games, long after the real games had ended. He knew when I rolled up a towel and slept in the trainer's room or the times I actually slept on the field underneath the glare of the stadium lights after a night game, the moon rising above the El, with the sparkling field stretched out before me. Mr. Steinbrenner understood all of this. More than anyone else he knew of my reverence for my "home away from home," and how I never stopped asking myself if the stadium was real.

"If there are spirits here in this stadium, then they'll find a way to get across the street, Ray. But you've got to understand, with time comes change," the Boss would say.

Two nights before we were to play our last game at the stadium, I was working out in the gym, halfway between the locker room and the batting cage, around 6:00 P.M., unusually late for me. We had a 7:05 game against the Baltimore Orioles that night. As I was leaving the gym I bumped into Derek.

He was just about to perform his routine: at 6:50 every evening he would go to the batting cage and take a few last-minute swings before the game. He then had the habit of smacking the gym door as hard as he could with his bat, his way of letting off steam. You could see by the marks and dents that he had given the door a good pounding over the years.

The new Yankee Stadium was rising beyond our left field wall. The old stadium, where the greats from Babe Ruth to Mickey Mantle to Alex Rodriguez to Derek had played, where so much history had been made over the last eighty-five years—since the Babe opened the ballpark in 1923, with a home run in a victory over the Red Sox—was to be torn down. For weeks, I had been watching the wrecking ball, poised to strike.

It hadn't been a good year for the Yankees. We weren't even going to be in the playoffs, the first time since 1993. Now I felt a sense of urgency. I didn't want to be a pest, but Derek just had to experience that mystical room. Just as he was about to whack the gym door, I opened it. Derek stood there, his bat held high, "Man, I almost hit you in the head."

"Derek, this is no coincidence. You know what I'm going to ask you—this is supposed to happen," I said.

"What are you talking about?" he asked.

"You know, I've been telling you about the Lou Gehrig room for years. Give me forty seconds, Derek."

I was suddenly feeling the spirit of Lou Gehrig, telling me to bring him the captain.

"Okay, Ray, but I've got to go to the batting cage, so let's make it quick."

I led the way as we headed to the underworld.

We dashed to Room 107 and stopped in front of the small storage space. Derek looked around at the broken chairs, the drums of disinfectant—and then he saw the mural.

He stopped and stared.

He didn't speak. Neither did I. I could see the taut muscles in his forearms bulging as he gripped his bat tightly. "It really is here," he said.

I stood quietly, allowing Derek time to sit in the chair, to take in the painting of the three captains. After about a minute, I walked out of the room.

A few seconds later, Derek followed behind me. "Thanks. Thanks for bringing me here." We continued to walk through the hallway. "Seriously, thanks," Derek said again.

He walked into the batting cage, turned to me, and for a third time expressed his gratitude. "Hey, thank you." The next day Derek returned with *New York Post* photographer Charles Wenzelberg and had his picture taken next to the pillar.

FOR WEEKS THE biggest question on every fan's mind before the night of September 21, 2008, seemed to be: who was going to hit the final home run in the old stadium? The Babe, in 1923, had had that question in mind, too, when he said, "I was glad to have hit the first home run in this park. God only knows who will hit the last."

It seemed like everyone had a favorite. I sensed it was a toss-up between Alex Rodriguez and Derek Jeter. But Derek wasn't having a great game. He went 0-for-5 on the last night. However, he would be the last Yankee ever to bat at our old stadium, with a groundout to third in the eighth inning. Joe Girardi pulled him for defense with two out in the top of the ninth, so he could give the fans one last curtain call.

Following an impressive send-off ceremony, honoring many of the greats who wore the Yankee pinstripes, Andy Pettitte turned out to be the winning pitcher. Mariano Rivera recorded the last out, and backup catcher Jose Molina hit the last homer, a two-run shot in the fourth inning. Our 7–3 victory over the Baltimore Orioles that cloudy, mild night had been an uneventful game, but the crowd nonetheless went wild.

Derek took a microphone behind the mound during the on-field ceremony and addressed the standing crowd, many of them wiping away tears.

"For all of us up here, it's a huge honor to put this uniform on every day and come out here and play," Jeter said. "And every member of this organization, past and present, has been calling this place home for eighty-five years. There's a lot of tradition, a lot of history, and a lot of memories. Now, the great thing about memories is you're able to pass it along from generation to generation. And although things are going to change next year, we're going to move across the street, there are a few things with the New York Yankees that never change—it's pride, it's tradition, and most of all, we have the greatest fans in the world. We're relying on you to take the memories from this stadium and add them to the new memories that come to the new Yankee Stadium, and continue to pass them on from generation to generation. On behalf of this entire organization, we want to take this moment to salute you, the greatest fans in the world."

The Yankees took a lap around the field, waving their caps to the fans as Frank Sinatra's rendition of "New York, New York" blared over the sound system. Policemen on horseback lined the field to make sure our treasured relics didn't start disappearing.

For months before the final game, I had been thinking that I had to do something special to say good-bye to this most sacred of stadiums—something that was mine and mine only. I knew that there was a beautiful ceremony planned, and I had enjoyed it all a few hours earlier. That just wasn't enough for me. I wanted the last hit in that park to be mine.

I had started working out in early June, getting my middle-aged body in shape. The stronger I became, the more I believed that accomplishing that last hit wasn't going to be enough. I had to hit the last *home run* in the stadium.

For twenty-eight years I had kept a promise to myself: I would never hit another ball in Yankee Stadium. I had achieved every boy's dream by hitting one out of the yard in 1980. That year, Graig Nettles was working his way off the disabled list, pushing hard to get back in the lineup. Our batting practice pitcher, Nick Testa, had been throwing to him, and Graig was knocking himself out. He finally dropped the bat and headed for the clubhouse. Instinctively, I started to pick up the equipment and take it back to the dugout.

"Come on, Ray, your turn. Hit a few," Nick called to me. I picked up a bat and stepped into the batter's box. At first I didn't notice him, but then I saw that he was sleeping out in the left field stands, his feet propped up on the seat in front of him—Mr. Wilson, head of Yankee Stadium security.

I popped up a couple of times before I could feel myself starting to get into the zone. Always a pull hitter, I started poking a few solid hits into left field. Now I was beginning to feel my inner strength. I wasn't a big strong guy, but my next hit, what I thought would be a routine fly ball to left, took off like a laser.

"Holy shit," I said. I dropped the bat just like Reggie did in the World Series. I looked up and saw Mr. Wilson. Even though I couldn't stand the guy, I didn't want him to get clocked. The ball landed right in front of him. He woke with a start and glared at me as I laughed while rounding the bases. I felt a sense of quiet satisfaction.

After I crossed home plate, I told Nick I was finished. As I walked to the dugout to replace Graig Nettles's bat, I made a decision. That was it for me. I told myself that I would never hit another ball in Yankee Stadium.

But now, in the wee morning hours after the Yankees had played their final game in the stadium, I was about to break my promise and step back up to the plate. I was going to be the last person to hit a home run in the House That Ruth Built. Alex Belth, a reporter from *Sports Illustrated*, wanted to follow my last days at the stadium, but he didn't know that he was going to get a much bigger story. I also enlisted my good friends Aris Sakellaridis, a lifelong Yankees fan, and Yankees scout Cesar Presbott. Then I told one other person my secret, my thirteen-year-old son, Ricky. I would find some way to get up in the stands and track down that ball. I would bring it home to my son and say, "See? Your old man hit the last homer."

It took forever to clear out the stadium. There seemed to be an ocean of tearful good-byes. Even the great Whitey Ford had to pause to dig up some precious dirt from the mound where he had once dominated a generation of baseball.

Finally I slipped away and headed for the weight room. I wanted to get in some time warming up and stretching before I picked up a bat again after all those years. Then Cesar and Aris went with me to the batting cages underneath the stadium to get in some practice swings before I hit the field. Cesar pitched to me. It took me a little while to get my timing back, but I felt more confident with each swing. I knew I could do this, but it had been a long day, and now I was exhausted. While Aris took a few swings, I fell asleep leaning on the bat.

I ended up sleeping in the training room, as I had done so many times as a batboy. Aris and Cesar kept watch, waiting for the stadium to clear out and for security to call it a night. At three in the morning, there were still a couple dozen people hanging around.

Cesar woke me up. "Hey, Ray, sorry, man, but I can't stay any longer. I gotta get home."

Aris sauntered over to me. "It's over. It ain't gonna happen." He looked tired and defeated.

But I wasn't ready to give up. After I packed my jacket and balls, I decided to try the field one last time. The sun was starting to rise. I couldn't remember how many hours I had been at the stadium. The place was empty except for some crew members silently cleaning up. It was almost six in the morning. The field, as if in a time warp, was mine again, but I didn't know how long I would have before someone from security would come along and chase us out. All I knew was that I was ready, and that I was going to make the most of the swings I could get in.

While Alex stood off to the side, Aris walked out to the mound with a bucket of balls. There was no catcher there, but as I dug my spikes into the dirt in the batter's box, I could feel Thurman Munson squatting behind me. I could sense him checking out my spikes, just as he had with Lynn Jones so many years ago. I could hear him talking to me. I was happy to have my old friend close to me again, if only as a reminder of how real the spirits at Yankee Stadium were.

The late September morning was chilly and damp, making the balls extra heavy. I hit a few to the wall. They would have cleared it on a sunny, dry day. I could feel myself pushing it now. I could see the white balls dotting the grass in left field—just as they had on that day in 1980. I still couldn't hit to the opposite field, but a home run in the left field seats would be just fine.

Yet something told me I wasn't going to get many more swings. I took a pitch that was way out of the strike zone. Aris was fading as quickly as I was. I got hold of the next one. The two of us watched as it sailed out to left field. My heart was pounding.

This was it.

Then I watched it hook and land in the seats to the left of the foul pole. A long strike. With each pitch that followed, I could feel myself pushing harder and harder. The muscles in my groin tightened. I knew I didn't have many more swings in me. The balls were getting wetter, and I couldn't lift them anymore. I could only manage a few choppy ground balls to the infield.

Derek Jeter could have turned two on any of them.

I could hear Thurman's voice as I tried to massage my groin muscles and stretch them for just a couple more swings.

You already hit a home run, buddy. That's enough. I knew he was right. Two or three more swings and I wasn't going to be able to walk off the field on my own. And Gene Monahan, the Yankees' trainer, was nowhere in sight to help. He was home in his nice warm bed, where I should have been. Aris was pushing for another ten pitches. There was nothing I wanted more than to keep hitting. Sure, I had gotten one into the seats, but it was a foul ball and that just wasn't good enough. But my body was telling me otherwise. Around the clubhouse, I might still have been known as the batboy, but the batboy was now a middle-aged guy with a couple of kids in college.

It was time to go home.

Aris wanted to leave the balls dotting the outfield, but I just couldn't do that.

"No, we gotta get rid of the evidence," I told him as I picked up the empty bucket and headed out to left field, sad that I wasn't headed up to the seats to retrieve my home run ball for my son Ricky. He would ask, and I would have to tell him, I just couldn't do it.

As we headed to the infield with the bucket filled with soggy balls, a security guard dressed in a navy blazer and gray slacks appeared. He was a day guy, and I didn't know him. I was sure we were about to get thrown out. Aris and I stopped.

"We're leaving," I said.

"Could I have one of your balls as a souvenir?" he asked.

"Sure," I said. Aris handed him two. He had probably just come on duty and missed out on all the activities the night before. I smiled at him as he took the balls. "I thought you were going to kick us out."

He smiled back. "Nah, I'm not going to throw you out. You're Steinbrenner's guy."

Then it hit me.

Thurman had been right.

I had hit a home run.

I thought back to all the times the Boss said, "You're somebody. Don't ever allow anyone to put you down. If I hadn't believed that you could do great things, I never would have given you a chance that day."

That morning I came to appreciate what the Boss meant more than ever. Someone I had never seen in my life recognized me and told me I was "Steinbrenner's guy." I listened to those words again, "Steinbrenner's guy." With the exception of not hitting that home run on that chilly morning, I had accomplished virtually everything I had set out to do. In April 2009, the Yankees would move into a new stadium and on to new challenges, and Ray Negron—Steinbrenner's guy—was ready to move with them.

EPILOGUE

I only wish that the spirits would have given me a sign that
day that this would be my last conversation with the Boss.

George Michael Steinbrenner III died at 6:30 a.m. on July 13, 2010, less than two weeks after his eightieth birthday. Ron Dock, my friend and the Yankees' counselor, called me at my home on Long Island. It was around eight in the morning.

"You don't know what's goin' on, do you?" he quietly asked me. "I've got something to say about a friend of yours."

"Oh, boy, here we go." I had been sleeping soundly, but now I jumped out of bed.

"Take it easy." Ron's voice was calm. "Unfortunately, Mr. Steinbrenner has died of a massive heart attack."

"Don't bullshit me," I yelled.

Silence on the other end.

"I'll call you back, Ron."

I hung up and dialed Hank Steinbrenner. We had been talking frequently because I was managing Hank's Yanks, the team that helps underprivileged New York–area youth that Hank and Herman Hernandez, my childhood friend, had started earlier that year. He was driving home from St. Joseph's Hospital in Tampa.

"Is it true?" I asked him.

"Yes, it's true." Hank's voice was weary, resigned. "He's gone. You know, the crazy thing was that when we got to the hospital this morning my father was still alive, and his eyes followed me around that hospital room. He asked me, 'You all right, pal?'"

"That doesn't surprise me. That's your father," I said. As I hung up the phone, my thoughts ran wild. My heart went out to Mr. Steinbrenner's family. I couldn't imagine what this enormous loss meant to each of them. Then an overwhelming fear gripped me.

"What's going to happen to me?" I asked myself over and over. I tried to push away my selfish reaction, but I couldn't shake my feelings. Inconsolable, I was deep in the anxiety of being in this new reality.

Eventually, later that day, my thoughts turned to Robert and Alex, two of the many members of a fraternity, a club of lost souls who had been saved by the Boss. His collection of "misfits"—some I knew, but most I didn't—was comprised of ex-cons, drug dealers, the disabled, alcoholics, and the poor.

"Folks who think these people are losers are really the losers themselves," the Boss once said to me. I was proud to be a member of his "club."

A few days later I called Robert to see how he was coping. Robert's mother had wanted her son to meet the Boss ever since they moved from Detroit to Tampa in 2004. Her friend, a waitress at a Tampa International House of Pancakes, had told her of Mr. Steinbrenner's habit of ordering the steak and eggs breakfast, which he always got with pancakes. On several occasions she had seen the Boss, after he finished his meal, call the manager.

"How many you got today?"

"Well, let's see, Mr. Steinbrenner, including the cook, I've got eight people working today."

"Okay, line 'em up," he'd say. Then he'd chat with each of the employees for a while. "How's your family? Your nephew still going to college? What are you doing for the holidays?" At the end of the conversation, he'd slip a fifty-dollar bill into each palm.

Robert's mother thought that maybe the Boss could somehow help her son, who had been struggling in school and getting into trouble. She asked her waitress friend to call Robert the next time that Mr. Steinbrenner came into IHOP.

Sure enough, before long Robert's phone rang. "Get over here, quick. Mr. Steinbrenner, you know, that man who owns the Yankees, has just walked in."

Meanwhile, she told Mr. Steinbrenner about Robert's struggles.

"Let me talk to him. Let me see what I can do," he said.

When Robert arrived at IHOP, he and the Boss instantly struck up a conversation. Fifteen minutes later, Robert had a job in the Yankee clubhouse in Tampa, helping the equipment people, but not before promising the Boss three things: he wouldn't sell drugs, he would show up on time for work every day, and he'd get his GED.

When the Boss told me about meeting Robert I asked him, "Why'd you help that guy out?"

"Didn't I help you out once?" he snapped.

Not surprisingly Robert fulfilled the first two of his promises, but he was having trouble passing the tests to get his GED. Finally, after his fourth try, he passed in the summer of 2010.

"My GED certificate is still at Ken Fagan's Frame Shop in Tampa," Robert said to me over the phone after I told him of Mr. Steinbrenner's death. "I was having it framed so I could show the Boss. Now he'll never get to see it."

"Well, Robert, when you have your low moments, you can be comforted that the most powerful man in sports took a true interest in you."

Then I laughed to myself, remembering how the Boss had said, "I've found another one of your pals, Ray," after he had offered Robert a job that day.

Epilogue

A few days later, I called Alex, now a student at Queens College and another youth I met through the Boss. Back on Old-Timers' Day in August 2000, Alex, then ten years old, and his father were standing outside the stadium, waiting for the Yankee greats to walk by so they could get autographs. They especially wanted to meet Phil Rizzuto, because Alex had dreams of becoming a sports announcer. Alex, a small boy as Phil was, had been born with one leg. He leaned on his crutch, a Rollerblade on his foot. He and his father weren't sure whether to approach the older gentleman with the neatly combed hair who passed by them that afternoon.

"Excuse me, sir," Alex said. "I'm trying to get Phil Rizzuto to sign this baseball. Would you know how I could find him?"

"Sure I do," the man said. "He's up in my suite."

The boy looked at the older man quizzically. "Well, would you sign my baseball?" he asked. He almost dropped the ball when he read the signature: George M. Steinbrenner.

"Thank you, Mr. Steinbrenner."

"Take them up to my suite," Mr. Steinbrenner said as he looked at one of the security guards. Then he was gone.

Alex and his father were led to the Boss's suite, where they watched the old-timers play against each other. Then they stayed and watched the Yankees play against the Los Angeles Angels. The Boss continued to take an interest in Alex, a spunky, curious young man, who now has his own internally televised show, *The Garrett Sports Report*, at Queens College. Alex and his father have had an all-access pass to Yankee Stadium ever since 2000, courtesy of the Boss.

"You okay?" I asked Alex on the phone.

"I'm sad, Ray. I'll never forget how good he was to me. He always told me to hang in there."

"Well, just keep going back to the stadium and feel his spirit. He's there with the rest of the Yankees. If you feel the spirits at the stadium, then you'll always be able to feel him."

The Boss left Robert, Alex, and me—and a countless trail of others from every walk of life—his personality, his fun, his enduring friendship, and his selflessness, a term rarely associated with the Boss. For years I had seen and talked to Henry Kissinger, a frequent guest of the Boss's at games. Mr. Kissinger would introduce me to his friends. "Tell my friend here about how George discovered you." I'd tell the story, and he'd laugh and say, "That's George, that's just George."

On the other hand, I'm certain that every single one of us had witnessed the other side of the Boss at some point in our lives.

"I WANT YOU to pack your bags," the Boss hollered, shooting up from his chair and wagging his finger in my face, "and get the hell outta here!" We were in the middle of our 1978 spring training camp in Fort Lauderdale.

Just an hour earlier, Billy Martin had approached me in the clubhouse as I was setting up for that day's game. "I've forgotten my notes, Ray," he said. "I'm going to need you to go back to my hotel in Boca and grab them. We're making cuts after the game, so I gotta have them. Take my car—and hurry!"

We had sixty players in camp, and little by little over the next couple of weeks some of them would be sent down to the minors. I understood how important Billy's notes were.

Mr. Steinbrenner, though, had just finished telling me not to go anywhere. "I've got several guests coming in this week. I'm going to need you to stay in the clubhouse so you can help me out, Ray. When I call you in the clubhouse, I want you to run up here. Understand?"

"Yes, Boss," I said.

However, the only assignment that Mr. Steinbrenner had given me all week was to bring him ketchup-and-relish-drenched hot dogs during the third innings of the last few games. I figured he wouldn't notice if I left the stadium for a short while to help Billy out.

Billy handed me his car keys. "Haul ass, Ray!"

I ran out of the clubhouse, climbed into his blue Lincoln Continental, and headed north on I-95, hoping to make the half-hour drive in less than twenty minutes. I floored the gas pedal and raced up to Boca. Billy's notes were right on his hotel room bed, just where he said they would be. I grabbed them, jumped back into his car, and returned to the stadium in less than forty-five minutes.

As I was parking Billy's car, our traveling secretary, Bill Kane, greeted me in the parking lot. "Where the fuck have you been?"

He tapped on his watch several times. Rumor has it that Graig Nettles had once witnessed Bill in an argument and nicknamed him Killer Kane. Now I understood why.

"The Boss has gone crazy. Get upstairs," he yelled. "I think you're done. You're done."

By this time, I had been with the Yankees for almost five years and I'd seen Mr. Steinbrenner's tirades. "Well, hopefully by the time I get up there, he'll be okay." I climbed the stairs two by two to his suite. When I approached the door, I heard his voice. "You fuckin' asshole. This guy can't play. Why am I paying you guys?" Silence. Al Rosen, a former third baseman for the Cleveland Indians and at that time our president and COO, and some other baseball personnel walked out of the office looking haggard.

"Good luck," Al said sarcastically.

I tentatively walked into the small suite. The Boss was sitting in a chair, looking out over the field.

"Where the hell were you?" He turned and glared at me.

"Billy asked me to go to Boca and get his game notes," I said.

"Who signs your checks?"

"You do," I said quietly.

"Uh-huh, okay, so evidently you work for me." The Boss stood up. "Okay, good. Now get your ass back to the hotel, pack your stuff. Bill Kane will have your airline ticket for you. I never want to see you at Yankee Stadium again. Understand me?" he said.

"Yes, I understand." I started backing out of his suite.

"Okay, good-bye," he said matter-of-factly.

"Good-bye." I bit my lip.

Bill Kane was waiting for me when I walked out.

"Ray, this is Charlie. He'll be driving you back to your hotel. Here's your airline ticket—your flight departs in three hours. And here's some cash for your cab to the airport."

The drive back up I-95 seemed to take forever. Charlie tried making small talk with me while I stared out the window, trying to comprehend what had just happened.

Back at the hotel I threw my clothes in my suitcase, jumped in a cab, and headed for Fort Lauderdale–Hollywood International Airport. I checked in with Eastern Airlines, bought a Coke, and sat numbly at the gate, waiting for my flight. I heard a woman's voice over the loudspeaker.

"Ray Negron to the white courtesy telephone." I stood up and looked for the phone. "Ray Negron to the white courtesy telephone." The man behind the check-in desk pointed to the phone a couple of feet away.

"Hello?"

"Where the hell are you?" the Boss shouted. I looked around.

"I'm at the airport."

"Good. Get your ass back here," he bellowed. "And when you get back here, come back to see me. Not Billy. Not Reggie. Come to see *me*. Good-bye."

In a daze, I hung up the telephone.

I retrieved my bags and climbed into a cab. "Fort Lauderdale Stadium," I said.

When I arrived, I sprinted through the clubhouse carrying my suitcase. Mr. Sheehy was sitting on a bench, sipping a cup of coffee, marking numbers on underwear. I put my bags down. He looked up, smiled, and said, "Welcome back," a rare hint of cynicism in his voice.

I ran upstairs to the Boss's suite, not sure what I would find. Four or five people, none of whom I knew, but probably some of his important friends, surrounded him as they watched the game.

"Hey, pal, how ya doin'?" He glanced up at me.

"I'm fine, how you doin'?"

"Taking BP tomorrow? Are you gonna get into uniform tomorrow?" Mr. Steinbrenner knew how I liked to work out with the team.

What the hell is going on here? I said to myself. "Yeah, yeah, I guess so."

"Oh, good. I'll see you later." He turned back to his friends. "If I need you, I'll know where to find you, right?"

"Oh, yeah," I said.

A COUPLE OF DAYS LATER, the Boss called me on the clubhouse phone. "Ray, I need you. Now." I tore up to his suite.

"Listen, pal, the most important thing in the world to me is my kids. I'm gonna give you a special assignment," he said. "My kids are coming in. You're gonna pick them up, drop the girls off at my condo, and you're gonna bring Harold to the ballpark. Treat him like a little brother. Be very careful with him. Okay, here are the keys to my car. By the way, I'm sure you know your way to the airport by now." He chuckled.

I did exactly as Mr. Steinbrenner instructed and brought Hal—everybody but the Boss called him Hal—then all of eight years old, to the ballpark. We ran out on the field and shagged fly balls. It was a beautiful spring day, and Hal was excited to be out on the field with the players. Afterward, we visited the Boss in his office, which was housed in a small trailer right on the players' parking lot. I let Hal run through the clubhouse, and he jumped into the whirlpool, pretending he was in a swimming pool.

Around six o'clock that night the Boss came looking for us. When he saw Hal, he stared at him, almost like it was the first time he was seeing him in years. Then he gently cradled Hal's little head in his arms. I thought how tough the Boss had been with me just a couple of days ago. Looking at the tender expression on his face as he interacted with his son, I found myself wishing that I had had just one moment like that with my real dad.

Mr. Steinbrenner, his arm around his son, glanced over at me. "You got a lot of guys in this clubhouse that really care about you, Ray. Don't ever forget that."

He had a gift for knowing what people were really thinking, for understanding, when no one else did.

.   .   .

At the end of the '95 season, the Yankees had made it into the playoffs, our first since 1981. Hopes were finally high. But then we lost in a heart-wrenching, eleven-inning game against the Seattle Mariners on October 8. In the bottom of the eleventh, the Mariners' third baseman and designated hitter, Edgar Martinez, lined a double to left field, bringing in two runners and winning the series, 6–5.

At the time the Boss had begun to take a big interest in thirty-year-old Dwight Gooden, who had missed most of the 1994 season and all of the '95 season with the Mets because of a drug suspension. The Boss believed that the once feared and dominant pitcher might have a future, even when the scouts were doubtful. I told him that I thought Dwight could be a good Yankee someday. As much as I liked Dwight, I knew I had to protect the Boss above anything else. I had to make sure that Dwight and I were doing right by him, but the enormity of my new responsibility weighed heavily on me.

"Help the guy, do whatever you can to make sure he doesn't fall off the wagon. Talk to Adele Smithers," the Boss had said to me in the beginning of the season. Adele advised me to find a good place where I could take Dwight to meetings. I discovered New Freedom House, where Dwight and I started attending Narcotics Anonymous meetings. I set up workout regimens for him. I also asked him to come into schools and talk about the dangers of alcohol and drug use. I began to understand that you have to share your story to be able to deal with it.

Attending the meetings with Dwight provided me with a stronger appreciation of just what addicts have to go through every single day to stay clean. I soon learned that everyone has a different story, yet there's a similarity about all the stories, too. Initially the Boss thought that the disease part of addiction was bullshit, but over time, after I told him what meetings were actually like and how Dwight was doing, he came to accept that addicts had cravings that were different from other people's. He began to use the term "disease" more freely when discussing Dwight's issues.

"I'll support you, I'll help you, Dwight. But if you mess with me, I'll be the worst friend that you could ever have," he told Dwight as we began the recovery work.

Dwight took the Boss's warning seriously. So did I. When the Boss got mad, you couldn't look him in the eyes, because his steely blues seemed to pop right out of his face as if they wanted to punch you. At that point, my life became Dwight Gooden. "Do whatever you have to do to keep him clean, even if you have to get physical with him," the Boss had said, realizing that Dwight could be his own worst enemy.

Now, within an hour of losing Game 5 to the Mariners, the Boss was on the phone, calling from Seattle. My four-year-old son, Joey, the first of my children to get to know and enjoy a relationship with the Boss, answered the phone before I could get to it. Joey was laughing as he handed me the phone.

"Ray, George Steinbrenner. What are you and Dwight doing tomorrow?"

"Just what we do every day, Boss," I said.

"Good, let's meet at Iavarone's for dinner tomorrow night. See you at seven," he said. "And I'm bringing Billy Connors along." Billy was the organizational pitching coordinator for the Yankees.

I called Dwight. "It's show time," I said. "The man called, and he wants us to meet him for dinner tomorrow night."

"Mr. Steinbrenner himself called?" Dwight was incredulous.

I told Dwight that we'd better dress well. "The Boss is always dressed up nice. No one dresses like the Boss." We arrived before the Boss and Billy. While we sat there and waited, the two men pulled into the parking lot and walked toward us. We had spent the entire day preparing for this evening. We got haircuts, picked out just the right shirts and suits, and had our shoes shined. The Boss and Billy were wearing jogging outfits and running shoes. The four of us looked at each other and started laughing.

The Boss sat next to Dwight, trying to determine if Dwight was going to be clean long enough to play for the Yankees.

"Do you have control over yourself? How's your family? I hear that your father's been sick. Try to include him in everything in your life, Dwight. You know, I don't have my father anymore, but I wish I did."

Dwight was deferential. "Yes, Mr. Steinbrenner, I want to be with the Yankees. Ray has told me so much about the team. I want to play for you. I want to be a Yankee."

As we left the restaurant that night, Mr. Steinbrenner offered to come to my house in St. Petersburg to discuss the details of potentially hiring Dwight. Knowing how much Dwight's father, Dan, loved his son and baseball, the Boss suggested that Dan join us. We all agreed that evening that we would do a contract ourselves, without an agent. Mr. Steinbrenner had been closely monitoring Dwight's recovery. There was no need to bring in an agent.

The next day we met the Boss in the conference room of his hotel, the Bay Harbor Inn. Dwight and I had discussed a number. On the drive to the hotel we talked to Dan. Weak from dialysis, he could barely walk from the parking lot to the hotel.

"Okay, Mr. Steinbrenner, we think that one million for the first year, two million for the second, with an option for three million for the third—that would be fair," I said.

"Lemme see, lemme see." The Boss glanced over at Dan. "You okay with this, Dan?"

"Uh, yeah," Dan said quietly.

"Don't push me now, Dan." Mr. Steinbrenner looked over at me and gave me a little smile. "So, Dan, you want this option, this third year, then?"

"Yeah, I think that would be good," Dan said.

"You're driving a hard bargain, Dan. You know I don't like to be pushed."

The Boss looked over at Dwight and me and winked. There had been a sweetness and lightness to the negotiations.

"Even though my son hasn't played in the last year, I hope that you are comfortable with that," Dan said to the Boss. "I need you to care for my son, be his friend. That's all I care about."

"Dan, Ray will tell you. I'm going to be here for this young man. I'll be a second father to him. I want him to try really hard to deal with his demons. Ray, you're gonna have to help me more than ever. I'm trying to learn . . ."

"I'm there for you and Dwight, Boss."

At that point the Boss and Dan shook hands. "I don't care about the money. I just care about my son," Dan said softly again.

When we got in the car Dan said, "I hope I did a good job."

The Boss continued to be hopeful and excited about his new pitcher. In March, during the '96 spring training, the Boss called me in the late evening to check in. "How you doin'?" he asked.

"Everything's fine, Boss," I said.

"How's Gooden?"

I swallowed hard. I hadn't been able to find Dwight that night. I had called his house constantly, but my frantic messages on his answering machine weren't returned. I was sure he'd had a relapse.

"You'd better find this guy, Ray," the Boss shouted and hung up.

I called Dwight a few more times. *Hi, it's Dwight. Leave a message after the beep.*

I slept fitfully, imagining that Dwight was going nuts in some rat-filled crack house. Early the next morning, I woke up exhausted and defeated, guessing I would have to drive to Legends Field by myself. What was I going to tell Mr. Steinbrenner? He had taken the biggest gamble of his career. When people told him, "Dwight can't be trusted. He just can't stay clean," the Boss had trusted me to prove the naysayers wrong.

I looked out the window. Dwight was sitting outside my house in his black Mercedes 500. He waved to me.

I threw on my clothes and climbed in the car. We began the trip to the stadium in silence. Then, as we were driving across the Howard Frankland Bridge toward the stadium, I turned to Dwight.

"Hey, man, I was worried about you last night. Why didn't you call?" I said, trying to control my anger.

"I am sick and tired of you babysitting me," Dwight screamed. "Why the hell do you always think that I'm gonna do drugs? Why?"

"Pull the car over," I snapped. "I've had it with your selfishness. Pull the goddamned car over right now."

Dwight looked at me like I was crazy. He swerved over two lanes to the inside lane and stopped the car in the middle of the bridge. We both jumped out of the car.

"You know what? I want to fight you!" I shouted. "The Boss said that if I have to get physical with you, then I should." I raised my fists in front of his face.

Dwight walked toward me and burst out laughing.

"What are you laughing at?"

"If the Boss told you to jump off this bridge, you would, wouldn't you?" he said.

"Yeah." I put my hands down by my sides.

"Well, don't feel bad. I would, too. He's why I'm gonna pass my drug test today. Now, let's go to work."

April was a rough month for Dwight's pitching. People close to Mr. Steinbrenner said that Dwight should be released, or at the very least be sent down to the minors and learn to be a relief pitcher. Had Dwight been with any other team, that would surely have happened.

Mr. Steinbrenner, however, knew that Dwight was dealing with his recovery. "I'm not going to send him down. It's one day at a time," he said. "Make sure you are keeping Smithers abreast of this, Ray."

By the beginning of May, Dwight had had a couple of good starts. Then David Cone came down with an aneurysm, and Dwight was asked to take over for him on May 14, even though his father was scheduled for open-heart surgery the very next day. "If you want, you should go home and be with your dad at the hospital," the Boss said to Dwight on the phone. "You know you can go home. I want you to have the strength to deal with this."

"No, I want to pitch and then I'll go home," Dwight said.

That night, an unseasonably cool one, Dwight pitched a no-hitter against the star-studded Seattle Mariners, a team that included Ken Griffey Jr. and A-Rod, winning the game 2–0. I watched from the stands as Dwight's teammates carried him off the field.

The next morning Dwight and I caught the first flight and arrived in Tampa. We went straight from the airport to the hospital.

When we walked in, the Boss was sitting right there in the waiting area. He stood up and hugged Dwight. "I was very proud to see you get carried off the field like that last night," the Boss said.

The three of us sat together and waited for the doctors to give us a prognosis. The doctor finally came to the waiting room. "We did the best we can."

"I'm going to need more than the best you can," the Boss said. Later that night Dwight handed his father the ball that he had pitched with the night before.

Seven months later, in early January of 1997, I was walking by the conference room at the minor league ballpark, Himes, in Tampa, where the Boss was conducting a meeting.

The Boss looked up as I walked by. "How's Dwight's father?"

"Not good," I said. "I don't know if he's going to make it."

"Excuse me." The Boss stood up. "I've got something more important to deal with, boys. I'll be back. C'mon, Ray, let's get to the hospital."

We climbed into the Boss's car and raced to St. Joseph's, where we found out that Dan was in the intensive care unit. As we approached the door a doctor said, "I'm sorry, Mr. Steinbrenner, we can't let you in, only family."

"Like hell you can't. And besides, I am family." The Boss walked right in, and I followed close behind.

Dwight, his two sisters, and Dwight's mother were standing by Dan's bedside. Dan looked up and saw the Boss and began to tear up.

"Hang tough, Dan," the Boss said.

Dan grabbed the Boss's hand and squeezed it tightly.

"You know I'm gonna take care of your son," the Boss said.

"Please," Dan whispered. Tears rolled down his cheeks.

I looked over at Dwight, who was sobbing uncontrollably.

DAN GOODEN DIED only a few days later, at age sixty-nine.

The Boss drove himself to the funeral in St. Petersburg. He walked into the church, packed with family and friends, and quietly took a seat next to Rego Garcia, an administrative assistant with the Yankees, and Eddie Robinson III, an administrative assistant and the grandson of the famous football coach Eddie Robinson.

Dwight had asked me right after his father died to say a few words at the service. This was one of the first times that I had ever spoken publicly; I wanted to make sure that I would be reaching Dwight's heart, even though I was speaking to a large group.

I stood up on the podium, looked out at the congregation, and said, "As much as Dan Gooden loved baseball, and as proud as he was that his son was a major leaguer, he would have traded all of that for Dwight to be sober and healthy." Rego later told me that when I walked off the podium, the Boss's eyes followed me all the way to my seat.

After the service, I walked toward my car, drained. The Boss was sitting in his car waiting for me. He leaned out of the window and said, "I was really proud of you today. I hope that your friend understands the message you were trying to convey. You spoke from your heart, Ray. I hope your friend doesn't forget what you said."

"Thank you, Boss."

"No. Thank you, Ray."

MY LAST CONVERSATION with the Boss was in late March of 2010. We were at one of the final spring training games. He appeared to be in a fine mood. I watched him early on in the day as he sat in his suite and sang show tunes with Jim Fuchs, a former Olympian and one of his dearest friends. They laughed about old times and talked about Jim's sons, Slater and Nicky, and his daughter, K.C. Along with William Walters, she runs the Silver Shield Foundation, a charity that Jim and the Boss started in 1982 that helps the children of police officers and firefighters killed in the line of duty. Later I was sitting in the stands and looked up to see the Boss and Reggie watching the game. I decided to run up to the suite and visit with the Boss.

"What's up, Boss?" I said and leaned on his shoulder.

"How are you, Ray?" he said. We talked about the game. Then he leaned over and said, "So, am I ever going to get to see that cartoon of yours?" He was referring to *Henry & Me*, the animated film based on my children's book series about a young boy's magical journey as he battles his illness.

"We're finishing it up," I said.

The Boss had asked me about it from time to time, and he was interested in the cast of voices, which included Richard Gere, Chazz Palminteri, Reggie Jackson, Danny Aiello, Yogi Berra, Alex Rodriguez, and many other celebrities, non-Yankees and Yankees. I had asked Hank Steinbrenner to be the voice of his father.

"Geez, you've been working on it forever. Is Hank gonna do my voice?"

"He did, Boss, and he was great."

"Oh, yeah? Hank's a better actor than I am."

"Yeah, and you're a pretty good one." Reggie couldn't help himself. We all laughed. Uncharacteristically, it would be the only time that Reggie joined in our conversation that afternoon.

"Well, I've got to get back to New York tomorrow," I said.

"Stay close to Randy Levine," the Boss said, referring to the Yankee team president, whom he implicitly trusted. "He'll protect you."

We watched the game some more. I turned to go, but the Boss stopped me.

"So, Ray, your newest book. It's not a children's book?"

"No, this one's called *Yankee Miracles*. It's all about the miracles that you've helped to create while you've owned the Yankees."

"You give me too much credit, Ray."

"Well, that's the way I see it," I said. "I want to use this letter that you wrote to me when my first children's book came out." I took out my wallet and unfolded a copy of the letter dated September 7, 2006, when my first book was published. I treasured that letter. The original was framed and hangs on my wall.

The Boss glanced at the letter. I watched his lips move as he read the first paragraph: "If I were to make a top-ten list of the most moving and emotional experiences with regard to the Yankees that I have had in the thirty-four years of my ownership, I would add your book to the top of my list." He looked up at me and smiled.

"I want to share that with the world."

"You should. That would be good," he said.

"You'd be okay with that, then?"

"Yeah, Ray. You know, I think your book is going to reach a lot of people." He paused. "Tell it right. Tell it good."

LOOKING BACK, it seems fitting that the Boss, Reggie, and I sat together that warm spring day, three survivors of the lunacy of the Yankees years in the '70s—Billy, Reggie, Thurman, the Boss, and, dare I add, me. Throughout his life, I saw the Boss as invincible, someone who changed the world. That's why when it came time to write this chapter I started dragging my feet. How could I possibly give the Boss the justice he deserved? How could I show others what this man had meant to me—and to others like me? I was terrified of writing about the person I respected more than any other.

"You're stressing out," my daughter, Toni, said as I drove her to work. "Why don't you let the spirits talk to you, the way you say they do?" She rolled her eyes and got out of the car. I turned on the radio to WCBS-FM, my favorite oldies station. Gladys Knight was singing "The Best Thing That Ever Happened to Me." I had often listened to that song since its release in 1974. Now I was quiet as I took in each word, one by one. Gladys sang that if she decided to write her life story, the person who meant the most to her would be right there between each line. I thought about what it had been like over the past year as I recorded my own story, only the Boss wasn't there.

That's when I heard his voice ringing in my head. "Ray, didn't I always tell you to confront your fears, to face your challenges? That's the only way you're going to get ahead in this world." The voice was so vivid, so undeniably the Boss's, that I began to smile. I even laughed a little.

Much has been written about George Steinbrenner, and more will be forthcoming, some flattering, some not. But I have put these words on paper so that people will remember a man with more heart and soul than any other human being I have ever known. I am proud to have called him my friend.

In telling this story, I have tried to stay true to his instructions, his very last words to me, "Tell it right. Tell it good." I only wish that the spirits would have given me a sign that day that this would be my last conversation with the Boss. I would have grabbed his hand and said, "Thank you for being the best thing that ever happened to me."

ACKNOWLEDGMENTS

Tᴴɪꜱ ʙᴏᴏᴋ ᴄᴏᴜʟᴅ not have been possible without the support of the following:

To sweet Lou Pinella . . . you made us love you. To David Boomer Wells, thank you for bringing back the Babe one more time the day you wore his hat for one inning in 1997—his spirit was with you.

Matthew, Michael, Malcom Valdez and all my Valdez relatives everywhere; the New York Yankees, Randy and Mindy Levine, Ray Bartoszek and RLB Holdings, Felix Lopez, Brian Cashman, Debbie Tymon, Lon Trost, Robert Brown and family, Debbie Nicolosi, Marty Roth, Joe Scafidi and family, Jean Catillo—for always taking care of the Boss; Stephanie Fullam, Sonny Hight, Brian Smith, Ben Tulibitz, Jason Zillo, Tony Morante, Rob Gomez, Eddie Fastook, Manny Garcia, Vanessa Rodriguez, John Sponar, Tony Bruno—your love of Munson inspires me; Diane Blanco, Dolores Hernandez, the Cucuzza family, and the Yankee clubhouse staff; Terry Jenkins—because you loved him; Richard, Carey, and Homer Gere; Russell and Daniel Hernandez and family; Max Solon—keep protecting our boy; Mary and George, Jackie Williams, Linda Cotney, Yunior Tabares, Alex Cotto, Damon Oppenheimer, Mark Newman, Billy Connors, Curtis Lane,

Phoebe Ozuah, Montifiore Medical Center, Greg Manocherian, RoeCo, Hackensack University Medical Center, David and Alice Jurist, Jack Szigety, Lenny Caro, the Bronx Chamber of Commerce, Lucky Riviera, Positive Workforce, Adele Smithers, Ray and Linda Aguila, Puerto Rico USA Imports, Bunger Surf Shop, the Giovinazzo family, James Lanzarotta, Charlie and Janet Bunger; Charlie, Kristin, Charles and Finn Bunger; Tom, Agnes, Olivia, and Thomas Bunger; Josef Hoppl, Greg Jagenberg, Ciaran Sheehan, Bill O'Connell, Curtis Cruz, Cali, Michael Rube, King & Spalding LLC, Cesar Presbott, Angelo Martinez and family, Robbie Alomar, Sandy Alomar, Bruce Zipes, Bruce's Bakery, Spalding, Hector Pagan, Josh Zeide, Darryl and Tracy Strawberry, Dave Valle, Brenda Bonini, Jim Madorma, Tom Hopke, Vincent Kenyon, Joey Gian, the Smithers Foundation, Maggie Hyde—February 9th; the Kremer family, the Sakellaridis family, Carl Ferraro, Tom Giordano, Robby Robinson, Miguel Montas, Amtrak, Larry Frank, Bob Klapish, the Keating family, the Dromerhauser family, the Hernandez family, John Larossa, Sue and Johnnie Larossa; Tony Melendez, the Murcer family, Michael Kay—in your own way you always told Bobby Murcer that you loved him; Raúl Ibañez—Gehrig's spirit is always behind you; Ron Dock, Diana Munson, Daniel Quintero, the Kips Bay Boys and Girls Club, Dr. Tom Haveron; Andrew, Tim, and the guys at Wish You Were Here; Lorne Michaels, for giving the Boss one of the best days of his life when he hosted your show; Sue Polino and Laura Casini, for putting my story in music; Steve Kalafer; Kassie Caffiero and my friends at Broadway Video; Scooter Honig, Quiksilver, Chris and Helene Lewis, Louis Ciliberti, Paul and Armi Viti—you were there from day one; Kim Berry, for keeping us healthy; the Gere Foundation, Bob Unger, Jon Lane, Billy Martin Jr. and family; Mort Fleischner, Maurice Friedman and family, Zaah Technologies,

ACKNOWLEDGMENTS

Keith Delucia, Al Sontag, Bill Laggner, Ed Arikian, Charlie Maher, Christian Pascale, Ark Restaurants; Brandon, Giselle, and my beautiful niece Savana Rae Boyd; Richard Seko, Reed Bergman, Sandy Kyrkostas, Wayne Hickey, Mike and Sue Studley, Joe Avallone, Creative Group, Barrett Esposito, Joe Castellano, Dan Halpern, David Lennon, Ken and Jonathan Davidoff, Jim Baumbach, Joe Auriemma, Father Thomas Gorman, the Silver Shield Foundation, KC Fuchs, William Walters, Ken Aretsky, Anna Deluca, Mott Haven Academy Charter School, George Ntm, Greg Hess and family, Mike Lavalva, the Feinstein family, Jane Rogers, Jon Hart, Joe Fosina, Eric Mays, Robert Narvarez, Under Armour, the Reale family, West Islip Little League, Bronx Grand Slam, the Profetta family, Larry Davis, Phil Tavella, the Nederlander family, Tom Barbagallo, Dom Scala, Matt Guiliano, Mark Wilson and family, Nick Giampietro, Mead Chasky, Michael Steinberg, the Watt family, Hank's Yanks, Leonel Vinas, Matt Duran, my friends at the YES Network, Charlie Santoro, Ken Fagan, Amy Chua—thank you; Dick Biley, Slater and Nicky Fuchs, Steve Fortunato, Kevin Brosnahan, Sy and Joanne Presten, Babylon Bean, where I spent many hours writing; Mr. D, Herb and Barbara Steier, Leo and Danny Caputo, Tommy Mattola—a legend, Yankee Tavern; Luis Torres, PS 55, Pete Curti, Beaver Bats, Tony Fantasia—another of the Boss's lost souls; Bronx Lebanon Hospital, St. Barnabus Hospital, Memorial Sloan-Kettering, Jacoby Hospital, Christian Hunter, Ralph and Linda Scordino; Alan, Mark, and Plessers; Coach Mike Turo—a high school legend; Bobby Hoffman, Joe Kelleher, Joe Simone, Ruben Diaz Jr., Alfred Zaccagnino, Joe Daglomini, Mulberry Street, Colony Records, Michael Grossbart; Emil Ferrand and Carrabbas in St. Petersburg; Lucie Arnaz and family; Hurley, Howard Goldin, and *Bronx News*; Terry Whitfield, Paul Schindler, the Pisanti brothers, Bobby Rossi, Ruth Eckerd Hall, Hector Florin, Julio Pabon, Latino Sports, Joe Appio, Play It Again, Send in the Clowns, TL Bats, Newsmax, and Chris Ruddy; Steve Sakellardis—your courageous battle will help others forever.

In the immortal words of Francis Albert Sinatra . . . "That's life!"

—Ray Negron

WE HAVE RECEIVED tremendous and support from a wide and wonderful group of friends, relatives and colleagues. Bob Weil, our extraordinary editor at Liveright Publishing Corporation / W. W. Norton, created miracles from the beginning and has been by our sides ever since. Philip Marino, assistant editor, carefully read several drafts of the manuscript and provided outstanding comments and suggestions. We owe Bob and Phil a huge debt of gratitude for their diligence, passion, knowledge, and attention to every phase of making this book. They are true aces. Also, our thanks to Peter Miller at Liveright for his energy and enthusiasm.

Special thanks to Aris Sakellaridis, a walking baseball encyclopedia, for sharing countless hours with me, recalling his vast baseball knowledge. Theresa Bunger's goodwill, energy, enthusiasm, and amazing kindness sustained me through many long days.

I can't possibly thank all of my talented and wise friends for their time, interest and generosity. If I have inadvertently omitted anyone here, I apologize. Gratitude to: Amy Archer, Laurence Bergreen, Bente Busby, Rob Castillo, Peter Canby, Susan and Carlo DeRege, Karen Doeblin, Stacey Farley, Wendy Gordon, Diane Ingersoll, Debby Jones, Jon Keenan, Katherine Leiner, Maryann MacDonald, Kate Manning, Kathy Marr, Trish Marx, Hope Matthiessen, Celia McGee,

Acknowledgments

Kate McMullan, Diane McWhorter, Marilyn Schwenk, and Bonnie Stockwell. My friends and colleagues at Project Sunshine inspire me every day.

My intelligent and dear mother read the manuscript from the beginning and offered her usual sage advice. My thoughtful siblings—Jeanne, Daniel, and John—and their families provided enduring interest and laughter. My children, Liz and Alex, and my husband, Bob, read several drafts of the manuscript. I am deeply grateful for the love and caring they show me every day.

A curtain call for Holly McGhee, our special agent. Her humor, wisdom, and friendship know no bounds.

—Sally Cook

RAY NEGRON TIMELINE

1973–1974	New York Yankees batboy
1975	Drafted by Pittsburgh Pirates; played for Bradenton Pirates in Rookie League
1976	New York Yankees batting practice pitcher
1977–1981	New York Yankees video operator; clubhouse and Boss assistant
1982	Actor, *Blue Skies Again*
1983	Actor, *The Cotton Club*
1984	Actor, *The Slugger's Wife* and commercials; sports agent
1986–1992	Tokyo Yomiuri Giants adviser
1989–1990	General manager, Port St. Lucie Legends, Senior Professional Baseball League
1991–1993	Tampa YMCA, coordinator/coach for children's afterschool programs
1994–1995	Dwight Gooden, Daryl Strawberry: devised rehabilitation program
1995–1997	Special adviser to New York Yankees owner George M. Steinbrenner
1998–2001	Cleveland Indians, worked with sports psychologist Dr. Charles Maher

2002–2004	Texas Rangers, worked with management and sports psychologist Don Kalkstein
2005–2010	Special adviser to George M. Steinbrenner; author, children's books; executive producer, animated film *Henry & Me*
2010–Present	Community adviser, New York Yankees

INDEX

INDEX

ABOUT THE AUTHORS

Ray Negron is the author of two New York Times best sellers, *The Boy of Steel* and *The Greatest Story Never Told*, as well as *One Last Time*. He is the executive producer of the animated film *Henry & Me*. He currently works with the New York Yankees as a community adviser. He lives in Florida. You can visit him at www.batboyhelps.com.

Sally Cook is the coauthor, with legendary coach Gene Stallings, of *Another Season*, a *New York Times* bestseller. She is also the coauthor, with James Charlton, of *Hey Batta Batta Swing! The Wild Old Days of Baseball* and the author of *Good Night Pillow Fight*. Sally, a special adviser for the Project Sunshine Book Club, lives in New York City. You can visit her at www.pippinproperties.com.